RELIGIOUS APARTHEID

RELIGIOUS APARTHEID

JOHN W. WHITEHEAD

MOODY PRESS
CHICAGO

ISBN: 0-8024-7891-3

3 5 7 9 10 8 6 4 2

Printed in the United States of America

To Alexis Irene Crow

Thanks for all your help.

BOOKS BY JOHN W. WHITEHEAD

The Separation Illusion

Schools on Fire
(with Jon T. Barton)

The New Tyranny

The Second American Revolution

The Stealing of America

*The Freedom of Religious Expression in
Public Universities and High Schools*

Home Education and Constitutional Liberties
(with Wendell R. Bird)

*The Right to Picket and
the Freedom of Public Discourse*

Parents' Rights

The End of Man

An American Dream

True Christianity

*The Rights of Religious Persons
in Public Education*

Home Education: Rights and Reasons
(with Alexis I. Crow)

Religious Apartheid

CONTENTS

PREFACE

*T*he United States is in the midst of a series of cultural wars that threaten to undermine its basic foundations.

These cultural wars include the continuing strife between the races (primarily black and white), the poor and the wealthy, orthodox and progressive beliefs,[1] the religious and the secular. It is the last category—the war between the religious and the secular—that is the concern of this book.

Unfortunately, America is moving toward what I call a system of religious apartheid. What is "apartheid" as a general definition, and why do I apply it to the United States? "Pronounced apart-hate, the word [means] apartness or separation."[2] In South Africa, it is an Afrikaans word, defining the public policy of separating the white race from all other races. Applied to the United States, the term describes the increasing hostility of secular concerns toward religious interests. Religion, especially public manifestations of Christianity, is being systematically separated from American society. From the removal of crosses and nativity scenes in public places to the prohibition of individual prayer in the schools, examples of this apartness and separation are occurring daily (sometimes hourly) throughout the country.

Where did this division start? Society in general began moving away from Christianity as early as the beginning of the twentieth century. However, there was no official governmental sanctioning of this apartness until 1947. That came in the United States Supreme Court's decision in *Everson v. Board of Education.*[3] In that case, Justice Hugo Black construed the First Amendment in a more restrictive fashion:

> The "establishment of religion" clause of the First Amendment means at least this: Neither a state nor the Federal Government can set up a church. Neither can pass laws which aid one religion, aid all religions, or prefer one religion over another. Neither can force nor influence a person to go to or to remain away from church against his will or force him to profess a belief or disbelief in any religion. No person can be punished for entertaining or professing religious beliefs or disbeliefs, for church attendance or non-attendance. No tax in any amount, large or small, can be levied to support any religious activities or institutions, whatever they may be called, or whatever form they may adopt to teach or practice religion. Neither a state nor the Federal Government can, openly or secretly, participate in the affairs of any religious organizations or groups and *vice versa*. In the words of Jefferson, the clause against establishment of religion by law was intended to erect "a wall of separation between church and State."[4]

This absolute definition of the First Amendment Establishment Clause went well beyond the original intent of the framers of the United States Constitution and paved the way for future cases that would further restrict religious expression in American public life. This ruling declares that *any* aid or benefit to religion from governmental actions is unconstitutional. As Justice Black said: "The First Amendment has erected a wall between church and state. That wall must be kept high and impregnable. We could not approve the slightest breach."[5]

Based upon this new interpretation, the Supreme Court held in a series of subsequent cases that prayer, Bible reading, and the mere posting of the Ten Commandments were unconstitutional in public schools. Even long-standing traditions with hundreds of years of history —such as graduation prayer—have been held unconstitutional and rightly to be separated from public life.

As this book will show, the effects of these cases have been far-reaching. Courts have largely eliminated prayer (even silent prayer) from public schools, often with decisions that offend common sense and traditional notions of First Amendment freedoms. For example, one federal appeals circuit court held the following prayer recited by kinder-

garten children to be an establishment of religion and thus unconstitutional:

> We thank you for the flowers so sweet,
> We thank you for the food we eat,
> We thank you for the birds that sing,
> We thank you for everything.[6]

In this case, God is not even identified. In another case, a federal court
ordered that there be *no prayer* by anyone under any circumstances at a
high school graduation ceremony.[7]

Now various liberal private interest groups, such as the American
Civil Liberties Union, often in conjunction with public schools and local governments, search the public arena for any reference to God or
Christianity and seek its removal. As one author, writing about the
South African situation, puts it: "This obsessional, anachronistic law-
making and its harsh policing are what constitute apartheid."[8] And this
is exactly what we in America are now facing—religious apartheid. This
obsessional "separation," or apartheid, would apply to *every* Bible, cru-
cifix, crèche, blessing, and prayer in the public realm.

What we are witnessing is the end of religion and morality in the public sphere.

As religious apartheid has gained a foothold in the culture, however, the threat to traditional practitioners of religion (such as Christians) has been made much worse by the decline in the moral principles
that have undergirded America since its inception. Moreover, those
who reject those moral values now dominate government circles and
governmental policymaking.[9] That has created a series of crisis points
that are having a great impact, changing the way people think and act.

For example, the doctrine of political correctness that has stamped-
ed across university campuses is now affecting the general culture. It
has created an aura of censorship and a climate of fear that is chilling
the very right to speak and think freely.

The family, once the bedrock of society, is under siege from state
agencies and the culture at large. As new forms of the family, such as
homosexual liaisons, gain more acceptance, the traditional family is
losing its authority.

The devaluing of human life continues unabated. Unborn children, as sanctioned by the Supreme Court, are the targets of private interest groups as well as state agencies that not only want to abort them but harvest their body parts as well.

The homosexual movement has blossomed into a national gay agenda that is altering politics, education, the church, the arts, and the family. The radical assertion of the rights of gays in all areas of American life will have far-reaching effects that we do not yet fully comprehend.

What we are witnessing is the end of religion and morality in the public sphere. As Christianity is driven further from the marketplace, American public life is increasingly vulnerable to radical lifestyles and options that make up the "closed loop" of a purely secular consensus.

Governmental institutions, such as the Supreme Court, the presidency, and the Congress do not shoulder the entire blame for these profound changes in the American cultural fabric. Far from it. Indeed, past generations of Christians and other religionists who were not involved in society or who sat silently by as the culture embraced the secular worldview are also greatly responsible. Thus, those who are threatened by the loss of freedom and influence due to religious apartheid must share the blame for the demise of a once great culture.

The thesis of this book is that if the Judeo-Christian principles that served as the source of all law governing this republic are not recovered in the near future, the conflict that will naturally emerge over the changes sweeping across the cultural landscape like a fire storm will destroy the structure of our country and its major institutions. As a cultural collapse due to opposing worldviews becomes more imminent, those supporting the system of religious apartheid in America will intensify the pressure, and oppression and even overt persecution of those holding a religious worldview may result.

JOHN W. WHITEHEAD

ACKNOWLEDGMENTS

I appreciate the research and editing assistance of Alexis Crow. The comments of Sheila McThenia and Nancy Reynolds were also very helpful. Carol Whitehead's typing and the technical assistance of Aaron Cook, Kim Lowe, Nancy Anderson, Brian Marinas, and Rita Woltz were of great assistance as well.

PART ONE
CONCERNS AND PRINCIPLES

The whole structure is now tumbling down, dethroning its God, undermining all its certainties. All this, wonderfully enough, is being done in the name of the health, wealth, and happiness of all mankind.

MALCOLM MUGGERIDGE
The End of Christendom

1

DE-CHRISTIANIZING THE AMERICAN PSYCHE

*O*n every side and in every phase of life, Judeo-Christian beliefs and practices are berated and denounced. Once the norm of society, the concept of Judeo-Christian absolutes, when not being discounted as untrue, is being deemed irrelevant to anything of importance. The moral, philosophical, and religious structures of Western society (including American society) have, as a consequence, been completely altered.

In the early 1900s, if one were randomly to gather a crowd of people and address them from a biblical perspective, most would generally understand and agree with what was being said. At least they would recognize basic biblical principles. However, gather a random crowd today and argue from the basis of Judeo-Christian principles, and many will not understand the meaning of what is being said.

Most of Western society is now largely biblically illiterate. Many people may comprehend or remember a few verses, but to attempt to communicate to contemporary society from a Judeo-Christian worldview will produce incomprehension or disagreement. The Bible is simply no longer the norm of belief and behavior.

Modern culture is prejudiced against the Judeo-Christian ethic. This predisposition and cultural derision is reflected in a *Time* essay: "The day after the 1992 election was supposed to be the first day of life without the religious right. Americans had finally, as Voltaire might have put it, crushed the infamy. The political theologians and theological politicians of the late unlamented '80's were no more."[1] Yet as the theologian William Barclay said twenty years ago, "there has never been a time when the discussion of the Christian Ethic has been more necessary and more relevant."[2]

THE NEW CONCEPT OF TRUTH

One may counter these propositions by indicating an increased activity in religion by certain segments of American society. Recent increases in some church memberships are often pointed to as a hopeful sign.

We are witnessing . . . the collapse of the Judeo-Christian ethic and the religious establishment that guided American society in the first two hundred years of its existence.

However, in 1962, polls indicated that at least 65 percent of Americans believed the Bible to be true. In 1992, polls indicate that only 32 percent do, while 50 percent say that they actually *fear* fundamentalists.[3] As Chuck Colson recognizes: "If the polls are right, our Judeo-Christian heritage is no longer the foundation of our values. We have become a post-Christian society."[4]

. There are worrisome trends which threaten to undermine the efforts of churches and to stall any spiritual momentum. Chief among these troublesome trends is a lack of the nation's religious heritage, the Ten Commandments, and the central doctrines of religion by those who call themselves Christians.[5]

Despite the fact that the majority of Americans say they accept the Bible as the Word of God, the comprehensive 1979 Gallup Survey found that only 49 percent of Protestants and 44 percent of Roman Catholics could name as many as four of the Ten Commandments and less than half of the respondents said they turn first to the Scriptures for guidance in times of crisis.[6]

We are, therefore, presented with a major *ethical* crisis of "illiteracy" as well as a theological crisis.

SHEDDING RELIGION

The process of "shedding" the Judeo-Christian religion gained its greatest momentum with the cultural revolution of the 1960s. As Chuck Colson states:

[This cultural revolution] exalted existentialism and a kind of "live-for-the-moment-God-is-dead-or-irrelevant" philosophy. Today, that Sixties philosophy has become mainstream; it is in the White House, it is in the poetry of Maya Angelou, it is in every walk of life. This is not to say that people aren't going to church. Forty-four percent of the American people still attend religious services regularly. But we live in a Donahue-ized culture in which we sit and watch, hour by hour, the banality that passes for knowledge on television, and we rarely think about issues in terms of Judeo-Christian truth.[7]

This new orientation not only explains present moral and ethical dilemmas but also explains the great chasm between living generations. This chasm has been created almost entirely by a change in the *concept of truth*. Wherever you look today, this new concept of truth, which is a post-World War II phenomenon, predominates.

Indeed, after World War II, schools began to teach ethics based on subjective standards without moral truths. C. S. Lewis challenged this, writing, "We make men without chests and we expect of them virtue and enterprise. We laugh at honor and we are shocked to find traitors in our midst. We castrate and bid the geldings be fruitful."[8] Colson concurs: "*We are taking away the spiritual element and abandoning morality based on religious truth,* counting instead on our heads and our subjective feelings to make us do what is right."[9]

This new concept of truth, one based on purely subjective standards, has created a secular consensus that governs contemporary society.

INTOLERANCE

What we are witnessing is the collapse of the Judeo-Christian ethic and the religious establishment that guided American society in the first two hundred years of its existence. With this collapse, a vacuum was created, and the shift in the view of truth from a Judeo-Christian base to a secular base occurred. I do not use the term *humanistic,* because classical humanism is compatible, in varying degrees, with Judeo-Christian thinking. In other words, it does not totally debase God.

> *The great chasm between the living generations . . . has been created . . . by a change in the concept of truth.*

But the Judeo-Christian religious beliefs and secularism are not compatible. Secularism is more than a philosophy. Indeed, as one noted theologian recognizes, it is an "ideology, a new closed world-view which functions very much like a new religion. . . . It is a closed ism."[10]

Like any religion that becomes the dominant view of those in power, secularism becomes a closed system. That poses a danger to the basic freedoms to profess and act upon traditional theistic beliefs. This is more so since the secular elite use the "organs of the State" to impose the secularistic dogma.[11] Thus, although the disciples of secularism preach against religious "dogmatism," they impose their own, because they forcibly separate religion from the state.

Secularism, then, is not a tolerant system. It seeks to be not only a dominant viewpoint but the *only* viewpoint. In America, as stated earlier, this has resulted in a form of "religious apartheid" in various segments of society.[12] In fact, the rise of secularism as the dominant American ethos has resulted in a form of intolerance that threatens freedoms generally thought to be essential to the survival of any society.

POLARIZATION

A survey conducted in the late 1980s, although not conclusive, indicates that a *tense polarization* has occurred in the United States between those who hold to a Judeo-Christian ethic and the secularists who reject it. This is seen in light of several factors.

First, the survey found that "as the political claims of the evangelicals have become more vocal in the last decade, so too, the social antagonism between [the secularists and the evangelicals] has grown."[13]

Second, the survey discovered that "[n]early one out of three academics (34%) said that evangelicals are 'a threat to democracy.'"[14] An academic, according to the survey, covers "university faculty members of the Ph.D.-granting departments of political science, sociology, history, and English."[15]

The results of the survey seem to indicate that the polarization of the two philosophical views is rapidly widening. As secularists continue to increase their control while in positions of authority, there will be an increase in restrictions on the religious freedom of Christians, Jews, and other religious persons, because they are viewed as "a threat to democracy." Moreover, as "evangelicals" and those labeled "fundamentalists" grow more strident in their own requests for fair representation, the reaction from the secularists will increasingly be negative. They will view such advocacy as an attempt to set up a state based on the religious beliefs of one group or another. The pattern will be especially significant as it is seen in those in positions of authority with the greatest impact on society: leaders in government, education, and media.

In the future, this antagonism will inevitably expand beyond evangelicals to include anyone believing in a supernatural deity who wishes to apply those beliefs in any way to the public sector. University professors, for instance, hold a tremendous sway over developing young minds. The secular bias can be demonstrated in many professions besides academia. This secularist bias against religious influence will have an enormous negative effect on the role of religion in American public life.

Judges play a key role in deciding the important issues of religion in public life. Judicial bias, as anyone who has ever tried a case knows, is an important factor in the outcome of legal battles. There is a secular bias in much of the judiciary, and it will continue to have a negative influence on religious liberty.

All this becomes a bit more frightening when one realizes, as the survey documents, that "only 1 in 3" American young people "in the 15 to 18 and the 19 to 22 age brackets" knows "that the freedom of religion is guaranteed by the First Amendment."[16] Knowledge of American constitutional rights and freedoms by those who are soon to achieve majority as citizens is, therefore, extremely shallow. This lack of awareness means that major cultural shifts, such as the loss of religious freedom, will continue to go largely unnoticed by a significant segment of uncon-cerned, uninformed, and apathetic Americans.

APARTHEID

This is indeed troubling when it becomes apparent that the very right to speak and act on certain religious beliefs in American public life is increasingly challenged in the United States. American secular society is systematically closing the door to virtually all forms of Judeo-Christian expression in public places. The annual lost battles over reli-gious displays (such as nativity scenes) and student-initiated prayer at graduation ceremonies attests to this.

The rise of secularism. . . has resulted in a form of intolerance that threatens freedoms thought to be essential to the survival of any society.

We are now seeing, so to speak, the de-Christianization of the American psyche. The denial to religious persons of equal access to the marketplace of ideas is epidemic. The noose is growing tighter around religious speech and its various expressions.

This censorship may be most visible in the "public" schools, where the rights of free speech of many religious teachers and students are restricted. The belief is that somehow religious persons who seek expression in the public schools should be reigned in and segregated. Thus, they do not receive equal treatment under the law. In certain cases, this ends in a form of discrimination that threatens the rights of an entire class of citizens.

Many, as stated earlier, are unaware of the broad implications of this controversy. That is due in large part to the fact that the cases and instances of religious censorship are generally unreported in the secu-lar media and receive only sporadic attention in the religious media.

It is increasingly clear, however, that if religious people do not re-tain their right to free speech in American public life, then theistic reli-gion will continue to be privatized, similar in some respects to the practice in the former Iron Curtain countries. There, "freedom of religion" was allowed only in a controlled church or other "specified" areas.

DE-CHRISTIANIZING THE AMERICAN PSYCHE

The secular onslaught has had a negative impact on the Christian psyche. As Colson says, "We hear carolers singing 'Silent Night' or an invocation at a public ceremony and we are filled with trepidation: we are worried that we are infringing upon the rights of nonbelievers. We see the symbol of the cross and we feel compelled to paint it out because it might violate the principle of separation between church and state. We exalt tolerance, not truth, as the ultimate virtue."[17]

As a consequence, over the past several decades we have witnessed the systematic removal of religious symbols from public places. Crosses and nativity scenes are embattled symbols every Christmas season.

In one instance, a group of citizens objected to a cross on a Christmas tree which was displayed on public property. When public officials broke the cross into pieces and reassembled it in the form of a Christmas tree and placed it on top of the Christmas tree itself, the threatened lawsuit was dropped.

In another example, Chicago city officials rearranged two crosses made from lilies at Easter after the American Civil Liberties Union objected that the exhibits were improper public displays of religion.

In still another example, a war memorial to University of Virginia law students killed in the Civil War was removed from the law school's hallway (after being there for many years) because it contained a message that was overtly religious.

The forced, systematic removal of religious symbols from public life has and will continue to have a tremendous effect on the American psyche and constitutional process. During the holiday season, public schools seldom refer to Christmas anymore in their activities and programs. Instead, terms and phrases such as "Winter Program" or "Winter Holidays" are used. This is a subtle form of censorship and discrimination, but it can have far-reaching ramifications on religion in society.

Religious symbols in public parks and buildings likewise have come under attack. Traditional street preaching has come under assault. Cases of street preachers being arrested and brought to trial are increasing—in a society that day-in and day-out preaches pluralism and tolerance.

THE WOLF AT THE DOOR

We have been told that pluralism, accommodation, and tolerance of theistic religion go hand-in-hand. To a certain extent, this may be true. However, with the rise of secularism and its continuing expansion by persons in positions of authority, we are now seeing that there are limits to this supposed accommodation and tolerance in a pluralistic society.

Finally, we must not forget that the real struggle is over what appears to be a nihilistic future, that is, a future with no absolute values. The crunch of technological nihilism, if not countered, will swallow secularists and evangelicals alike. In the words of professed atheist Michael Harrington:

> The committed believers and unbelievers now have the same enemy: the humdrum nihilism of everyday life in much of Western society. . . . I think that in the late twentieth century serious atheists and serious believers have more in common with one another than the mindless, *de facto* atheists (who often affirm some vague and sentimental God) and routine churchgoers.[18]

2

THE
FIRE STORM

*T*he most striking and unusual feature of the present moment is the speed at which change is taking place. A brief review of history reveals that in cultures of the past, change occurred very slowly and such cultures have, in some instances, endured a thousand years or more.

Today, however, the passing of a couple of decades brings incredible changes, so that the 1970s, for example, stand in sharp contrast to the 1990s. Moreover, a look at those young people who grew up in the 1970s will reveal that they have little in common with the youth of today.

The development of technology has much to do with the rapidity of change. The changes that are occurring, however, do not relate simply to speed of communications or the ease with which we can do our work. Indeed, the rapid changes that are rushing toward us are altering basic structures undergirding the entire culture.

IDENTITY CRISIS

The vacuum created by the decline of Judeo-Christian thought in our society has created a parenthesis in time. Into this parenthesis new and ominous ideas are flooding. Chuck Colson puts it well: "We are in the middle of an identity crisis in which we are attempting to redefine our basic values all over again. We can no longer assume that right and wrong have clear meanings or that there is universal truth. After all, pollsters tell us that sixty-seven percent of the American people say there is no such thing."[1]

As the Judeo-Christian values of our society have been removed, the door has been opened for numerous possibilities. The unthinkables of several years ago are now not only thinkable but doable. A simple comparison of the sexual activity, adultery, language, and violence on television during family viewing hours with the television of the 1970s is testimony enough to this fact. Twenty years from today, what may now seem obscene or evil could be operative in a very different society.

The Judeo-Christian worldview dominated the West for centuries. Judeo-Christian principles, however, were not taught as *mere truths.* They were taught as *the* truth. This teaching formed the religious base as well as the cultural, legal, and governmental foundation of society.

The Judeo-Christian worldview prevailed not only because it was inculcated from youth but also because it answered the fundamental questions of humanity. *Where did I come from? What is my purpose? Where am I going? Who is God? What is God like?* It also provided meaning to core issues such as the significance of human life and how people should relate to one another.

In this way, the Judeo-Christian ethic formed a general cultural consensus and provided the basic moral and social values by which things were judged. The decline of Judeo-Christian theism began in the early twentieth century. Judeo-Christian values, however, maintained a foothold in American culture through the 1950s and retained some vigor even after the cultural revolution of the 1960s. Since then, the rapid disappearance of Judeo-Christian values is one of the most salient features of our present culture. Moreover, the outright rejection of Christianity is a tenet of the modern age.

It is as if a nuclear blast (the rejection of Christianity) has occurred and the resultant fire storm is consuming any sense of absolute moral values. This fire storm (the religious apartheid we experience) transforms culture, and, as these words are written, the Judeo-Christian foundations that have nourished freedom around the world are being burned away. Those foundations are turning to ashes.

For perhaps the first time in human history, countries worldwide have no idea of what their future will be. The Manifest Destiny of the United States is no longer pervasive or viewed as inevitable. Nations once determined to expand their commercial influence or their religious doctrines are now imploding in orgies of political correctness, ethnic cleansing, tyranny, and selfishness. Other countries are simply overwhelmed by corruption or self-doubt. Governments with no real sense of destiny or purpose turn from their responsibilities and offer a myriad of so-called rights to citizens who reflect their same purposelessness.

Politically, economically, and morally, Western countries in particular have become broken reeds. The old forms in society that once predominated, such as traditional religion and family structures, are being revised with no consensus regarding the goals for revision. The idea of moral absolutes is, for the most part, obsolete. Most see all situations and ideas as relative. Even the value of human life is increasingly seen in relative economic and quantitative terms.

Beset by numerous crises, men and women in virtually every society stand paralyzed, unable to act effectively. As a consequence, the present age is characterized by confusion, chaos, decay, and death.

DEFINING AWAY HUMANITY

On the other hand, some believe that the human race stands on the dawn of a new civilization.[2] Indeed, in technological terms, humans now have the ability to transform not only their society but their personal selves as well.

But technology also now possesses the awesome power to annihilate human life as it is presently known. With its human cloning,[3] genetic tinkering, "test-tube babies," amniocentesis, sociobiology, and behaviorism, modern science has reopened Pandora's box. Medical ethics are increasingly challenged by economic constraints and the demands of consumers with shifting values.[4] Human worth is viewed primarily in terms of its usefulness to society.

Science is outpacing religion. Indeed, the creature once thought to be "fearfully and wonderfully made" is now considered without value except in the utilitarian terms.[5] The trend in modern medicine often appears to hold that a human being is merely the sum of his or her body parts—a sum that is subject to revision as body parts are redistributed as needed, it no longer being important whether the donor is alive or dead. A "brave new world" hovers in the wings for humanity and civilization. But it is no new golden age. It is merely the old tyranny

27

disguised and revitalized by science. Technology often acts as a new religion.

Human beings are quickly becoming irrelevant. Compared to the computer, what is one person's worth? Is a person qualitatively different than a thinking machine? After all, a mere decade ago *Time* magazine nominated the computer as its "man" of the year.

These are questions that our society must soon answer for the simple reason that people, as humans, are being defined away. We have become but a shadow of our former selves, a reflection of our environment. That is to say, *modern culture has no view of humanity in the age-old, traditional sense.*

The older Christian idea that human beings alone and as a species have unique dignity and worth is gone. This is the argument of the late Harvard behaviorist B. F. Skinner in his book *Beyond Freedom and Dignity.*[6] Skinner first argued there was hope for humans, but only through an environment controlled by a statist elite. However, in his later years, Skinner became pessimistic. In his new pessimism, Skinner saw no hope at all for the human race. To him, humankind was unredeemable.

KILLING HUMANITY

The loss of the uniqueness of people has also led to the pervasive anti-life philosophy of many cultures around the world. This expresses itself in abortion, infanticide, and euthanasia. Even in countries such as Ireland, which remain officially pro-life, pro-abortion forces relentlessly seek to alter the law.

The matter of a "woman's right to an abortion" was articulated a mere three decades ago. As feminist Betty Friedan notes:

> [D]espite the well-laid plans of the male abortion politicos and medicos, the right of woman was spelled out as the basis of the abortion movement. . . . [The] right to sexual privacy and the control of our own bodies in the matter of childbearing and abortion was more basic than many of the rights spelled out in the Bill of Rights, as it was written of, by and for men.[7]

Thus, at the First National Conference for Repeal of Abortion Laws in Chicago in 1969 (four years before the decision in *Roe v. Wade*[8]), Friedan posed the question of abortion as a civil right: "The right of woman to control her reproductive process must be established as a basic, inalienable, civil right, not to be denied or abridged by the state—just as the right of individual and religious conscience is considered an inalienable private right in both American tradition and in the American Constitution."[9] Betty Friedan thus grounded the right to abortion in tradition and the American Constitution.

Following her lead, the United States Supreme Court "searched" the Constitution, and, in 1973 in *Roe v. Wade,* decided that, while the state has an "important and legitimate interest in protecting the potentiality of human life,"[10] that interest must be subordinated to a woman's right of *privacy.*[11]

In *Roe v. Wade,* the Supreme Court excluded unborn babies from humankind and denied them their God-given rights for essentially one reason: *convenience.* Maiming and murdering unborn children—and using pieces of their bodies for medical treatment and experimentation—are now legal because American law regards an unborn child as only the "potentiality of human life."

In its attempt to create a new "right" for women, the United States Supreme Court shifted the very source of rights and has, in the process, laid the foundation for the destruction of all rights. There is presently no basis to protect the very right to life in America and, thus, no basis for protecting any right.

Many have placed their hopes in a medical profession ostensibly sworn to preserving life and giving no abortive remedy. Yet, abortionists with medical degrees maim, dismember, and kill those whom they regard as mere "tissue," entities they define as not capable of "being harmed" by their actions.

Others have placed their faith in a judiciary they believed would support life. Yet several decades after *Roe v. Wade,* in *Planned Parenthood v. Casey,*[12] the so-called conservative American Supreme Court ratified the *Roe* position.

However, in *Casey,* the Supreme Court made a deadly shift. The basis of the abortion right moved from privacy to *liberty:*

The importance of this conceptual shift cannot be overemphasized. For rather than having abortion limited to a right of privacy protecting a rather traditional area of mental and family values, we now have abortion justified in the light of an argument geared to defend homosexual

29

liberty. . . . Indeed, every analogy the triumvirate [the writers of the decision] use for the right to abortion (including the franchise itself) is something that qualifies as a fundamental right. In its migration from privacy to liberty, abortion gains a firmer foothold in the judge-made law than it had before. . . . It is as free-floating as the Court might wish to understand "liberty." . . . The triumvirate's second argument . . . also suggests that autonomous liberty is crucial to the proper functioning of society.[13]

It is undeniable that women have civil rights, including rights with respect to sexual privacy and some control over their bodies. Yet, contrary to the view of Betty Friedan and the Supreme Court, the only rights that are "basic" and "inalienable" are those rights flowing from the Creator. One implication of this point is that *all* human life, as a gift from God, is sacred. This principle, as reflected in the Declaration of Independence, is a founding tenet of American government. The cataclysmic rejection of this principle led directly to the destruction through abortion of some 30 million American lives in the twenty years since 1973, and the holocaust continues.

America now has in place a judicial and cultural concept of autonomous liberty, *liberty that is to be defined by each individual* in society: "In the face of this self-definitive liberty and its social implications, what interest can the state hope to assert? . . . [The *Casey* decision] encourages Congress to exercise its [constitutional] powers to prohibit the states from enacting laws that uphold traditional morals in any number of areas."[14]

In its attempt to create a new "right" for women, the United States Supreme Court shifted the very source of rights and has, in the process, laid the foundation for the destruction of all rights. There is presently no basis to protect the very right to life in America and, thus, no basis for protecting *any* right. As abortion becomes more pervasive as a philosophical and legal feature of American life, the number of threats and assaults on other individual freedoms, including religious freedom, continues to grow.

Therefore, less than twenty years after the Supreme Court's decision in *Roe,* American society is permeated with the *Roe* philosophy. *Roe* is the new American way. Most Americans now understand what is meant by the term "products of conception" and the meaning of signs that read, "Don't Count My Eggs Before They're Hatched." The implications of a *Roe* culture are thus terrifying: If human beings, whether through legislation or judicial redefinition of rights, are defined out of humanity, then they have *no* rights and can lawfully be disposed of or treated in any manner that serves the purpose of the day.

This is true despite the efforts of the pro-life community. Although those opposed to abortion have resisted the *Roe* mentality in virtually every way possible, 1.5 to 1.6 million unborn babies have been killed each year in America since 1975. Again, that amounts to approximately 30 million dead babies in America as a result of the simple redefinition of humanity.

Thus, it must be recognized that *Roe v. Wade,* and all it stands for, is now the American philosophy. General support for the "right to choose," although perhaps not throughout the entire term of pregnancy, is nearly universal in America, Canada, Great Britain, and other countries.

We must also realize that the *Roe* epoch is, in many ways, similar to the Prohibition Era in America. During that time, many people in America manufactured, sold, and consumed alcohol despite—or to spite— American law. There was no widespread American moral imperative supporting Prohibition.

It must be remembered that before Adolf Hitler killed a single Jew, he murdered 275,000 adult handicapped people.

So it is with abortion. In today's moral climate, even if *Roe* were overruled, there is no question that abortion would still be widely practiced. This means that the cultural support for the *Roe* philosophy of individual rights even over the lives of others will continue to predominate in our torn world.

THE RIGHT TO DIE

The *Roe* philosophy blends unmercifully into one of the most critical issues in contemporary technological societies. It is called the "right to die."

Distinctions between death and the dying process have become blurred. Basic human dignity has been compromised by technological prowess. Pain, once a common part of every person's life, is now to be avoided, even at the expense of life.

The phrase "right to die" is, of itself, absurd since no human being has the power *not* to die. Nonetheless, in today's proliferation of rights, increasing numbers of political and religious leaders support the legal option to terminate one's life, or that of another with permission, on the basis of factors that ignore the simple moral fact that life itself, on any terms, is sacred.

Euthanasia, or mercy killing, is a concept already accepted by many in the Western nations. Although no country has yet officially legalized euthanasia, popular support for the practice is growing. For example, in the Netherlands, thousands of terminally ill patients are being euthanatized under a law allowing for doctor-assisted suicides. There were indications before the enactment of this law that some physicians in the Netherlands were killing conscious patients without their consent. Too few are resisting these actions.

In America, voters in various states have placed the right to die on the ballot. Although these efforts have been unsuccessful to date, it is becoming increasingly common, and thus acceptable, in the United States and other Western nations for politicians to discuss the "allocation of medical resources" as a necessary goal for contemporary societies, thus limiting assistance to those who are terminally ill. In the end, the most efficient way to implement such a concept is simply to dispose of those for whom there is no justification for an "allocation."

Legalized euthanasia is, in the end, simply another manifestation of the devaluation of life. As with abortion, life becomes the question, and the answer is determined by weighing the quality of the life, the economic considerations, and, brutally, the convenience of it.

It must be remembered that before Adolf Hitler killed a single Jew, he murdered 275,000 adult handicapped people. Prior to this, abortion had been prevalent in Germany for more than twenty years; next there was infanticide; and then followed the destruction of 275,000 adult handicapped people. From there, it was only a short step to the killing of six million Jews for the sake of the Fatherland.

Another example may be found in Japan, where abortion has been allowed for decades. Economic pressures resulting from the destruction of much of the younger generation through abortion are now creating pressure to kill the elderly and "defective." The parents have been killing the children, and now the children are killing the parents.

Jack Kevorkian, known as "Dr. Death," is a man who assists people allegedly wanting to end their lives. In our present cultural climate, there are other potential "Dr. Deaths" who are waiting for a better climate in which to operate.[15]

THE DENIAL OF RIGHTS

If the right to life, which is the foundational right, is not protected, then no right in and of itself will be protected in the end. For example, as abortion becomes more pervasive as a philosophical and legal feature of American life, the number of incidents and current cases involving other individual freedoms, such as religious freedom, is also increasing. Unfortunately, in addition to supporting abortion, the so-called conservative American Supreme Court has actually provided new rationales for excluding religion and religious belief from public view and public consciousness.

The United States Supreme Court historically understood that America was founded upon Christian principles and that Americans have always been, in the Court's words, "a religious people."[16] But that Court is gone.

> *A teacher in Colorado was told that he could not read his Bible silently even during his free time.*

Supreme Court Justice Anthony Kennedy (an appointee made to the Court by former President Ronald Reagan) is a jurist who many traditionalists believed would defend their rights. However, Justice Kennedy, writing for the majority in *Lee v. Weisman*,[17] held that school-sponsored graduation prayer is unconstitutional in public schools and asserted that religion belongs in what he termed the "private sphere."[18] In dissenting from Kennedy's decision, Justice Antonin Scalia asserted that the *Weisman* Court would have religion, "like pornography," be indulged only in private.[19]

Many Christians also hoped that Justice Scalia would defend the constitutional rights of religion. Yet in the so-called peyote case, *Employment Division v. Smith*,[20] Justice Scalia said that freedom of religion is a right that is secondary to other rights.[21]

In another instance, a teacher in Colorado was told that he could not read his Bible silently even during his free time. When he appealed the school's decision to the Supreme Court, the "conservative" justices refused to hear his case.[22]

Lower state and federal courts are following the lead of the Supreme Court. For example, public school students across America are told that they may not distribute Bibles to classmates who request them. Book reports and essays involving religious beliefs are excluded from public school classrooms. School boards continue to refuse to include Bible clubs among permitted after-school activities—despite a federal law requiring them to do so. A kindergartner asking God's blessing on her lunch was tapped on the shoulder by her teacher and told that she must not do that at school. Following a school board decision to rename a school's Christmas program a "Winter Program," teachers in one school district even began to forbid their students to say the word "Christmas" on school grounds![23]

Public school districts across the United States spend thousands of dollars on lawyers and lawsuits to prevent students from initiating their own prayers around school flagpoles or at their sports events. Yet some seem to look the other way when guns, knives, and drugs are used on the school grounds by students who have no idea how to pray.

As religious apartheid has become more commonplace, the systematic attack on and prohibition of all religious expression in America's public places has become the rule rather than the exception. Early challenges to Christmas displays on public property and the "plastic reindeer decisions" that followed were merely the forerunners to the "sanitization" of America's public arena. It must not be forgotten that these cases looked relatively benign at the time. After all, said some, a crèche at the courthouse wasn't really all that important.

Thus, litigation across America now ranges from attacks on historical religious symbols on municipal seals and religious city names such as "Corpus Christi" in Texas to attempts to ban individual poster displays of "John 3:16" by fans at professional athletic events. Historical pictures and plaques with any Christian meaning or message are being purged from public schools and universities throughout America.

No religious reference or symbol in public is too minor to escape the current cultural revisionism America is undergoing. A glance at relatively recent history reveals that this is exactly what happened in the former Soviet Union after the Bolshevik Revolution and again at the disintegration of the U.S.S.R.

THE AGE OF MANIPULATION

Media analyst Marshall McLuhan once said that American society moved into "1984" (or the authoritative state) in the 1930s, but no one noticed. He asserted that the basic groundwork (ideas and technology) for the modern authoritarian state had been laid by the early 1930s. All that remained necessary was for someone or something to put the needed elements together for control of the people. McLuhan's assertions were validated by the Communist regimes formed in such countries as made up the former Soviet Union.

With the recent splintering of the Soviet Union and its totalitarian regimes, many see hope for the future of "democracy" as the main avenue to freedom. However, when traveling this avenue there is the danger of chaos and, therefore, more inhumanity.

This may be seen in the "ethnic cleansing" that went on in Yugoslavia while the international community debated whether rescue of the victims was consistent with the policies of the United Nation.

A nyone looking for black shirts, mass rallies, or military displays will miss the telltale clues of what has been called "creeping fascism."

The new "freedom," with its lack of boundaries and its chaotic inhumanity, has, during the past few years imperiled the Azerbaijanis and Armenians, Muslims in Bosnia-Herzegovina, Iraqi Kurds, Mozambicans, Peruvians caught in the middle of the battle between Shining Path and the Peruvian government, Muslim Rohingyas in Burma, starving Somalis, Sri Lankans, South Sudanese, and Tuareg refugees in the Sahara. Moreover, the chaos created by the lack of real democratic institutions in countries formerly a part of the Soviet Union threatens the very existence of the newly formed countries and their dreams of democracy and freedom. These countries have changed regimes, but they are not truly free under a thriving bureaucracy.

We must remain mindful of the control of the media and governmental bureaucracies, especially in the West, where technology and its extensions are prevalent. Citizens increasingly feel powerless to act. Indeed, modern governments often pose a threat more serious than the older ones because government has become even more pervasive. The modern "welfare" state controls more and more of the totality of life—often in response to the demands of its citizens that it do so. An attorney from the former Soviet Union once remarked to me that the real power of the state resides in its bureaucracy—the unresponsive mono-lith that seems unaffected by history or change.

Thus, the old forms of governmental authoritarianism will most likely fade from contemporary "free" societies. Instead, the modern authoritarian state will more likely be a *manipulative* government. Modern governments have tools of manipulation that the world has never known before, from mass communication resources to faceless computerized bureaucracies that disburse government rewards for housing, parenting, schooling, working, farming, and believing as the government desires.

For example, Hitler was powerful, but think what he could have accomplished if television had been available to him—or, for that matter, if other modern technological devices such as the computer (including digitized manipulation of photo reality) had been at his disposal. Television and computers have boundless potential for manipulation and control.

Therefore, in Western countries such as the United States, Great Britain, Canada, and others, there will probably be no overnight revolution culminating in totalitarianism. Rather, the current trend of government, media, and public state-controlled education toward greater control and manipulation of the individual citizen will continue.

With the advent of the electronic media, the mechanism for manipulation has arrived. Television more than any other medium of mass communication, forms public opinions. This was clearly evident in the 1992 American presidential elections. Many have said that the media elected Bill Clinton as the American president through its coverage of the candidates. Indeed, President George Bush himself admonished the electorate to "Annoy the Media—Vote for Bush," as one bumper sticker suggested. The media, moreover, has convinced Americans that the wholly unrestricted right to abortion is critical to freedom, even though surveys indicate that the majority of Americans do not personally support abortion on demand through the full nine months of pregnancy.

The media does more than affect public opinion—*it alters the consciousness and worldview of entire generations.* Anyone looking for black shirts, mass rallies, or military displays will miss the telltale clues of what has been called "creeping fascism." Bertram Gross says: "In America it [will] be supermodern and multiethnic—as American as Madison Avenue, executive luncheons, credit cards, and apple pie. It [will] be fascism with a smile. As a warning against its cosmetic facade, subtle manipulation, and velvet gloves, I call it friendly fascism. What scares me most is its subtle appeal."[24]

Sweden, with its "benevolent" socialism, has shown us that relatively crude indoctrination by television and public education provides tremendous opportunities for the authoritarian state. Through the medium of television, the Swedes have also demonstrated a kind of powerful semantic manipulation, not unlike Orwell's "Newspeak" in which words are more or less gradually changed to mean something else. In this way, concepts undesirable to the state may be redefined in accordance with the state's ends. Thus, as journalist Roland Huntford demonstrates in his book *The New Totalitarians,* the word *freedom* does not yet in Swedish mean exactly "slavery." It does, however, already imply "submission" and is therefore being effectively neutralized as a rallying word in the vocabulary of forces that oppose servitude to the state.[25]

Nations, it must be remembered, have not been terrorized by despots proclaiming themselves as such. Instead, totalitarian regimes have acquired power while asserting their dedication to liberty, equality, and fraternity—for *and* at the expense of the untouchables designated by the victors. This was true of the French Revolution of the eighteenth and the Russian Revolution of the twentieth century, and it is equally true of modern Communism and third-world Socialism. It also applies to the emerging democracies of Eastern Europe. The potential for manipulation, though more crude because there are fewer resources, is there. In Latin America, where some governments are attempting to write new constitutions providing greater freedom, the potential is the same.

The people must be ever mindful of the art to which politics and governmental manipulation have developed. The media, in all of the examples just listed, is a very powerful channel for these subtle yet vast changes.

SURRENDER

Some might feel uneasy about increased government control and manipulation, but as our modern secular culture continues to expand, will such people be able to control the limits—for themselves and their society? This limit-setting will be in tension with the desires of those who speak of civil liberties but who also support the state's authority and responsibility for solving all problems. In a time of overwhelming societal pressures, feelings of unease may well be submerged and certain limitations of power may well be set aside. In any case, the skeptics will likely be lost in the clamor for "rights" and the rush to claim the benefits offered by the pervasive state.

There is still enough of the older ethical base in some countries—what has been called the "Christian memory"—so that people will resist if they understand that their values are being seriously threatened. But if this trend toward government control through manipulation continues to move slowly and quietly, there may be less resistance, because perceived change is gradual.

As the state gradually assumes more control, calls to the people for allegiance will come from the right as well as the left. However, in the end, political concepts such as "right" or "left" will make little difference (as may be seen in the violence of Germany's Nazis and the left-wing response). There is no substantive difference between an authoritarian government from the right or the left. In their extreme forms, they are only two means to the same end. And the negative results are the same—loss of liberty.

Many people cannot cope with the contemporary difficulties of managing their own lives. With this lack of responsibility they may be surrendering their minds and their civil liberties to those who "can explain the world to them anew."[26] As William Irwin Thompson puts it, "When the individual's consciousness is made up of a moving collage of televised fragments, his state of anxiety makes him prey to 'the recollectivization through terror' of the fascist state."[27] Therefore, confused and manipulated by their own technology, people, in an act of faith, surrender to the explanation given them by technology's interpreter, the media.

Off in the distance, we can hear a stamping boot coming closer and closer. It is the same old boot, but it has been resoled. And it is stamping to the beat of seemingly different, yet really the same, music.

"There is, of course, no reason," Aldous Huxley once wrote, "why the new totalitarian should resemble the old. Government by clubs and firing squads . . . is not merely inhumane . . . it is demonstrably inefficient, and in an age of advanced technology, inefficiency is the sin against the Holy Ghost. A really efficient totalitarian state would be one in which the all-powerful executive or political bosses and their army of managers control a population of slaves who do not have to be coerced, because they love their servitude."[28]

THE DEVILS

Albert Einstein, in discussing hatred against the Jews, retold an ancient fable:

The shepherd boy said to the horse: "You are the noblest beast that treads the earth. You deserve to live in untroubled bliss; and indeed your happiness would be complete were it not for the treacherous stag. But he practiced from youth to excel you in fleetness of foot. His faster pace allows him to reach the water holes before you do. He and his tribe drink up the water far and wide, while you and your foal are left to thirst. Stay with me! My wisdom and guidance shall deliver you and your kind from a dismal and ignominious state."

Blinded by envy and hatred of the stag, the horse agreed. He yielded to the shepherd lad's bridle. He lost his freedom and became the shepherd's slave.[29]

In America today, the state is the shepherd boy promising that, if the people will only accept the bridle, the government will deliver them from the restraints upon their liberty that are represented by the Judeo-Christian principles that once structured the nation. Similarly, as with the horse, Americans suffering the tribulations of hatred, bigotry, powerlessness, poverty, and ignorance are also gullible prey for the easy fix of the state's "benefits."

But without a system of moral absolutes, how will tyranny deal with Judeo-Christian opposition? C. S. Lewis describes the problem:

Of all tyrannies a tyranny sincerely exercised for the good of its victims may be the most oppressive. It may be better to live under robber barons than under omnipotent moral busybodies. The robber baron's cruelty may sometimes sleep, his cupidity may at some point be satiated; but those who torment us for our own good will torment us without end for they do so with the approval of their own conscience. . . . In reality, however, we must face the possibility of bad rulers armed with a Humanitarian theory of punishment. . . . We know that one school of psychology already regards religion as a neurosis. When this particular neurosis becomes inconvenient to government, what is to hinder government from proceeding to "cure" it? Such "cure" will, of course, be compulsory; but under the Humanitarian theory it will not be called by the shocking name of Persecution. No one will blame us for being Christians, no one will hate us, no one will revile us. The new Nero will approach us with the silky manners of a doctor. . . . [W]hen the command is given, every prominent Christian in the land may vanish overnight into Institutions for the Treatment of the Ideologically Unsound, and it will rest with the expert gaolers to say when (if ever) they are to re-emerge. But it will not be persecution. Even if the treatment is painful, even if it is life-long, even if it is fatal, that will be only a regrettable accident; the intention was purely therapeutic. . . . But because they are "treatment," not punishment, they can be criticized only by fellow-experts and on technical grounds, never by men as men and on grounds of justice.[30]

Thus, limiting government's power will necessarily be in tension with those who speak of or act in the name of civil liberties but who also support the state's authority and responsibility for solving all the social problems of the day.

The point is that, in the process of seeking perhaps even worthy goals, the foundational principles of freedom are being destroyed in America. Playwright Robert Bolt poses the dilemma in *A Man for All Seasons:*

> SIR THOMAS MOORE: Yes. What would you do? Cut a great road through the law to get after the Devil?
>
> ROPER: I'd cut down every law in England to do that!
>
> SIR THOMAS MOORE: . . . Oh? . . . And when the last law was down, and the Devil turned round on you—where would you hide, Roper, the laws all being flat? . . . This country's planted thick with laws from coast to coast—man's laws, not God's—and if you cut them down . . . d'you really think you could stand upright in the winds that would blow then? . . . Yes, I'd give the Devil benefit of law, for my own safety's sake.[31]

Sir Thomas Moore's logic applies as well when the "Devil" is racism, bigotry, or personal autonomy. America is currently cutting great roads through its very Judeo-Christian foundations to get after its modern devils, and this is the heart of the problem.

TO JUDGE RIGHT AND WRONG

Some have asserted that every generation has had its devils and that each has appeared overwhelming. Yet, the present fire storm of change is different.

For almost 2,000 years, humanity has had a basis upon which to formulate solutions to the pressing problems of the day. Judeo-Christian principles provide a unified view of truth. Its absolutes do not vary according to circumstances and political norms. As historian Paul Johnson notes, the "primary purpose of Christianity is not to create dynamic societies . . . but to enable individuals to achieve liberation and maturity in a specific and moral sense. It does not accept conventional yardsticks and terrestrial judgments."[32] Against this truth, citizens— Christians or otherwise—could judge the right or wrong of their decisions, individually and collectively.

Christianity, then, provides the basis for both self-correction and value systems by which to limit the actions of government. Johnson writes:

> The nature of Christianity gave Europe a flexible framework of intellectual and moral concepts, and enabled it to accommodate itself to eco-

nomic and technological change, and seize each new opportunity as it arose. . . .

[Christianity was] designed to . . . set targets and standards, raise aspirations, to educate, stimulate and inspire. Its strength lies in its just estimate of man as a fallible creature with immortal longings. Its outstanding moral merit is to invest the individual with a conscience, and bid him follow it. . . . and it is the Christian conscience which has destroyed the institutional tyrannies Christianity itself has created—the self-correcting mechanism at work. The notions of political and economic freedom both spring from the workings of the Christian conscience as a historical force; and it is thus no accident that all the implantations of freedom throughout the world have ultimately a Christian origin.[33]

In America today, these Judeo-Christian principles, the touchstone of truth and the basis for judgment, have been rejected. The pragmatism motivating today's solutions may create the tyranny in face of tomorrow's problems, but there will be no standard with which to judge that tyranny as morally wrong. There will be no vehicle to establish the truth.

Without Judeo-Christian foundations, individual conscience is invalidated as a social norm. There is no longer a basis for challenging institutional tyrannies and the "compulsory society."

To be sure, history is replete with totalitarian excesses as well as misdeeds performed in the name of Christianity. Yet, Johnson continues:

[M]ankind without Christianity conjures up a dismal prospect. The record of mankind with Christianity is daunting enough, as we have seen. The dynamism it has unleashed has brought massacre and torture, intolerance and destructive pride on a huge scale, for there is a cruel and pitiless nature in man which is sometimes impervious to Christian restraints and encouragements. But without these restraints, bereft of these encouragements, how much more horrific the history of these last 2,000 years must have been! Christianity has not made man secure or happy or even dignified. But it supplies a hope. It is a civilizing agent. It helps to cage the beast. . . . In the last generation, with public Christianity in headlong retreat, we have caught our first, distant view of a de-Christianized world, and it is not encouraging. We know that Christian insistence on man's potentiality for good is often disappointed; but we are also learning that man's capacity for evil is almost limitless—is limited, indeed, only by his own expanding reach.[34]

The view of a "de-Christianized world" is no longer distant. America is hastily recreating its culture, one that is based upon man without God. Christianity is being rejected. The new American god is our personal and collective "rights," and it is replacing the Judeo-Christian God and His demand for moral absolutes.

IT IS HAPPENING HERE

Western societies, therefore, face the obliteration of an entire value system going back nearly two thousand years. As James Dobson has written: "Traditional Judeo-Christian values literally hang in the balance [in America]. They can be 'forgotten' in a single generation if they are not taught to children and teenagers. That loss of spiritual consciousness has already occurred in Great Britain . . . [where only 4 percent attend church]! A generation of young people is growing up with no memory of the Christian faith. . . . It could happen here if we don't defend what we believe."[35]

3

JUDEO-CHRISTIAN PRINCIPLES

*R*ejecting the transcendental truth given to us by Judeo-Christianity is tantamount to committing national suicide. A secular state cannot—as we see in our present cultural crisis—cultivate virtue.

Indeed, the opposite takes place, as Chuck Colson observes: "In his classic novel, *The Brothers Karamazov,* the nineteenth-century Russian novelist Dostoyevsky asked, essentially, 'Can man be good without God?'. In every age, the answer has been no. Without a restraining influence on their nature, men will destroy themselves."[1]

To preserve true freedom basic Judeo-Christian principles must be restored and practiced. Although ridiculed today, Judeo-Christian theism established a system of presuppositions and principles that ably provided both boundaries and freedom for Western societies.

From the acknowledgment that Judeo-Christian absolutes are a source of objective norms, however, it does not automatically follow (as some may assume) that such norms should be enforced through any state mechanisms (such as governmental edict, legislation, and so on). To the contrary, if such absolutes are practiced consistently by those people who advocate them, then, by the principle of cultural absorption, they will serve society well.

A BASIC SOURCE

Our world is, of course, structured by ideas. Our presuppositions and ideas create the worldviews through which we evaluate reality. This was true of all those who came before us, including those who established the structures that embodied the Judeo-Christian principles under which many still live their lives.

Judeo-Christian theism includes a unified view of truth. Its principles include absolutes that do not vary according to circumstances and which appropriately govern the actions of people as they respond to constantly changing conditions.

A qualifying statement is appropriate here. Although Judeo-Christian principles represent absolute norms, they have never been applied perfectly because people, being fallen, have never carried them out perfectly. However, when these principles have been administered with some consistency, they have nonetheless brought about positive results. This is evident, as we have seen, with the freedoms that were established in the United States and other countries.[2]

Of course, that raises important questions. For example, to what extent are we now living on moral capital accumulated over many centuries but no longer being replenished? To what extent is this capital already severely depleted?

We are told daily by advertisers, public institutions, planners, and other purveyors of popular wisdom that the world, as people become more "politically correct," is an increasingly better place to live. In other words, "consume," acquire material things, conform to a uniform way of thinking, and satisfaction will come. This, however, belies the everyday intimidation, oppression, tragedies, and terror that surround our otherwise "happy" lives.

Because Judeo-Christian principles are important to the operation of free societies, we will now examine some basic premises of this theistic system. Keep in mind that, being fallen, no one practices these principles perfectly. However, as noted, if practiced with at least some consistency, they bring about positive results.

CREATEDNESS AND *IMAGO DEI*

Judeo-Christian theism first posits that all people are *created* in the image of God (or *imago Dei*). The concept of people made in the image of God can be summarized by saying that people, like God, have personhood, a measure of self-transcendence, intelligence, morality, love, and creativity. This, of course, raises people, contrary to much contemporary environmentalist thinking and much non-Christian theology, above plant and animal creations.

Being created in God's image means that people reflect the Creator. They demonstrate the characteristics of God. That affords people the greatest dignity and worth. It also means that people, instead of being one-dimensional machine-entities, are three-dimensional body, soul, and spirit beings.

THE EXALTED INDIVIDUAL

That brings us to one of the major premises of all Judeo-Christian social and political thinking: the concept of the *exalted individual*. The concept manifests itself clearly in Judeo-Christian theology and in the dichotomy of creature/Creator. The exalted individual has dignity and worth. That exalted status is only derived from an exalted Creator.

When the apostle John wrote that "God so loved the world, that He gave His only begotten Son,"[3] he illustrated the fundamentally "sacrificial" character of divine love. This is the essential element of *agape:* it is *entirely selfless.* Professor Glenn Tinder observes:

> If one could love others without judging them, asking anything of them, or thinking of one's own needs, one would meet the Christian standard. Obviously, no one can. Many of us can meet the requirements of friendship or erotic love, but *agape* is beyond us all. It is not a love toward which we are naturally inclined or for which we have natural capacities. Yet, it is not something exclusively divine, like omnipotence, which human beings would be presumptuous to emulate. In fact, it is demanded of us. *Agape* is the core of Christian morality.[4]

Of course, the nature of *agape* stands out starkly against the background of contemporary social existence. Although *agape* receives much lip service, it is scarcely practiced. To the contrary, present-day societies throughout the world are judgmental, are self-serving, and encourage a focus on self-interest. *Agape,* however, means refusing to indulge in such practices.

The exalted individual, as it relates to createdness, is best exemplified, of course, in Jesus Christ. Speaking of Jesus Christ's resurrection, the Bible indicates that "He is the image of the invisible God, the firstborn over all creation."[5] And, concerning people, the Bible states: "Therefore, if anyone is in Christ, he is a new creation."[6]

When Christians speak of the exalted individual, phrases such as "the dignity of the individual" and "the infinite value of the human being" are often used. However, because contemporary society has lost the concept of *createdness*, these terms are trivialized and no longer evoke the mystery and importance of their meaning.[7]

However, if the Christian concept of the exalted individual is taken seriously, then people are seen as possessing great value and worth. People, as such, may no longer be treated as "throwaways," or expendable. The Christian concept of the exalted individual, then, places an absolute value on life.

> *O*nce Western culture began diminishing Christian principles of the Creator/creature relationship and the concept of the exalted individual, the worth and dignity of people correspondingly began to diminish.

Also, Professor Tinder writes, "the concept of the exalted individual implies that governments—indeed, all persons who wield power—must treat individuals with care." He continues: "This can mean various things—for example, that individuals are to be fed and sheltered when they are destitute, listened to when they speak, or merely left alone so long as they don't break the law and fairly tried if they do. But however variously care may be defined, it always means that human beings are not to be treated like the things we use and discard or just leave lying about. They deserve attention."[8]

This Christian criterion demands that the state practice certain standards. *Equality* is one of them. "No one, then, belongs at the bottom, enslaved, irremediably poor, consigned to silence; this is equality. This points to another standard: that no one should be left outside, an alien and a barbarian."[9]

46

This Judeo-Christian principle of *equality* was powerfully expressed by Paul: "There is neither Jew nor Greek, slave nor free, male nor female, for you are all one in Christ Jesus."[10]

Once Western culture began diminishing Judeo-Christian principles of the Creator/creature relationship and the concept of the exalted individual, the worth and dignity of people correspondingly began to diminish. In contemporary society people are often valued as consumers to be manipulated and formed into the images desired by the advertising industry. Devaluation is also reflected in the denigration of human life through abortion, infanticide, euthanasia, and "physician-assisted" suicide. Basic human dignity is disregarded, as pieces of aborted babies are injected into the brains of Parkinson sufferers, the remains of the babies then being hauled off in garbage bags to the toilet or to incinerators.

DEVALUATION FACTORS

The loss of the Judeo-Christian concepts of the created and exalted qualities of humankind ultimately results in the de-deification of God.

First, science, redefined to exclude any concept of a Creator or intelligent design, became not just inherently secularistic but also a potent *secularizing force.* Modern science does not resemble the presuppositions of the science practiced by Newton, Pascal, and others. To the contrary, modern science and the so-called death of God movement are symbiotic. As Lucien Goldman notes, the death-of-God phenomenon is "related to the most important scientific conquest of the age, the discovery of infinite geometric space, and counterposes the silence of God to it. God does not speak any more in the space of rational science, because in order to elaborate that space, man had to renounce every ethical norm."[11] In fact, any mention of God is generally suppressed in modern science or even in the classroom, because this discipline has excluded all possibility of divine intervention in a universe supposedly governed by natural laws.[12]

Using this naturalistic philosophy, science postulated secular interpretations of natural events and interruptions in natural laws and substituted them for religious interpretations. If these secular interpretations could not *disprove* God, they at least were attempts to restrict the Creator's realm.

Second, certain philosophies that attempted to discredit Judeo-Christian theism had a great impact initially on major social institutions and secondarily on the general populace. These were the philosophies of Friedrich Nietzsche, Karl Marx, Sigmund Freud, Charles Darwin, and others.

Nietzsche's thinking, for example, was grounded in a bitter repudiation of Christianity. He argued strenuously against the Christian standard of love and the concept that every human being deserves respect. Instead of equality and exalted individuals, Nietzsche argued for the "super man" or superhumans who should rule over inferior ones. The rise of Nazism later reflected this philosophy.

Marx, bitterly anti-Christian, argued for the entire transformation of human life and nature. He sought superstatus for the mass proletariat. This superstatus was to be reflected in the state's ownership of everything.

Freud repudiated the Christian concept of sin and theorized that all human disorders are scientifically explicable and capable of cure by way of therapy. "The soul was thus severed from God (for Freud, a childish illusion) and placed in the province of human understanding and action."[13]

Finally, Darwin's theory of evolution, as accepted and propounded by modern science and philosophy, completed the secularization of the Western world. Evolution theorizes that everything is the product of impersonal natural processes. From that point, it becomes easy to posit the silence and nonexistence of God.

However, if God is silent or nonexistent there is no objective standard to measure worth and dignity for the individual's place in the universe. This logically leads to people being the product of impersonal forces, merely a part of the workings of "nature," without purpose, souls, or absolutes.

Thus the secular state, as a product of evolution and all that follows from it, is antihuman. This is exhibited in two ways, according to James Hitchcock.

> One regards man as totally insignificant, a mere speck in a vast universe. At various times, mechanistic philosophies have proposed that man lacks any spiritual dimension and is merely a kind of advanced automaton. In recent times this anti-humanism has often predicted that man will be "replaced" by robots, computers, and other machines which will render him obsolete. The other form of anti-humanism dwells on all that is sordid, animalistic, and degraded in human existence, not to seek to elevate it but to proclaim in triumph, "See! Man has a high opinion of himself, but when you strip away the trappings, this is what he is."[14]

ABSOLUTES

Judeo-Christian theism teaches that an absolute standard exists by which all moral judgments must be measured. The character of the Judeo-Christian God (love, mercy, and justice) is the absolute standard.

Furthermore, Christians and Jews hold that God has revealed His character in the various laws or principles expressed in the Old and New Testaments of the Bible—such as the Ten Commandments, the Sermon on the Mount, and the apostle Paul's ethical teaching. In these and in many other ways, the Creator has expressed His character to His creatures. There is, therefore, a detailed standard of right and wrong, and people who want to know it can do so.

The spurning of absolutes also accompanied the contemporary repudiation of the Judeo-Christian God. Instead of absolutes, Western culture now generally holds to a system of moral relativism, which means that an idea or action must be judged true or false according to its utility in a particular situation. Relativism, then, is based on the premise that there is no absolute truth.

> *odern thinkers [who refuse to explain the inhumanity of man in terms of the Fall] have no real answer to the fact that the . . . noble attributes of people are undercut by selfishness, cruelty, and vice.*

This philosophy is reflected in such current applications as situational ethics and values clarification. Values clarification takes hypothetical moral dilemmas and provides solutions on the basis of what is expedient rather than what is right. What works today in one situation may not work tomorrow in another. Everything is arbitrary, depending on its usefulness. This ethical process is currently taught in much of American public education. Teachers are compelled to ask their relativistic-oriented students only, "What would have been a *better* choice?"

Relativism has been an important part of twentieth-century philosophy and politics. In *Mein Kampf,* for example, Adolf Hitler writes that "everything must be examined from this point of view and used or rejected according to its utility."[15]

Thus, we have come to the point in Western culture where the only absolute is that "there are no absolutes." As such, modern people no longer have any meaningful understanding of right and wrong.

This philosophy is devastating for young people, in particular. It may explain the hopelessness and high rate of suicide among youth in Western societies. It also creates a society in which people believe that they can bring about their moral vision at any price. Joseph Stalin, for example, held a similar philosophy. He once remarked that in order to make his omelette he would have to break a few eggs. By this, Stalin meant killing and maiming people and forcing them into concentration camps to achieve the rulership of the working class.

On the other hand, the Judeo-Christian system of absolutes demands accountability. People are held accountable to the standards of the Creator. Accountability and responsibility are the result of a clear understanding of the dignity of people and the sovereignty of God.

The destruction of the absolute principle of accountability to the Creator has led, in many respects, to the birth of the modern state. Modern states are accountable to no absolutes. Without those absolutes, any state can become authoritarian and even totalitarian. In the end, that means that the state is the *only* absolute.

THE FALL

Judeo-Christian theism explains the inhumanity of man in terms of the Fall. Many modern thinkers deride this concept and argue that people are basically good. However, such thinkers have no real answer to the fact that the supposedly noble attributes of people are undercut by selfishness, cruelty, and vice. As a consequence, many modern people, deeply aware of their flaws, oftentimes see themselves and their actions as absurd and futile. In the words of Albert Camus: "I proclaim that I believe in nothing and that everything is absurd."[16]

The paradox that human beings are exalted—possessing great worth and dignity—and yet are morally degraded is a difficult proposition for many to accept. Most secular philosophies hold that, although some people are "bad," most people are morally upright and good. However, this philosophy is antithetical to true Christianity, which holds that no one is inherently good because of the taint of the Fall and sin. It is the discussion of "sin" that often causes the most problems. Glenn Tinder writes:

> Nothing in Christian doctrine so offends people today as the stress on sin. It is morbid and self-destructive, supposedly, to depreciate ourselves in this way. Yet the Christian view is not implausible. The twentieth century, not to speak of earlier ages (often assumed to be more barbaric), has displayed human evil in extravagant forms. Wars and massacres, systematic torture and internment in concentration camps,

have become everyday occurrences in the decades since 1914. Even in the most civilized societies subtle forms of callousness and cruelty prevail through capitalist and bureaucratic institutions. Thus, our own experience indicates that we should not casually dismiss the Christian concept of sin.[17]

The Christian doctrine of sin holds that people's evil tendencies are not problems that may rationally be comprehended or deliberately solved. As such, this concept of sin indicates that people are inclined toward evil and that this inclination is primarily for people to exalt themselves rather than allowing themselves to be exalted by God. As Professor Tinder writes: "We exalt ourselves in a variety of ways: for example, by power, trying to control all the things and people around us; by greed, accumulating an inequitable portion of the material goods of the world; by self-righteousness, claiming to be wholly virtuous; and so forth."[18]

However, there is an irony to the nature of sin. "In trying to ascend, we fall. The reason is not hard to understand. We are exalted by God; in declaring our independence from God, we cast ourselves down. . . . By sin we cast ourselves into a degraded sphere of existence, a sphere Christians often call 'the world.'"[19]

The political repercussions from the loss of Judeo-Christian absolutes are . . . profound and disturbing. With the loss of absolutes, all logical grounds for attributing an ultimate and immeasurable dignity to every person . . . disappears.

In sin, then, is the way human beings relate to the world. People "look at one another as objects; they manipulate, mutilate, and kill one another. . . . [T]hey continually depersonalize themselves and others. They behave as inhabitants of the world they have sinfully formed rather than of the earth created by God."[20]

In the atoning work of Jesus Christ, Christianity provides the answer to what most see as the futility of life. The fatal infection is cured, even though some pain remains. We will never reach perfection in this life. The believer, then, needs the guidance of the Creator's absolute laws along with the Spirit's power, in order to overcome his fallen nature.

The proposition that people are inherently good, as noted above, can lead to great deceptions. We must develop a healthy skepticism and be careful not to follow the Pied Pipers of "if it feels good" or tolerance of others' behavior (even if these come in the guise of Christianity) without a proper understanding of the Fall and redemption. Otherwise, we will fall prey to the mistakes of past generations. Those mistakes have resulted in, for example, the Holocaust, the atrocities of Joseph Stalin, the ethnic cleansing in Yugoslavia, and the currently rising nationalism of a unified Germany.

POLITICAL CONSEQUENCES

The political repercussions from the loss of Judeo-Christian absolutes are both profound and disturbing. With the loss of absolutes, all logical grounds for attributing an ultimate and immeasurable dignity to every person, regardless of character, disappears. Glenn Tinder claims, "Some people may gain dignity from their achievements in art, literature, or politics, but the notion that all people without exception—the most base, the most destructive, the most repellent—have equal claims on our respect becomes as absurd as would be the claim that all automobiles or all horses are of equal excellence."[21]

As a consequence, society is defined in terms of the "struggle for the fittest," where the weak and failing, if they are to have any rights at all, exact from the strong a deference that they do not logically deserve. Clearly, then, if "the principle of personal dignity disappears, the kind of political order we are used to—one structured by standards such as liberty for all human beings and equality under the law—becomes indefensible."[22]

This fact was recognized by Francis Crick. An avowed atheist, Crick, along with James D. Watson, discovered the DNA code. In a speech made in March 1971, Crick said:

> [Y]ou must realize that much of the political thinking of this country is very difficult to justify biologically. It was valid to say in the period of the American Revolution, when people were oppressed by priests and kings, that all men were created equal. But it doesn't have biological validity. It may have some mystical validity in a religious context, but . . . [it's] not only biologically not true, it's also biologically undesirable. . . . We all know, I think, or are beginning to realize, that the future is in our own hands, that we can, to some extent, do what we want.[23]

IDOLS

Nietzsche argued convincingly that a society cannot give up the Christian God and go on as before. The loss of the Christian God means also that a society will lose Judeo-Christian morality, absolutes, and the exaltedness of people. In the process, however, a vacuum is created. And, of course, the question becomes: who or what will fill the vacuum?

Fyodor Dostoyevsky asserted in his writings that people cannot live without worshiping "something." God made us to seek after Him. A person is inherently religious, whether he be a believer, an agnostic, or an atheist.

Primitive man bowed before stone and wooden representations of gods and demons. The Greeks and Romans personalized their gods so that they could manipulate them. Thus, their gods became reflections of the humans who made incantations to them. These gods were mere extensions of human beings, or what would be called "amplified humanity." Humanity has a long history of worshiping its "extensions."

The Hebrews, and later the Christians, broke with tradition and proclaimed that a transcendent God existed. This God was not a mere extension of humanity or the creation of humanity. This God was viewed as the Creator of the universe and one who disdained gods made in the image of their people. As the source of existence, He demanded tribute be paid to God alone. The Hebrew God went so far as to restrict the building of altars of hewn stone, lest they be tainted by human hands and become extensions of people. Later in history, the apostle Paul, drawing upon Jesus Christ's teachings, took this principle a step further in proclaiming that we are temples of God Himself.

Jesus Christ confounded the elders of Israel, announcing that God must be worshiped in Spirit and truth and would be found *in* the believer. Imprinted by the *imago Dei* and indwelt by the Spirit, as was intended in the beginning (but negated by the Fall), Christians would now embody the essence of true religion.

It is curious, then, that modern society, with its break with the Judeo-Christian concept of God, inevitably turns to the idolatry of primitive peoples. Although those who deny God will still worship an idol, that idol is not necessarily a wooden or metal figure. For example, "[i]n our time we have seen ideologies, groups, and leaders receive divine honors. People proud of their critical and discerning spirit have rejected Christ and bowed down before Hitler, Stalin, Mao or some other secular saviour."[24]

Unfortunately, when disrespect for individuals is combined with political idolatry, the results can be disastrous. Professor Tinder says:

Both the logical and emotional foundations of political decency are destroyed. Equality becomes nonsensical and breaks down under attack from one or another human god. Consider Lenin: as a Marxist, and like Marx an exponent of equality, under the pressures of revolution he denied equality in principle—except as an ultimate goal—and so systematically nullified it in practice as to become the founder of modern totalitarianism.[25]

Under such political idolatry, freedom vanishes. When the state becomes god, it becomes difficult to protect freedom since there is no God to justify and sanctify protection of the individual. In such an instance, when society is ruled by a state-god, as Dostoyevsky recognized, *everything may be permitted.* And although the state may proclaim good intentions for equality and liberty, there is always a gap between intentions and results. Oppression is usually the final consequence.

MAN DISAPPEARS

Secularism, based upon an impersonal genesis without the intervention of the Creator, can give no real explanation of personality. In a very real sense, the ultimate question for all generations is "Who am I?"

When I look at the "I" that is me and then look around to those who face me and are also humans, one thing is immediately obvious: Humans possess attributes the rest of creation lacks. That is to say, people have a conscience, a soul, an imagination, and an otherwise nonmaterial side to them. Francis Schaeffer puts it well: "The assumption of an impersonal beginning cannot adequately explain the personal beings we see around us; and when men try to explain man on the basis of an original impersonal, *man soon disappears.*"[26]

Materialistic philosophy relieves one of responsibility to anyone—whether it be God or humans. Atoms have no morals. If atoms are humanity's progenitor, then people are not so much *im*moral as *a*moral. Once this is the accepted philosophy of a society and its government, the implications can be grave.

Secularistic philosophies, therefore, provide no sure foundation upon which to base freedom, or for that matter, upon which to secure oneself against tyranny. Secularism, moreover, as it erases all traces of Judeo-Christianity from society, poses a series of life-threatening crisis points that seem insurmountable. To these crisis points we now turn.

PART TWO

CRISIS
POINTS

*I*n the city of man, there is no moral
consensus, and without a moral
consensus there can be no law. Chairman
Mao expressed the alternative well: in his
view, morality begins at the muzzle of a
gun.

CHUCK COLSON

4

THE NEW
CONCENTRATION
CAMPS

*F*or religious people and those with a traditional moral view, the world is becoming a smaller and smaller place each passing day. Indeed, a type of concentration camp is being built to house such deviants. This time, however, these concentration camps are being erected with words and social ostracism.

This is illustrated by recent events and the growth of the political correctness movement. As a consequence, there is an icy chill in the air and people are afraid to act and speak as before.

THE NEW LEADERS

American colleges and universities are training the youth of today to be tomorrow's leaders. With the current political atmosphere, however, our future leaders will be motivated by impulses different than their forebears.

For example, a sophomore at the University of Connecticut placed a sign on her dormitory room listing "people who are shot on sight." Among those named were "preppies," "bimbos," "men without chest hair," and "homos." The University of Connecticut's gay community had the student brought up on charges of violating the university's student behavior code. The code, subsequently rewritten, prohibited "posting or advertising publicly offensive, indecent or abusive matter concerning persons . . . and making personal slurs or epithets based on race, sex, ethnic origin, disability, religion or sexual orientation."

The student was found guilty of violating the behavior code and was ordered by the university to move off-campus and was forbidden to enter any of the university dormitories or cafeterias.[1]

Other examples of such codes may be found in universities and colleges throughout the United States. In a well-publicized case at the University of Michigan, a graduate student was charged with violating the school's Discrimination and Discriminatory Harassment of Students in the University Environment Policy for stating during class "his belief that homosexuality was a 'disease' and that he intended to develop a counseling plan for changing gay clients to straight."[2]

At another college, "three students were punished under the school's code for calling the assistant director of campus ministry a 'feminazi' and a sufferer of 'penis envy' in their independently published newspaper."[3]

A campus minister was threatened with removal of his ministry from the university unless he signed a statement pledging that he would not discriminate against homosexuals. The minister readily agreed not to discriminate because it was his hope that homosexual students *would* seek his help through his ministry. Nonetheless, the minister was threatened with banishment from the campus because he would not also agree to stop saying that he viewed homosexuality as a sin.

Incidents are not limited to violations of actual university "speech codes." At Harvard University, dining hall employees were denounced by the dean for having a back-to-the-fifties party because segregation still existed at that time in history.[4]

An editor of a UCLA newspaper was suspended for publishing a cartoon satirizing affirmative action in the hiring of minorities. Following the event, a student columnist for the *Daily Sundial,* a California State University paper, was suspended from his editorial position for publishing without permission an article that criticized UCLA officials for their action.[5]

"FAHRENHEIT 451"

The "unacceptable" action in the foregoing instances was that the speech or action involved was not "politically correct."

The doctrine of "political correctness," or "PC," is now in full force in America. Although it originated on America's college and university campuses, the PC movement is spreading through the mass media and into the workplaces, churches, public schools, and social gatherings of America. Its result has been discrimination and censorship of both speech and speech-related behavior.

Ostensibly, the goal of political correctness is to eliminate prejudice. However, under the PC agenda, it is not, as *Newsweek* magazine reports, "enough for a student to refrain from insulting homosexuals or other minorities. He or she would be expected to 'affirm' their presence on campus and study their literature and culture alongside that of Plato, Shakespeare and Locke. This agenda is broadly shared by most organizations of minority students, feminists and gays."[6]

This is the crux of the problem. The elimination of prejudice is a worthy goal. But the motivation for eliminating prejudice, so far as speech is concerned, must be *internal*. When the *state* changes language and suppresses speech to accommodate its political agenda, freedom is imperiled.

In the 1979 afterword to his book *Fahrenheit 451*, Ray Bradbury wrote:

> The point is obvious. There is more than one way to burn a book. And the world is full of people running about with lit matches. Every minority, be it Baptist/Unitarian, Irish/Italian/Octogenarian/Zen Buddhist, Zionist/Seventh-Day Adventist, Women's Lib/Republican, Mattachine/Four Square Gospel feels it has the will, the right, the duty to douse the kerosene, light the fuse. . . . Fire-Captain Beatty, in my novel *Fahrenheit 451*, described how the books were burned first by minorities, each ripping a page or a paragraph from this book, then that, until the day when the books were empty and the minds shut and the libraries closed forever.[7]

The temperature at which books burn is 451 degrees Fahrenheit. It was Ray Bradbury's prediction that it would be books that future societies would burn in order to conceal the truth. However, with political correctness, contemporary society is attempting to suppress *ideas* before they can be spoken or written. Therefore, in the end, the crucial question concerns those who are politically "incorrect"—those who intentionally or unintentionally fail to conform to the "community spirit."

Society should be an even playing field for each and every group to make and change laws. As long as there is a balanced perspective and tolerance for the expression of all views, diversity and thus freedom survive. However, once any group takes the helm of political power to the exclusion of others—whether they carry a swastika, hammer and sickle, peace symbol, Bible, or a pink triangle—then, as we have seen in the past, the nonconformists become outcasts and outlaws.

Although the PC movement may have begun in the good faith belief that speech restrictions would foster equality for minorities and oppressed groups, the end result has largely been the suppression of free speech.

Even though courts have ruled some hate speech codes and hate crimes laws unconstitutional,[8] PC continues virtually unabated on both a formal and informal basis. For example, even though the University of Michigan's hate speech code was declared unconstitutional, many university codes are still in place (even though the constitutional validity of such regulations is uncertain), or the speech codes are being revised so as to pass constitutional muster.

A controversy in the music industry provides a clear example of the vitality and informal power of PC:

[Steve] Vaus's song "We Must Take America Back," a response to deteriorating conditions in his adopted hometown of San Diego, was pulled from the airwaves in late July 1992 by RCA, which had signed a contract with Vaus for the rights to his ten-song album less than one month before. RCA was initially enthusiastic about the tune, which had risen to the top of call-in request charts in cities around the United States following its release last spring. But objections from programmers at major radio stations to the "controversial philosophical content" of the song [a call for citizen action] led RCA to dump Vaus' album, cancel his contract, and prevent him from rereleasing or even recording his material for five years. . . .

[Vaus asks:] "Since when does a record company allow anyone to dictate the content of its releases? . . . Ice-T's singing about killing cops, and Sister Souljah's rapping for genocide, and I can't sing about God and country?"

As this episode makes clear, Congress and criminals are not to be criticized, but the violence and obscenity advocated by "artists" like Ice-T and Sister Souljah, as well as 2 Live Crew, Public Enemy, Madonna, and most recently 2Pac, are protected under the First Amendment. From 2 Live Crew's graphically and misogynously sexual 1990 album *As Nasty As They Wanna Be* to Public Enemy's 1991 video for the rap "By the Time I Get to Arizona," which depicted the shooting and poisoning of public officials who declined to approve a public holiday honoring Martin Luther King, Jr.; from Madonna's fall 1992 release of the aptly named "Erotica" to Ice-T's infamous "Cop Killer," which Time Warner, the parent company of his record label *Sire,* pulled from his album *Body Count* only after Ice-T himself gave in to popular pressure —these examples of "creative expression" make any protest about the "controversial philosophical content" of Vaus's lyrics seem absurd. Indeed, in comparison to the words of "Soulja's Story" by rapper Tupac Amaru Shakur, known as 2Pac, Vaus's ditty is mere child's play. "Cops on my tail so I bail till I dodge 'em/They finally pull me over and I laugh/Remember Rodney King and I blast on his punk a—/Now I got a murder case." *These* lines, which incited one Ronald Howard to fatally shoot a state trooper who had pulled him over for a routine traffic stop near Victoria, Texas, last year, are controversial.[9]

"NEUTRAL" TERMINOLOGY

While criticism is growing concerning the merits of the PC movement, it was originally viewed as an ongoing impetus for making academic institutions more open, diverse, and egalitarian. The use of terms such as "Native American" instead of "Indian" or "African American" instead of "black" was offered to help combat prejudice by using people's chosen terms for identifying the groups to which they belonged.[10] As stated by one author, "Common courtesy dictates one should address people by the names they prefer."[11]

Further studies showed that gender-neutral language or references to prominent figures in casebooks and children's storybooks could make a difference in perceptions.[12] Thus, the use of "neutral" terminology was thought to positively affect the perceptions about the group referred to as well as other listeners.

> *An indivisible concept of free speech is the premise that words which are merely offensive may not be prohibited.*

The PC movement was ostensibly only an attempt to include all the elements of America's culture through manipulation of its common language. For example, expanding the university curriculum and magazine contents to include "multiculturalism" could arguably add to the enrichment of students and readers, especially those previously limited to studies based on European history. Educating people about the numerous components of society could, it was argued, only be beneficial in an increasingly diverse society and interconnected world.[13]

With this goal, so-called hate speech codes were adopted at universities across the country.[14] Numerous explanations could be found with what some consider the best of intentions. Many asserted that the codes were in response to a concern about the rising number of acts of violence and harassment that have been occurring on college campuses.[15]

Furthermore, the codes were justified on the grounds that racist speech "creates an intimidating, hostile, or demeaning environment" that "interfere[s] with an individual's academic efforts [and] participation in University sponsored extra-curricular activities."[16] Some proponents argued that racist speech caused discrete and serious harm to racial minorities and other victim groups.[17]

Finally, it appears that the adoption of racial harassment policies is often to affirm symbolically a university's commitment to tolerance and nondiscrimination.[18]

But something has gone wrong. Although some of the original intentions of the PC movement may have been worthy, the negative implications of the movement are far-reaching.

THE COURTS AND FREE SPEECH

As a critical element of a free society, free speech in a university setting is especially protected.[19] For example, Supreme Court Chief Justice Earl Warren once wrote:

> The essentiality of freedom in the community of American universities is almost self-evident. No one should underestimate the vital role in a democracy that is played by those who guide and train our youth. To impose any strait jacket upon the intellectual leaders in our colleges and universities would imperil the future of our Nation. . . . Teachers and students must always remain free to inquire, to study to gain new maturity and understanding; otherwise our civilization will stagnate and die.[20]

More recently, Justice William Brennan has written:

> Our Nation is deeply committed to safeguarding academic freedom, which is of transcendent value to all of us and not merely to the teachers concerned. That freedom is therefore a special concern of the First Amendment, which does not tolerate laws that cast a pall of orthodoxy over the classroom. . . . The classroom is peculiarly the "marketplace of ideas." The Nation's future depends upon leaders trained through wide exposure to that robust exchange of ideas which discovers truth "out of a multitude of tongues, [rather] than through any kind of authoritative selection."[21]

Thus, the United States Supreme Court has repeatedly prohibited public schools from suppressing the expression of certain types of views even if they were found to be offensive to some.[22]

An indivisible concept of free speech is the premise that words which are merely offensive may not be prohibited.[23] For example, in striking down the Texas flag desecration laws, which received a good deal of national attention,[24] the Supreme Court stated: "If there is a bedrock principle underlying the First Amendment, it is that the government may not prohibit the expression of an idea simply because society finds the idea itself offensive or disagreeable."[25] After all, the Court said, "one man's vulgarity is another's lyric."[26]

In another case,[27] despite the city's restrictions otherwise, a Nazi march was permitted through a predominantly Jewish neighborhood where many Holocaust survivors lived. Although the march would have been offensive to most people, the Constitution and its free speech requirements made it necessary for the parade to proceed.

Finally, restrictions on speech may not be based on viewpoint. Under the Constitution, "the government may not allow the expression of views it finds acceptable while suppressing those views it finds less favorable."[28] For example, the Supreme Court affirmed a lower court decision to strike down an antipornography law that defined pornography as the "graphic sexually explicit subordination of women"[29] because it favored the view of men and women being equals in sexual relationships over the view of sexual subordination by men over women.

Thus, the very principles underlying political correctness violate the First Amendment. For example, although racist or sexist or "heterosexist" comments may stir emotions, these comments should not be suppressed by the state, especially when comments of an opposing view are permitted.

Unfortunately, despite the lip service of the Supreme Court concerning free speech, as a social movement political correctness continues to gain momentum.

STIFLING TRUTH

Perhaps the most serious threat posed by the PC movement is that it stifles the development of truth. Free speech is the best way to determine truth.[30] By allowing a free marketplace of ideas, open to even the most offensive ideas and expressions, the truth should ultimately triumph as long as an unrestricted marketplace is available.[31]

Speech codes and the PC movement destroy the free flow of ideas. Individuals are often afraid to speak up for fear of being ostracized or perhaps even being punished under some speech code. For example, many students fear going before a college speech tribunal because of possible career-jeopardizing punishment.[32] For example, it has been reported that a male Brown University sophomore was suspended from the university for four and a half years for leaving three vulgar messages on a female student's answering machine after a dispute.[33] As Benno Schmidt, Jr., president of Yale University, states:

> When offensiveness is ground for suppression, a lethal and utterly open-ended engine of censorship is loosed. Its impact will be felt not only by those whose speech is punished; the greater problem is the vastly greater number of speakers who will steer clear of possible punishment by steering clear of controversial or unpopular views. The chilling effects of vague powers to punish offensive speech are likely to be far more damaging to freedom of expression than the actual application of such rules.[34]

A CULTURE WHERE QUESTIONS ARE FORBIDDEN

Speech restrictions, therefore, are already having a serious adverse effect on the marketplace of ideas. A Wesleyan University student has written:

> These incidents and many others make it clear that student judicial boards have become increasingly politicized to punish those who dare to stray from the prevailing ideological hegemony. . . . The vagueness of the offenses and the possibility of ominous, complicated proceedings before the mock courts have created the desired air of uncertainty and intimidation, in writings by students, in oral presentations in class, in physical relationships, and in private dealings with another student who might report to the speech police.[35]

As a result, truth and freedom suffer. Indeed, commentators have noted that the new rules at universities are "fostering a decline in tolerance and a rise in intellectual intimidation."[36]

Regardless of actual speech code requirements, the mere threat of being rebuked can have a serious chilling effect even on classroom discussions. At George Mason University law school, students themselves launched a petition drive seeking to ban a particular word from all classrooms under all circumstances after a law professor illustrated a "discussion of hurtful speech that might merit litigation."[37] As one author has observed: "Law school professors report an enormous unwillingness among students even to argue hypothetically for the 'wrong' side in matters that touch upon [political correctness] because of a fear of being labeled an -*ist* of some sort: racist, sexist, heterosexist, classist, ableist."[38]

---

*A*t Harvard University, two professors stopped teaching a course on race relations after being accused of insensitivity . . . because one professor read from a plantation owner's diary without giving equal time to the recollections of a slave.

This "culture forbidding questions" is continuing.[39] The editor of a student paper at the University of Wisconsin at Milwaukee found students less willing to discuss frankly the school's code once it went into effect.[40] As Nat Hentoff recounts, a Brown University graduate student felt compelled to tell incoming students that "there are some things that are simply not discussed here."[41] In some cases, students are pressured into majoring in areas that are in accordance with their race and gender and other elements of their "background."[42]

The pressure to conform to "PCness" and thus limit the free flow of discussion in the classroom is not limited to students. At Harvard University, two professors stopped teaching a course on race relations after being accused of insensitivity, among other things, to African Americans because one professor read from a plantation owner's diary without giving equal time to the recollections of a slave.[43]

At the University of California at Santa Barbara, sexual harassment charges were filed against a professor who, in referring to the movement to call pets "animal companions," noted that women posing for *Penthouse* were not yet called "animal companions."[44]

EXTREMIST STEAM VALVES

Regulating speech creates resentment and resistance to consideration of the underlying issues. Further, censorship measures often have the effect of glorifying extremist speakers.[45] Attempts at suppression result in attention and publicity that otherwise would not have been garnered.

Studies have shown that governmental attempts to censor speech, for whatever reasons, often make the speech more appealing.[46] As one writer notes: "Advocates of hate speech regulations do not seem to realize that their own attempts to suppress speech increase public interest in the ideas they are trying to stamp out."[47]

This idea is validated by the extreme popularity of diverse radio and television speakers such as Rush Limbaugh, Howard Stern, and others. These act as steam valves in speaking for those who no longer dare to speak for themselves.[48]

UNDERGROUND THOUGHTS

With regard to the supposed beneficiaries of the PC movement and hate speech codes, such approaches are viewed as paternalistic by some. For example, some African-American scholars and activists have suggested that "an anti-racist speech policy may perpetuate a paternalistic view of minority groups, suggesting that they are incapable of defending themselves against biased expressions."[49] One minority commentator stated amazement at being "told that white folks have the moral character to shrug off insults and I do not."[50]

Another has commented that "politically correct" efforts insult minorities by efforts such as affirmative action, which can often make minorities feel they are only the "best minority applicant" instead of the "best applicant."[51]

Pressure from the PC movement also forces thoughts underground that are viewed as politically incorrect and removes a measurement on the true attitudes of society. Thus, it becomes difficult to predict to what extent racist attitudes, for example, pervade.

Some argue: "Racist speech can be used as a 'social thermometer' that allows us to 'register the presence of disease within the body politic.'"[52] Ideas that are seen as wrong and unjust, therefore, are much more difficult to respond to when they are not openly admitted.[53] Knowledge about the extent of racism may be of use in determining what some call the best "healing" measures, whether they be in the form of education, anti-discrimination laws, or more economic opportunities.[54] Past experience has shown that the public airing of racist comments has resulted in community efforts to redress the bigotry that underlies the expression.[55] The alternative is to pretend the sentiments do not exist, thus permitting them to fester and grow. Sooner or later, the underground tension erupts. Racial riots, such as those in Los Angeles in 1992, may at least partially be a manifestation of this.

As noted by an author discussing hate speech laws and codes, "by targeting the most superficial expressions of such deep-seated attitudes, the codes apply a band-aid to a problem requiring major surgery."[56] Generally, the democratic process works best when critical discourse is allowed. Group discussion allows the airing of concerns, which in turn helps to combat them.

Further, permitting racist or other negative or harmful speech actually helps strengthen tolerance and restraint. A society hesitant to overreact against provocations such as racist speech will be less quick to bypass moral standards in times of stress or danger.

Another concern raised by the PC movement is that it can lead to a subtle form of "mind control" by seeking to bestow certain virtues upon individuals by not permitting the development of others.

An example of this can be seen during the 1950s when people were quick to label fellow workers and friends as "Communists" in order to avoid being blacklisted. "Only a tolerant society can be counted on to refrain from the frenzied search for scapegoats so characteristic of human experience."[57] Both those imposing political correctness and those silenced will have to relearn the lesson of tolerating diverse or conflicting views in order to prevent a "McCarthy era."

MIND CONTROL

Another concern raised by the PC movement is that it can lead to a subtle form of "mind control" by seeking to bestow certain virtues upon individuals by not permitting the development of others. For example, the Ohio State University preamble states that "acceptance, appreciation of diversity, and respect for the rights of others must be institutional values for a major public university and are *values that it must impart to its students and to society as a whole.*"[58]

Further, the addition of hate speech codes at universities that already have codes of conduct prohibiting harassment, without defining it in terms of the victims, leads one to think the schools are attempting to coerce particular virtues rather than merely to maintain an atmosphere of civility.[59]

The application of such regulations provides the best evidence for the validity of such an argument. As stated by one author, "Sanctions seem to depend not so much on the speaker's civility (or lack of it) as on his or her political viewpoint. Moreover, rude speech is apparently perfectly acceptable as long as it does not betray wrongheaded ideas."[60]

Examples of speech that would or would not be prohibited were given by one advocate of hate speech regulations. They included: "anti-white speech by blacks would be permitted, but not anti-Semitic speech by blacks or whites. Zionism would be permitted only to the extent that it 'aris[es] out of the Jewish experience of persecution,' but not where it is a statement of white supremacy."[61] It seems that the extolling of virtues could be the only reason for such detailed and, in a sense, discriminatory examples.

WHO DECIDES WHAT SPEECH IS "POLITICALLY CORRECT"?

Although many people have some idea as to what comments would be derogatory or insulting to certain groups of individuals, acceptable language is forever changing. The difficulties in ascertaining "preferred" terminology can be seen by the entry in the *Dictionary of Cautionary Words and Phrases* for the term *Afro-American,* which contained the cautionary note, "Preferred by some, but not universally accepted."[62] Thus, someone who used the term *Afro-American* could be shunned for using a term not universally accepted by the people it describes.

Determining what terms are and are not acceptable is not the only problem. A similar issue involves the question of where the line should be drawn. There are obvious discrepancies in what can and cannot be said under hate speech codes.

Racist comments are not allowed by white individuals but may be permitted by black individuals. For example, the Whitney Museum's Biennial Exhibit in New York once featured this statement in cut-out letters two feet high: "In the rich man's house the only place to spit is in his face." Also, tags that visitors received in exchange for their admittance fee (which ostensibly must be worn as evidence that one's admission fee has been paid) contained fragments of the sentence "I can't imagine ever wanting to be white."[63] There is little doubt that substitution of the word "black" for "white" would have generated a response adverse enough to shut down the exhibition.

Under PC, may a man who holds pro-life views make negative comments about a woman who holds pro-abortion views? One could argue that his comments are aimed at the woman's view on abortion, while another could argue that his comments are sexist based.

What about a Black Muslim who disparages an African-American Baptist?

Another example includes the use of the word *community.* Once again, the *Dictionary of Cautionary Words and Phrases* contains a warning concerning the use of this word. "[The term *community*] implies a monolithic culture in which people act, think, and vote in the same way. Do not use, as in Asian, Hispanic, black, or gay community. Be more specific as to what the group is: e.g., black residents in a northside neighborhood."[64]

Moreover, some choices of words that were thought demeaning may actually be favored by some. For example, an article in the *New York Times* reported some gay rights activists preferred the term "queer" in that it was thought to be defiant and empowering.[65]

Examples taken to the extreme include the "politically correct" wording "hair disadvantaged" or "follicularly challenged," which means baldness, or the term "vertically challenged," which means short.[66] A deputy prosecutor in Hawaii was sanctioned for "sexist" remarks during a trial because he assumed a co-worker of a member of the jury pool was a "mailman."[67] This is not to downplay the importance of respecting the wishes of minority groups in their choice of descriptive words, but the examples above demonstrate some of the extremes of political correctness and its potential for abuse.

To be meaningful, freedom of speech must include freedom for all speech and not just the promulgation of one view as the only and correct one. "Our experience . . . informs us of a guiding principle—namely that no one group, and no one set of values, has a monopoly on truth."[68]

THE MEDIA AND "FUNDAMENTALISTS"

The bombing of the World Trade Center and the deaths of Branch Davidians and federal agents in Waco, Texas, gave ample fodder for the media to equate "cultists" with "fundamentalists" and lump them all together as lunatics who should be locked up or otherwise disposed of. Being a religious fundamentalist of any type means being politically incorrect.

The killing of a doctor in March of 1993 at a Pensacola abortion clinic was also an opportunity to assert once again that abortion protesters are dangerous. Anthony Lewis, a *New York Times* columnist, wrote that "most antiabortion activists" are "religious fanatics" who think "the end justifies any means."[69] As John Leo of *U.S. News & World Report* writes:

> The words "terrorists," "cultists" and "fanatics" rained down on all sides. These are words that the abortion-rights lobby pushes journalists to use, and they do. . . . Syndicated columnist Ellen Goodman . . . wrote that radical antiabortion groups like Operation Rescue and Rescue America have to be dealt with as domestic terrorists as deadly as the ones who blew up the World Trade Center and as fanatic as the cultists in Waco.[70]

As we witness the growing rejection of religion, and Christianity in particular, few could deny that the media has played an important role in the stigmatization of religion as evil. Given that the majority of those who control mainstream media in the United States are rigorously secular, it is no surprise that religion is being derided and removed from American public life. One commentator has suggested that secular liberals have, in part, contributed to religious radicalism itself: "Some religious people sense that they are 'being shut off from civic participation.'"[71]

Indeed, Christians are the only remaining people who may be publicly defamed with impunity. One apparent example involves the labels used by the media (and even the government) to describe Christians. One such label is "sectarian," a term that is hardly flattering, since one of its dictionary meanings is "a narrow or bigoted person." As Cornell professor Richard A. Baer, Jr., comments,

> [I]t is disturbing to note that the mass media regularly use the term to describe and label individual Americans and groups of Americans. Even more disturbing, however, is its use by the U.S. Supreme Court. Since roughly the end of World War II the highest tribunal of our land has used the term in a wide variety of cases as a synonym for the word *religious*.[72]

"[The term *sectarian*] is caste language," Baer continues, "a phrase that has been used throughout American history to keep the religious 'untouchables' in their proper place."[73]

> Just as ruling elites have used racial and sexual epithets to put down blacks and women, so they have used *sectarian* to exclude and marginalize those individuals and groups whose religious beliefs and practices did not correspond to their own vision of what was appropriate in the cultural marketplace.[74]

Labeling—and therefore dooming anything as politically incorrect —is extremely dangerous in a society that is controlled by the electronic media. The way the media shapes public opinion (even to the point of electing presidents) brings into question the entire concept of free speech. As Dr. Judith Reisman writes:

> Speech is "permitted" by a wealthy oligarchy that controls and directs a media monopoly through various techniques, one of which is censorship. . . . Through a successful public relations effort conducted by this corporate oligarchy, censored and controlled communications have been used to paralyze freedom of speech and of the press, causing these to become mere illusions, a part of a mythology the oligarchy strives to perpetuate.[75]

"SO WE CAN SPEAK LOUDER"

Throughout the history of our country, speech has been the springboard to freedom. Indeed, the United States was founded on the concept of freedom of religion, assembly, and speech.

The free expression of ideas was important, for example, to the women's suffrage movement. During the 1960s, the civil rights movement depended on free speech principles. Martin Luther King, Jr., and other civil rights champions spoke loudly and often, gathering others to support their causes. It was the principle of free expression that allowed those individuals to carry their message to the nation, even to those who found their message highly offensive and threatening to their values and way of life. Members of the civil rights movement were in danger of losing their jobs and, in some cases, their lives as they were equated with Communists, subversives, and criminals by government officials. Indeed, "[o]nly strong principles of free speech and association could—and did—protect the drive for desegregation."[76]

Because of this freedom of speech, blacks are gaining equal place and equal voice in the American marketplace of ideas. However, at some point those concepts were viewed as extreme or "incorrect."

Any restraint on speech holds the opportunity to endanger those who most need the ability to express their views. Thus, Aryeh Neier, a survivor of the Holocaust, decided to defend the American Civil Liberties Union's decision to fight for the rights of Nazis who wanted to march in a Jewish neighborhood; otherwise his free speech could be endangered as well. Aryeh Neier says:

> If the Nazis are free to speak, they may win converts. It is possible that they will win so many adherents that they will attain the power to abolish freedom and to destroy me. . . . The restraints that matter most to

me are those which ensure that I cannot be squashed by power, unnoticed by the rest of the world. If I am in danger, I want to cry out to my fellow Jews and to all those I may be able to enlist as my allies. I want to appeal to the world's sense of justice. I want restraints which prohibit those in power from interfering with my right to speak, my right to publish, or my right to gather with others who also feel threatened. Those in power must not be allowed to prevent us from assembling and joining our voices together so we can speak louder and make sure that we are heard.[77]

A more fitting example of the need to protect free speech cannot be found. The right to cry out for justice is too great and too necessary to prohibit it even for those who are most despised.

It may be true that certain forms of speech are spiteful, demeaning, and perhaps just plain ignorant. But expressions of such speech will undoubtedly do more to change minds than the repression of it. Many of the ideas that come forth may be discomforting, but the ideas of equal rights for minorities and allowing women to vote, to name but two, were concepts once considered taboo and wrong. America cannot endure if its citizens are unable to challenge the status quo.

Although many would argue that the PC movement is not an attempt to stifle the free exchange of ideas but only the attempt to be more courteous to those around one, the end result is *still* censorship. Political correctness and hate speech codes strike at the heart of the First Amendment. Time and time again, examples can be found of people afraid to speak up because of fear of reprisal. Individuals often feel it is best just to remain quiet. Their speech is, therefore, iced.

Thus, although the PC movement may have some laudable goals, the cost of achieving them in the manner the movement prescribes is too high. Suppressing speech, whether intentionally or unintentionally, is not the answer.

As American society continues its drive to be more politically correct, and as religion and other forms of expression that deviate from the socially accepted norm are increasingly deemed politically incorrect, we can only expect new concentration camps without actual walls. Those camps will be built on a form a paranoia where men and women are afraid to speak lest they be found to be insane in a world masquerading as the epitome of sanity.

5

UNCLE SAM'S CHILDREN

*T*he family is in trouble, even as lip service to "family values" is being paid to its importance from both the left and right of the political spectrum. Under the swirling current of this double-speak, the all-out attacks on the traditional family continue unabated.

What is new is the breadth and depth of the attack in the United States, a country that once prided itself on its family-oriented society. Unfortunately, the traditional family is not currently the preferred social unit it once was.

As a consequence of such open attack, the family unit in American life has unquestionably suffered. In addition, the entire social fabric of America is being torn apart as a result of deteriorating family life and the conditions that undermine care for our children.

The decline of the traditional family unit has been accompanied, and perhaps hastened, by the transference of duties (such as education, health, and welfare services) once provided and managed by the family to other institutions, primarily the state. The family, which is a critically important institution in shaping our children's minds, values, and behavior, has become in many instances merely the ward of the state.

Much concern has been voiced over the crisis in the American family. Little, however, has been done to facilitate a return to a family-oriented society. On the contrary, many government agencies, including the courts, have not only undermined the family but have also endorsed programs and policies antagonistic to the traditional family unit.

THE AUTONOMOUS FAMILY

Historically, the American family fared much differently than its modern counterpart. From its earliest beginnings, the importance of the autonomous family cannot be overstated. Indeed, most of the basic functions of society in the early days of America were carried out by independent families, not the state. Thus: "Family issues of marriage, divorce, children, inheritance, education, mutual support, and welfare were not questions for the new federal government. They were questions reserved to the states, where Christian conceptions of patriarchy, charity, and shared obligation and common law understandings of family and community governance could, and did, hold sway."[1]

> *But without the autonomous family and its permanent and insoluble lifetime commitments, democratic self-rule and ultimately civilized society will cease to exist.*

For the good of America, if for no other reason, concepts of "family" and "family rights" were well established in America's constitution and history. Moreover, the family was always viewed as important for moral and practical reasons. A court wrote in 1952:

The family is the basic unit of our society, the center of the personal affections that ennoble and enrich human life. It channels biological drives that might otherwise become socially destructive; it ensures the care and education of children in a stable environment; it establishes continuity from one generation to another; it nurtures and develops the individual initiative that distinguishes a free people.[2]

76

Today, however, the state is increasingly taking responsibility away from the family and, therefore, parents, for nurturing and developing the individual initiative that "distinguishes a free people." Perhaps even more significantly, many families are *giving* this responsibility to the state in exchange for materialistic manna, termed state "benefits."

No longer the unquestioned bedrock of American society, the autonomous family functioning under Judeo-Christian principles has given way to so-called organizational preferences, or voluntary groupings prompted by sexual orientation, convenience, and transitory desires. But without the autonomous family and its *permanent and insoluble lifetime commitments,* democratic self-rule and ultimately civilized society will cease to exist. Barbara DaFoe Whitehead makes this point in an article on the family:

> Increasingly, political principles of individual rights and choice shape our understanding of family commitment and solidarity. Family relationships are viewed not as permanent or binding but as *voluntary* and *easily terminable.* Moreover, the family loses its central importance as an institution in civil society, accomplishing certain social goals such as raising children and caring for its members, and becomes a means to achieving greater individual happiness—*a lifestyle choice.* . . .

> Yet the family serves as the seedbed for the virtues required by a liberal state. The family is responsible for teaching lessons of independence, self-restraint, responsibility, and right conduct, which are essential to a free, democratic society. If the family fails in these tasks, then the entire experiment in democratic self-rule is jeopardized.[3]

When viewed as nothing more than a "lifestyle choice," the concept of "family" will be defined by the agenda of the state to coincide with the spirit of the "new" age.

THE CHILD SAVERS

Radical critics of traditional society have long condemned the institution of the family and the claim of family rights.[4] The family, in their view, stands for and perpetuates narrow self-interest. If social equality is ever to be achieved, according to these critics, the traditional family must be abolished and, with it, the social classes supporting it.

They often argue that in place of child rearing by parents who lack training and a sense of communal responsibility, the state should intervene in child rearing on the basis of an egalitarian social agenda. Thus, by abolishing the traditional family, conditions of equality may be better perpetuated and the public interest better served.[5]

According to Thomas Fleming,

The first child protection laws were devised by well-meaning English statesmen who wished to save the lives of children. Beginning with Peel's Health and Morals of Apprentices Act (1802), Parliament passed a series of acts to protect working children. The first blow against family integrity was not struck by politicians who passed child protection statutes but by a social and economic system that drove mothers and children from the sanctuary of their homes, not into the marketplace but into the bowels of mines and factories.[6]

The American "Child Saving Movement" of the mid-1800s sought termination of parental rights without regard to the important difference between children who were poor and children who were neglected and/or delinquent. These advocates argued: "May not the natural parents, when unequal to the task of education or unworthy of it, be supplanted by the *parens patriae,* or common guardianship of the community?"[7]

Joining with the social workers and their progressive spirit, the "child savers" attacked the shield of natural parental rights and began the juvenile justice system: "'Parents could no longer shield themselves behind natural rights,' one early enthusiast said. Without a formal hearing or other consideration of due process, hundreds of thousands of American children would be seized by the Child Savers and incarcerated in reform or 'industrial' schools, all for 'the welfare of the child,' a lone actor in an individualistic world."[8]

The denial of the existence of natural parental rights largely obscured the real cause of child abuse, which was the demise of the intact, autonomous family.

From this position, "late 19th century proponents of mandatory state schooling, for example, ridiculed attention to the sacred rights and privileges of parents. Court decisions on mandatory attendance laws ruled that the principle of *parens patriae* took precedence over the rights of parents."[9]

By 1930, the "parenting state" had emerged and labeled "Uncle Sam's Child" as a human being "who belongs to the community almost as much as to the family, a 'new racial experiment,' and a citizen of a 'world predestinedly moving toward unity.'"[10]

Although the American family typified by Ozzie and Harriet Nelson and Ward and June Cleaver reappeared during the brief period from 1946–61,[11] its appearance was sustained, according to one commentator, only by America's distraction by the post-World War II economic boom and anti-Communist frenzy.[12] Allan Carson writes:

> This halcyon age collapsed in the 1960s . . . and the old trends and their parasitical "professions" came roaring back. Marriage rates tumbled while divorce rates soared. Illegitimacy spread rapidly among white Americans (it was already common among blacks), while marital fertility collapsed. The "sexual revolution" came out from under the covers, where it had been heating up since the American libido was drafted in 1942 to do battle with the arthritic and thinning legions of Christian decency. The family itself fell into disrepute, pummeled by neo-Malthusians, neofeminists, neo-Marxists, and neopagans alike.[13]

The disappearance of America's autonomous families quickened: divorce, the sexual revolution, women's liberation movement, and technology were taking their toll. According to an article in *The Atlantic Monthly*, in the postwar generation, more than 80 percent of children grew up in a family with two biological parents who were married to each other. By 1980, only 50 percent could expect to spend their entire childhood in an intact family.[14] Thus:

> The emerging late 20th-century American mind, awash in sensation and cheap sentiment, lurched to the proffered solution. Between 1963 and 1967, all 50 states adopted "reporting laws," requiring doctors, teachers, and social workers to report suspected cases of child abuse. Like the "Child Saving" tools of the past, these laws essentially denied the existence of natural parental rights and the Common Law. Accused parents faced a presumption of guilt (often involving seizure of their children) until they could prove their innocence.[15]

The denial of the existence of natural parental rights largely obscured the real cause of child abuse, which was the demise of the intact, autonomous family. As noted above, "awash in sensation and cheap sentiment," America "lurched" to a remedy for child abuse that had little if anything to do with the cause.

Thus, today there is little doubt that child abuse is increasing, or at least being identified and reported, at a frightening pace. Yet, the machinery of the child savers is too often directed at the *intact family*—a "special kind of terror unique to the sentimental totalitarianism of late

20th-century America."[16] As George Orwell chillingly forecast, "education" and the ever-vigilant state has begun to scrutinize every family *just in case* there might be child abuse:

> The family could not actually be abolished, and, indeed, people were encouraged to be fond of their children in almost the old-fashioned way. The children, on the other hand, were systematically turned against their parents and taught to spy on them and report their deviation. The family had become in effect an extension of the Thought Police. It was a device by means of which everyone could be surrounded night and day by informers who knew him intimately.[17]

Lest one believe that George Orwell was an extremist, consider the following case. In Michigan, a public school district conducted so-called counseling sessions with a young child that included questions such as these: "A girl was listening through the keyhole of the closed door of her parents' bedroom. Here [sic] parents were talking and didn't know she was there. What did she hear them saying?"; "What sorts of things are too personal to discuss with your parents?"; "How do you feel after you've gone to the toilet?"; and "What 'turns you on,' that is, what excites you?"[18] In its decision in the lawsuit filed by the parents to protest such activity by the school, the federal court said, "[I]t is clear that schools have broad authority to maintain discipline—often at the expense of a student's (and family's) privacy rights."[19]

CHANGING SITUATIONS

The decline of freedom in America will continue as long as families fail to function as families. As Cornell University Professor Urie Bronfenbrenner writes,

> While the family still has the primary moral and legal responsibility for the character development of children, it often lacks the power or opportunity to do the job, primarily because *parents and children no longer spend enough time together in those situations in which such training is possible.* This is not because parents do not want to spend time with their children. It is simply that conditions have changed.[20]

Professor Bronfenbrenner supports his conclusion by a twenty-five year survey of child-rearing practices in the United States.[21] Originally, his data was interpreted as indicating a trend toward universal permissiveness in parent-child relations, especially in the period after World War I. He notes: "The generalization applies in such diverse areas as oral behavior, toilet accidents, dependency, sex, aggressiveness, and freedom of movement outside the home."[22]

Years later, however, Bronfenbrenner recognized that the data pointed to another interpretation, consistent with the parental trend toward permissiveness, but going beyond it. He writes: "The same facts could be viewed as reflecting a *progressive decrease*, especially in recent decades, *in the amount of contact* between *American parents and their children*."[23]

Like their parents, children are not home much anymore. They leave early on the school bus, and it is close to dinner time when they get back. There may not even be anyone home when they get there: "If the mother is not working, at least part-time . . . she is out a lot because of social obligations—not just to be with friends, but to do things for the community. The men leave in the morning before the children are up. And they do not get back until after the children have eaten supper. Fathers are often away weekends, as well as during the week."[24]

THE STATE-SCHOOL

If a child is not with his parents or other adults, where does he spend his time? He or she is with other children—in school, after school, over weekends, and on holidays.

However, even this contact has become restricted. The passing of the neighborhood school in favor of "educational advantages" made possible by consolidation and homogenous grouping by age and more recently by "ability" has set the pattern for other activities. Thus, from preschool days onward, a child's contacts with other children in school, camp, and neighborhood tend to be limited to youngsters of his or her own age and social and/or academic characteristics.

Built on the nineteenth century factory model, mass public education ostensibly taught basic reading, writing, and arithmetic, a bit of theory, and other subjects. However, as Alvin Toffler points out, this was only the "overt curriculum":

> Beneath it lay an invisible or "covert curriculum" that was far more basic. It consisted—and still does in most industrial nations—of three courses; one in punctuality, one in obedience, and one in rote, repetitive work. Factory labor demanded workers who showed up on time, especially assembly-line hands. It demanded workers who would take orders from a management hierarchy without questioning. And it demanded men and women prepared to slave away at machines or in offices, performing brutally repetitive operations.[25]

Therefore, from the mid-nineteenth century on, one found a relentless educational progression. American children started school at a younger and younger age, the school year became longer and longer (it

81

climbed 25 percent between 1878 and 1956), and the number of years of compulsory school attendance increased.[26]

This has had a profound effect on family patterns, Toffler notes.

> By setting up mass education systems, governments not only helped to machine youngsters for their future roles in the industrial work force (hence, in effect, subsidizing industry) but also simultaneously encouraged the spread of the nuclear family form [away from the extended family]. By relieving the family of educational and other traditional functions, governments accelerated the adaptation of family structure to the needs of the factory system.[27]

Mass compulsory school attendance also rigorously promoted a uniform and therefore monolithic approach to education. With the older one-room schoolhouse, all ages interacted. With mass education, segregation by ages began and classroom materials and curricula became more uniform. The *diversity* of earlier educational settings was lost.

---

*A*merica is moving very rapidly toward a society that is segregated not only by race and class, but also by age.

The mass educational system also produced the professional educator and education bureaucrat. This new type of educator (the "educrat") not only allegedly knew more about education, but in the end also *completely replaced parents as the educators of their children*, because he was considered an "expert."

Thus, as a state-financed institution, the public education system began more and more to duplicate, and eventually replace, many family functions in addition to education (such as recreation and extracurricular activities).

SOCIALIZATION:
REPLACED WITH AGE SEGREGATION

A primary function of public schools, sociologists argue, is to provide for a "uniform orientation at the societal level."[28] Accordingly, a major part of the *socialization* process of America's future citizens has been assumed by the public schools. But mass state schooling has forced children into horizontal peer relationships that have largely displaced the traditional vertical relationships with adults. The result has been a move away from parental relationships to peer relationships along with all the negative influences of "peer pressure."

Compulsory public schooling has provided peer groups that occupy a place of primary importance in the life of the student. As Professor James Coleman has noted,

> This setting-apart of our children in schools—which take on ever more functions, ever more "extracurricular activities"—for an ever longer period of training has a singular impact on the child of the high-school age. He is "cut-off" from the rest of society, forced inward toward his own age group, made to carry out his whole social life with others his own age. With his fellows, he comes to constitute a small society, one that has most of its important interactions *within* itself, and maintains only a few threads of connection with the outside adult society.[29]

In essence, this means that the child's primary relationship is no longer parent-child or, for that matter, even child-child. Instead, it is child-state to the extent that the parent's role has been usurped or otherwise filled by the state-controlled public school system.

Because of this aspect of mass compulsory education, America is *moving very rapidly toward a society that is segregated not only by race and class, but also by age.*

Amazingly enough, this age segregation occurs everywhere, even in institutions that formerly encouraged relationships across age lines. Church Sunday schools, for example, are invariably grouped in such categories as preschool, early grades, teens, singles, young marrieds, adults, divorced people, and senior citizens. Groupings such as these effectively destroy relationships between younger and older people. Is it any wonder that there is a lack of "community" in churches and Christian groups?

PEER PRESSURE

A negative effect of public school socialization is its requirement for persistent conformity.[30] The pressure for conformity to the behavior and beliefs of fellow students is very strong. Sometimes conformity becomes an obsessive drive of students. It almost always has a harmful effect on parent-child relations.

A further negative effect is that the rare nonconforming student who attempts to withstand such socialization pressures is generally, as psychological and sociological studies show, rejected as a deviant or stigmatized in various ways. That can have severe emotional effects on such students when religious beliefs are involved. In fact, one research study indicates that "doubting religious doctrines is the source of much mental anguish and emotional stress on the part of the adolescent."[31]

The religious student, of course, faces this more and more since the full-blown arrival of the so-called, but almost universally misunderstood, separation of church and state doctrine, which, as it precludes the state schools from teaching religion, also fragments the process of education.

ALIENATION

Mass public schooling, along with the urbanization process and other societal forces, has simply alienated children and parent-adults. For example, one study of 766 sixth-grade children indicated that children, during a weekend, spent an average of two or three hours a day with their parents. During the same period, they spent more time than that with their friends. In short, they spent about twice as much time with peers, either singly or in groups, as with their parents.[32]

The entire concept of the neighborhood is lost.

Moreover, their behavior apparently reflects preference as well as practice. "When asked with whom they would rather spend a free weekend afternoon," writes Bronfenbrenner, "many more chose friends than parents."[33] However, analysis of the data on the child's perception of his parents, his peers, and himself has led researchers to conclude that "peer-oriented" children were more influenced by a *lack* of attention and concern at home than by the attractiveness of the peer group. "In general, the peer-oriented children held rather negative views of themselves and the peer group. They also expressed a dim view of their own future."[34]

Finally, peer-oriented children report engaging in more antisocial behavior, such as "doing something illegal," "playing hooky," lying, teasing other children, and the like. In summary, "*[I]t would seem that the peer-oriented child is more a product of parental disregard than of the attractiveness of the peer group*—that he turns to his age-mates less by choice than by default. The vacuum left by the withdrawal of parents and adults from the lives of children is filled with an undesired—and possibly *undesirable*—substitute of any age-segregated peer group."[35]

NO NEIGHBORHOODS

The entire concept of the neighborhood is lost. Rarely can a child see people working at their trades. Everyone is out of sight. Children can no longer listen to community talk at the post office or on the park bench. And there are no abandoned houses, no barns, no attics that children may safely explore. It is a bland world for children to grow up in. Forced to remain behind locked doors by the many dangers of an empty home and neighborhood, after-school children while away their hours by interacting with their computers and video games. Cyberspace has replaced the neighborhoods familiar to their grandparents.

Families used to be larger—not in terms of more children so much as *more adults.* This included grandparents, uncles, aunts, and cousins. Moreover, those relatives who did not live with the family at least lived nearby.

There were community visits, dinners, and get-togethers. People knew one another, all of them—the old folks, the middle-aged, the older cousins. And what's more, they knew everyone else. This had its good side and its bad side:

> On the good side, some of these relatives were interesting people, or so you thought at the time. Uncle Charlie had been to China. Aunt Sue made the best penuche fudge on the block. Cousin Bill could read people's minds (he claimed). And they all gave you presents.

> But there was the other side. You had to give them all Christmas presents. Besides, everybody minded your business. They wanted to know where you had been, where you were going, and why. And if they did not like what they heard, they said so (particularly if you had told the truth).[36]

Relatives were not the only ones concerned about children. Everybody in the neighborhood minded each other's business. Again, this had two aspects. Children were watched by neighbors. If they walked on the railroad trestle, the phone rang at their parents' house. Children also had the run of the neighborhood. Children could, without the parents worrying, play in the park and go to the stores alone.

The stable world of the small town has been absorbed by an ever-shifting suburbia. As a consequence, children are growing up today in a different kind of environment.[37] Urbanization has reduced the extended family to a nuclear, atomistic one with only *two adults*—and sometimes not even that many. The functioning neighborhood—where it has not decayed into an urban or rural slum—has withered to a small circle of friends, most of them accessible only by car or telephone. Paradoxically, although there are more people around, *there are fewer opportunities for meaningful human contact.*

Whereas previously the world in which the child lived consisted of a diversity of people in a variety of settings, now, for millions of American children, the neighborhood is nothing but row upon row of buildings where "other people" live. One house or apartment is much like another—and so are the people. As Professor Bronfenbrenner writes:

> They all have more or less the same income, and the same way of life. But the child does not see much of that life, for all that people do in the neighborhood is to come home to it, have a drink, eat dinner, mow the lawn, watch television, and sleep. Increasingly often, today's housing projects have no stores, no shops, no services, no adults at work or play. This is the sterile world in which many of our children grow, and this is the "urban renewal" we offer to the families we would rescue from the slums.[38]

This is a by-product of a variety of changes, all operating to decrease the prominence and power of the family in the lives of children. These social changes include "[u]rbanization, child labor laws, the abolishment of the apprentice system, commuting, centralized schools, zoning ordinances, the working mothers, the experts' advice to be permissive, the seductive power of television for keeping children occupied, the delegation and professionalization of child care."[39]

Thus, over the years, the decline in family vitality has resulted in a shift of responsibility for the upbringing of children away from the family to other settings in the society—such as schools, state and private institutions, and individuals who attempt to simulate the original family setting (for example, foster parents).

THE WITCH HUNT

It is logical that the shift in responsibility for children away from the family would bring state intervention. It is also evident that the Judeo-Christian worldview affected English law concerning parental rights and the early development of the law on parental rights in America. These early views tolerated state interference only where it was *clear* that the parents had forfeited their rights.[40]

However, despite the judicial standard, the modern child savers demand that parents who have had their children taken away, even without strong evidence of misconduct, be required to provide "concrete evidence of their positive motivation toward being a parent and the steps they are taking in that direction . . . *before* they get their children back."[41]

Essentially, the child savers are saying that the burden of proof should be shifted to the parents to prove they are fit, rather than the state having to prove they are unfit. In other words, instead of "innocent until proven guilty," the standard is now "guilty until proven innocent."

Similarly, many contemporary child advocacy groups contend that the focus should be on tightening the standards for termination of parenting by lowering the evidence the state is required to meet for termination.[42]

This relates directly to the problem of child abuse, which is undoubtedly a significant concern. But all too often, the social welfare bureaucracies include legitimate parental actions within their range of abuses. The witch hunt mentality prevails that marks *all* parents as suspected child abusers. This ranges from the social worker who investigates suspected child abuse to the lawmaker crafting abuse legislation.

According to Dr. Richard A. Gardner, a clinical professor of child psychiatry at Columbia University and an expert on the sexual abuse of children, the basic problem with child abuse legislation is that the system is biased.[43] Dr. Gardner has this to say:

> State and Federal money is available for the treatment of children who are found to have been abused, but no funds have been specifically allocated for the protection and treatment of those who have been falsely accused. Nor has money been available for another special and growing group—children who have suffered psychiatric disturbances because they have been used as vehicles for the promulgation of a false accusation. . . . Evaluators who conclude there has been abuse set in motion events that bring their offices both state and federal funds. If they conclude there was no abuse, their facilities receive no funding for further evaluation of treatment.[44]

The child abuse establishment also furthers its own agenda. Mental health facilities, child protection services, and investigating agencies (including police, detectives, and prosecutors) all depend on one another. It behooves them to work together because the greater the number of referrals, the greater the justification for the requisite funding. The current system generates an endless stream of referrals for investigators and "validators." All this predictably fuels sex-abuse hysteria, hysteria in which an accused individual's constitutional due process protections are commonly ignored.[45]

In this respect, all fifty states and the District of Columbia have passed mandatory reporting laws. Most states require reporting of suspected child abuse by physicians, educators, psychologists, and others likely to come in contact with children.[46] One has a duty to report even if there is only a mere suspicion of abuse, in other words, "less than probable cause."[47] Most statutes use words such as "reasonable cause to believe," "cause to believe," or "known or suspected abuse."[48] The statutes of all jurisdictions provide some immunity from civil or criminal liability for those who, in good faith, report suspected abuse or neglect.[49]

In 1991, 49,163 children in Virginia were the subjects of investigation for child abuse or neglect.[50] Of those, 13,894 were "founded" or were "reason to suspect" child abuse cases. The rest, 35,269, were "unfounded," that is, the social worker found no reason to believe that abuse or neglect occurred.[51] As one report recognizes, for those 35,269 families who were needlessly investigated by social workers, "it was an embarrassing and complex web of administrative formulas, perceptions and questions about their parental skills."[52]

New avenues for "abuse" determinations are developing:

> In less than a decade, new fields of law and psychotherapy have sprung up around the theory that children can repress memories of sex abuse and later, as adults, retrieve them. Since 1988, courts and legislatures in more than 25 states have responded to pleas from women's rights advocates and to public outrage about child sex abuse by creating a legal mechanism for both criminal and civil actions based on recovered memories.[53]

As Loftus and Rosenwald write, "The consequences of recovered-memory therapy often extend far beyond the patient, to family members, friends and neighbors. When an adult 'discovers' memories of past sexual abuse, the response often is to confront the alleged perpetrator or sever relations. . . . Unfortunately, families and reputations are shattered, and the most venomous divorces and custody battles ensue."[54]

The child savers have too often been allowed to "justify state intervention not just in cases of real abuse but even when the choice is only between *good* and *better* environments for a child."[55]

The result of these combined influences is a frightening increase of cases where parents are erroneously accused of abusing their children. As a consequence, children are taken away from their parents, and the entire family is emotionally ravaged, perhaps irreparably destroyed, by state legal mechanisms.[56]

In the process, a new class of people—children with the state as their protector—has emerged. The state is continuing to expand its role —apparently no matter is too trivial for the state's attention. For example, a court recently based a custody decision on the fact that the father smoked.[57] A brief review of areas once unquestionably the domain of parents illustrates this continuing trend all too well.

MARRIAGE

Currently, most states require parental consent for marriage of children prior to the age of eighteen,[58] even where the child is pregnant or has a child of her own and wishes to marry the father of her child.[59]

Yet our society does not absolutely prohibit minors from obtaining an abortion. So these marriage consent requirements do not logically appear to be immune from challenge. Moreover, our society no longer regards marriage as a permanent commitment, and minors are indoctrinated and equipped for unmarried sexual relations at school (in many cases despite parental objection); thus, such restrictions seem, at best, irrelevant. After all, if a minor can legally have sex and a married person can get a divorce for any or no reason, why require parental involvement in the decision to marry? This, combined with older laws, such as prohibition of sodomy, demonstrates certain inconsistencies in our legal system. Unfortunately, the newer rulings tend to override the older ones.

CHILDREN AND ABORTION

Parents do not have the same authority with regard to abortion that they currently have with respect to marriage by a minor.[60] The courts have, in effect, held the right of a minor to obtain an abortion to be of more significance than the right to marry.

In *Hodgson v. Minnesota*,[61] a 1990 decision, the Supreme Court reviewed a Minnesota statute[62] requiring an unemancipated minor[63] to notify both of her parents[64] of her intent to obtain an abortion at least forty-eight hours[65] before the procedure was performed.[66] The Minnesota legislature incorporated a judicial bypass proceeding whereby a mature or "best-interests" minor could seek court approval of her decision instead of notifying her parents.[67] The Supreme Court held that the primary two-parent notification requirement alone was unconstitutional[68] but that the two-parent notification requirement coupled with a judicial bypass alternative would withstand a constitutional challenge.[69]

In sum, the judicial bypass procedure enables a judge to authorize an abortion without parental consultation or consent if a pregnant minor can demonstrate her "maturity" and understanding of the nature and consequences of her decision to abort, or if she can show that, *even absent maturity,* the abortion is in her best interests.

The Supreme Court is thus saying that parents may not constitutionally deny a minor's *right* to an abortion!

SEX AND CONTRACEPTION

The child savers promulgate school-based "health" clinics as a method of reducing adolescent pregnancy rates and birthrates.

For example, in St. Paul, Minnesota, school-based clinics, among the first in this country, provide a full range of reproductive health services including education, decision making, counseling, physical examinations related to birth control, prescriptions for birth control methods, and pregnancy testing. The reported initial success of the St. Paul clinics in reducing birthrates contributed to the rapid increase in the establishment of school-based clinics nationwide.

However, recent data indicate that school-based clinics do not significantly reduce birthrates. The failure to find consistent decreases in birthrates after the clinics were established should not be surprising, partly because numerous studies have indicated that it is difficult to change adolescent sexual behavior.[70]

According to the Committee on Child Psychiatry, the age of attaining puberty has currently moved down from thirteen or fourteen to eleven or twelve.[71] The discussion goes on to say:

> [However], the capacity for making wise judgments has not moved downward in a like way. Moreover, the emotional end of adolescence appears to be moving up the chronological scale. This is manifested by teenagers' continuing financial dependence on their parents and delay in entering the workforce. Thus, youngsters are left in a mental and emotional no man's land between the ages of 12 and 22; they are physically mature, but emotionally and intellectually unformed. The sexual revolution of the 1960s has added to this problem. Sex is fully available, yet the capacity for reason and emotional control evades many of our adolescents.[72]

The obvious solution—to leave the matter with parents, where it belongs—appears to be the only solution that is unacceptable to the child savers.

RELIGION

The First Amendment guarantees to all citizens the right to freely exercise their religion. The degree to which this right applies to children, independently of their parents, is currently unclear. The Supreme

Court has ruled that when the parent and state conflict over the religious upbringing of children, the parents' interest should control.[73]

Although the Supreme Court has not yet decided whether parents can force children to practice their choice of religion, New York courts, for example, have found that once children reach early adolescence, they can make their own religious decisions.[74]

However, the Supreme Court's position on the right of minors to have an abortion, even in the face of sincerely-held religious views of parents to the contrary, would seem to conflict with the Court's earlier holdings that the religious interest of the parents should decide in situations of conflict.

The matter of school-based sex education is still in flux. Some schools require parental consent, whereas others proceed despite the lack of it. For parents with sincerely held religious views on premarital sex, there should be no legal question about the matter. Yet, it appears that the child savers, using the rhetoric of "public interest" and "AIDS prevention," will continue to erode this important right of parents exclusively to transmit their religious beliefs and values to their children.

RIGHT TO DIVORCE PARENTS

A Florida state court judge ruled that eleven-year-old Gregory Kingsley had legal standing to petition to terminate his parents' rights so he could be adopted by his foster parents.[75] Two months after the judge's decision, Gregory Kingsley "divorced" his parents—and attained his "freedom."[76]

The Florida decision is one of major consequence because it allows a child, rather than the state, to have standing to sue for termination of the rights of his or her parents. Essentially, children may now be allowed to make a decision that was previously made by a collective number of *adult* officials of the state.

The notion that a child should have a right to terminate a relationship with his or her parents has, for some, "evil and frightening" ramifications for families.[77] It seems axiomatic that "lots of kids, at some point in their lives, would probably rather have somebody else for a father than the one they've got. If a child has a right to choose his family, then all parents are in trouble."[78]

New York University law professor Martin Guggenheim notes: "The terrible thing would be if Gregory gets what he wants and ten years later suffers an emotional breakdown" because he chose one set of parents over another.[79] "The Gregorys of the past were free from these sorts of pressures."[80]

91

From another perspective, what about instances of a child being given the right to make a decision that is clearly not in his best interests? An article in *Newsweek* highlights this issue:

In Chicago, . . . lawyers recently waged battle over the rights of a 13-year-old who, like Gregory, wanted to have her say. The horrific events at the center of the case make the court's ultimate decision especially difficult. In 1987, the girl's stepfather was convicted of aggravated criminal sexual assault against her. The girl was sent to live with her maternal grandmother. The stepfather served four years of an eight-year sentence. After his release, the girl was allowed seven unsupervised overnight visits with her mother and stepfather. But this spring [1992], upon hearing that the parents were now denying the sexual abuse had even occurred, the child's court-appointed attorney, Patrick Murphy, demanded that the overnight visits cease. The child, who wants the visits to continue, two weeks ago won the right to her own attorney in the case.

Murphy was appalled by the decision. "Though I've spent a quarter century arguing for children's rights in the Supreme Court and every court on down, I think lawyers who argue that children are co-equal with adults are doing children and families a great disservice." Yet the girl's position demonstrates how far children will go to preserve even pathological ties to their families.[81]

The child savers assert that misparenting lawsuits by children will not proliferate as a result of decisions like the Gregory Kingsley decision. They appear to be wrong. For example, in Virginia, a twelve-year-old boy who wanted to live with his mother hired an attorney to wage the custody fight.[82] In New York, a sixteen-year-old girl won $142 a month from her father, who had locked her out of the house because she refused a drug-related psychiatric evaluation.[83] Kimberly Mays's termination of the rights of her natural parents in the summer of 1993[84] is yet another tragic case destined to make laws having negative consequences.

ARE THINGS BETTER?

There is little doubt that the traditional two-parent family adhering to Judeo-Christian principles generally provides stable and productive children.[85] The demise of such families and the surrender of family responsibilities to the state are largely to blame for the decline in economic conditions and education and the rise in teen suicide, teen pregnancy, abortion, and crime. Thus:

According to a growing body of social-scientific evidence, children in families disrupted by divorce and out-of-wedlock birth do worse than children in intact families on several measures of well-being. Children in single-parent families are six times as likely to be poor. A 1988 survey by the National Center for Health Statistics found children in single-parent families to have emotional and behavioral problems. They are also more likely to drop out of high school, to get pregnant as teenagers, to abuse drugs, and to be in trouble with the law. Compared with children in two-parent families, children from disrupted families are at a much higher risk for physical or sexual abuse. . . .

If we fail to come to terms with the relationship between family structure and the declining child well-being, then it will be increasingly difficult to improve children's life prospects, no matter how many new programs the federal government funds. Nor will we be able to make progress in bettering school performance or reducing crime or improving the quality of the nation's future work force—all domestic problems closely connected to family breakup. Worse, we may contribute to the problems by pursuing policies that actually increase family instability and breakup.[86]

THE CHILDREN'S REVOLUTION: WHAT LIES AHEAD

Until recently, the child savers operated on the premise of *parens patriae,* or the state acting as the parent. The state, operating through its child savers, usurped traditional family responsibilities or convinced families to delegate their duties to the state.

Today, the demise of parents' rights, and thus families, is shifting into its final phase. Children will have rights that they may assert independently of either their parents or of the state acting on their behalf. As noted above, this shift may be clearly seen in the Gregory Kingsley case. Thus, today's child savers are promoting legislation that will institutionalize such rights.

On an international level, this may be seen in the United Nations Convention on the Rights of the Child. The Convention on the Rights of the Child[87] was adopted by the United Nations General Assembly without vote on November 20, 1989. The treaty contains a number of human rights which have never before been protected in an international treaty —including many new "rights" for children.

These rights have been classified into thirteen categories, namely: (1) rights to life, survival, and development; (2) rights concerning identity; (3) rights against interference with family life and rights to support services for families; (4) rights to freedom of expression, association, and information; (5) rights to protection from abuse, neglect, or exploitation; (6) rights concerning health care; (7) rights concerning education; (8) rights to social security and adequate living standards; (9)

rights of disabled children; (10) rights of refugee children; (11) rights of children in substitute care or alternative family care; (12) rights of children in minority communities or indigenous people; (13) rights in the administration of justice.[88]

The possible interpretations of the Convention's decrees range from radical divergence from current state practices to simply reasserting, clarifying, and strengthening customary practices.[89]

Parents should be most concerned with the specific grant of "participation" rights,[90] which recognize the right of children to freedom of expression; freedom of information; freedom of thought, conscience and religion; freedom of association and assembly; and freedom from arbitrary and unlawful interference with privacy.[91]

The assertion of these child rights is virtually a libertarian charter of children's rights which, at best, dilutes and, at worst, could seriously impair the parental control of children. Concurrently, by reducing parental rights and powers, government agencies could increase their powers over children through the mechanism of "enforcement" of their new rights.

This Convention is the result of ten years of work on the part of "experts" appointed by the United Nations Commission on Human Rights.[92] One reason cited for the necessity of the Convention was to "lay down precise obligations for States."[93] Therefore, the nations that ratify the Convention could be obligated to use the guidelines in the Convention as a minimum standard for the rights of children. Laws of the ratifying nation that provide lesser rights for children could be declared invalid.[94]

Considering the increasing participation of the United States in affairs of the United Nations, this Convention should be given careful consideration by all citizens who either are, or will be, parents. Of course, Congress would have to ratify the Convention, and it would have to satisfy constitutional standards in order to be lawful in the United States. But, given the quickening demise of families and their rights in America, it is no longer certain that the Convention would fail to pass Supreme Court scrutiny.

AMERICA'S NEW DIRECTION

Hillary Rodham Clinton, wife of President Bill Clinton, has been a board member of the Children's Defense Fund, which, among other things, advocates giving children the standing to sue their parents.[95] Mrs. Clinton has been quoted as saying that "children should have a right to be permitted to decide their own futures."[96]

Hillary Clinton is not just referring to children who are abused and neglected. She also refers to such matters as "abortion, schooling, cosmetic surgery, employment, and others where the decision or lack of one will significantly affect the children's future."[97] The *National Review* article of October 19, 1992, clarified this:

> In Mrs. Clinton's world, there will be a children's rights bar, legal counselors in the junior high schools, a growing library of legal treatises on juvenile rights, five-part Supreme Court tests for determining which parental decisions "significantly affect" children's futures, Ivy League law-review essays on youthful self-esteem and the due process clause, and bipartisan congressional initiatives to enforce the latest judicial emanation on the entitlements of children.

> The social impact of all this will be subtle in the same way that the social impact of earlier legal revolutions in obscenity, school prayer, abortion, welfare, and divorce has been subtle. The state will have a basis for wanting to know more about the family life of children, third parties will be encouraged to intrude more quickly, and parental authority will be eroded as such practices as corporal punishment and restrictions on social relationships are questioned throughout well-publicized lawsuits.[98]

According to Mrs. Clinton: "The law is not unresponsive to societal values, and decisions are frequently influenced by notions of conventional morality, occasionally reflecting acceptance of changing morality."[99]

In a society that protects a minor's "right" to an abortion, provides birth control and sex education over parental objections, mandates state education heading toward affective outcomes, what could be left for Mrs. Clinton to give our children?

Mrs. Clinton has answered this question theoretically:

> [There are] two persistent, general problems of legal theory which children's rights advocates seek to overcome. First, legal policy is ambivalent about the limitation of parental control and the assertion of state control over children. There is an absence of fair, workable, and realistic standards for limiting parental discretion and guiding state intervention. Second, the state generally fails to evaluate a child's independent interests, giving a competent child the chance to articulate his interests for himself.

> Ascribing rights to children will not immediately solve these problems, or undermine the consensus which perpetuates them. It will, however, force from the judiciary and the legislature institutional support for the child's point of view. . . . Children's rights cannot be secured until some particular institution has recognized them and assumed responsibility for enforcing them.[100]

95

Mrs. Clinton has proposed several very specific ways to "resolve the theoretical problems" arising out of parental control of their children:

First, the "legal status of infancy, or minority, should be abolished and the presumption of incompetency reversed."

Second, all "procedural rights guaranteed to adults under the constitution should be granted to children whenever the state or a third party moves against them, judicially or administratively" (third parties, remember, includes *parents*).

Finally, the "presumption of identity of interests between parents and their children should be rejected whenever the child has interests demonstrably independent of those of his parents (as determined by the *consequences* to both of the action in question), and a competent child should be permitted to assert his or her own interests."[101]

This agenda of Mrs. Clinton may well be reflected in the governmental policies and court decisions of the 1990s and far beyond.

Indeed, President Clinton's Attorney General Janet Reno is reportedly "a vocal backer of a new American Bar Association working group report called 'America's Children at Risk: A National Agenda for Legal Action' that urges lawyers to give free legal services to children."[102] Unmistakably, the thrust of this agenda is that parents and their rights will be viewed as largely irrelevant and generally as an impediment to the assertion of "rights" by America's children. "Nintendo deprivation" lawsuits are just the beginning.

FOR THE CHILDREN

There is little doubt that America's children are in trouble. There is little doubt that America's families and parents are in trouble and that the problems are becoming more complicated.[103] Hopefully, it is not too late to recover some sense of the vibrancy and stability of the traditional family that adheres to Judeo-Christian values.

One thing is clear, however. The family will not revive overnight. It will take hard work based on love, patience, and courage—so often missing in the family setting.

Moreover, recovery will be painful because so many of the familial bedrocks and connections have been shattered. However, we must recover families' and parents' rights for the sake of our children and our children's children.

Barbara Bush summed it up well: "Our success as a society depends not on what happens in the White House but inside your house."[104]

6

THE
KILLING FIELDS

*D*uring the 1800s, a Christian missionary to China despairingly
      reported:

> When I reached Amoy thirty-two years ago, there was a pond in the
> center of town known as the *Babies Pond*. This was the place where
> unwanted little ones were thrown by their mothers. There were always
> several bodies of innocents floating on its green and slimy waters and
> passersby looked on without surprise.[1]

This is what a world without a clear, uncompromised Christian Gospel leads irrevocably toward.

The United States Supreme Court's decision in *Roe v. Wade*[2] institu-
tionalized "babies ponds" in America. In his attempt to define the issue
underlying abortion, Harvard constitutional law scholar Lawrence
Tribe, a "pro-choice" advocate, describes the problem as a "clash of
absolutes, of life against liberty."[3]

But the matter of abortion is not about a clash of life against liberty.
Although the abortion debate is, indeed, about a clash of absolutes, the

absolutes are: life against death. Liberty has never been, and never will be, absolute. Liberty, in its essence, involves values and limits. And it involves sacrifice. The "liberty" of a mother to abort her child requires the death of an innocent and unconsenting person each time it is exercised.

Yet in its never-ending search for unlimited liberty—the freedom to do what is convenient for one's own selfish interests—America has chosen death and given birth to a new, essentially hedonistic, American philosophy.

The right to life is no longer sacred—whether one is unborn, elderly, handicapped, or perhaps, someday, just bored—and must now be *justified* in the context of convenience, gender, liberty, quality, and a myriad of other considerations viewed as "relevant" to the circumstances. America has thus become the killing fields for the inconvenient.

WHEN DID THE RIGHT TO LIFE CHANGE?

Although it is claimed that "pre-quickening" abortion (before the fetus could be felt in the womb) was relatively common in the early history of the United States, it was not until the mid-nineteenth century that restrictive abortion laws were enacted in America. These laws were largely the result of "lobbying by the organized medical profession [which] reflected increased professionalization of the practice of medicine."[4] Though disagreeing that morality was a primary motivation for the profession's stand against abortion, Professor Tribe nonetheless admits:

> A moral component to the doctors' campaign cannot be denied. The movement to end competition for abortion services by having abortion declared criminal was motivated by a reluctance to perform abortions. On a professional level, adherence to the Hippocratic oath and to the ethical vision it implies underlay an important part of the movement to distinguish the regulars from other providers of medical services during this period. The oath expressly forbids giving a woman "an instrument to produce abortion," and it has been interpreted to forbid inducing abortion by any method.
>
> In personal terms, advances in science had given many doctors moral misgivings about abortion. Specifically, their more science-based view of human development as a continuous process rather than as a sudden event led them to question the relevance of the distinction between quick and nonquick fetuses.[5]

Thus, anti-abortion laws were enacted throughout the United States, and, as Tribe says, "the early twentieth century was remarkably free from debate about abortion, remarkably so because it appears that women continued to have abortions in roughly the same proportions as they had before criminalization. Although the data on this subject are not completely reliable, it seems that as many as one in three pregnancies was terminated by induced abortion during this era."[6]

Apparently, many abortions during this period were performed by physicians who were willing to interpret exceptions for therapeutic abortions as "broadly or narrowly as conscience demanded,"[7] and "poverty" and "psychiatric reasons" generally qualified as threats to the mother's life sufficient to justify abortion.[8]

The thalidomide tragedies of the 1950s and 1960s and the German measles outbreak of 1962–65 (which resulted in some fifteen thousand babies born with birth defects) challenged the restrictions limiting abortions to those necessary to preserve the "life of the mother" (however this term is defined) and revitalized the abortion question: the medical profession "now mobilized in favor of easing the restrictions, on the basis of the belief of doctors that on many levels abortion might be less tragic than childbirth."[9]

Although consideration of the *quality of the baby's life* represented a dramatic shift in the historic justification for abortion, "faced with the possibility of legal liability in an area that they had always considered the domain of professional judgment," according to Tribe, "physicians now pressed legislatures to codify the practices the profession had engaged in for the preceding decades."[10] Thus:

> In 1967 the AMA issued a statement favoring liberalization of the abortion laws, and in 1970 it recognized the legitimacy of abortion, limited only by the "sound clinical judgment" of a physician. . . . Indeed, a majority of doctors around that time appear to have favored the right to abortion on request.[11]

In that same year:

> [T]wenty-one members of the clergy made a stunning announcement, reported on page one of the *New York Times,* offering to refer women to doctors they knew to be performing safe and legitimate abortions. Their organization, the Clergy Consultation Service on Abortion, soon spread across the country with thousands of clergy participating as "gentle lawbreakers," referring women to doctors in Puerto Rico, in Great Britain, and even within the United States. In Michigan alone, a hundred members of the clergy, including a few Catholic priests, gave such referrals.

> These clergy served as a form of *Consumers Report* for abortion. . . . This movement among the clergy also lent moral legitimacy to those who would reform the law of abortion.[12]

In contrast to some early feminists,[13] American women during the 1960s came to see abortion rights as the touchstone of their "liberation" and thus intensified their efforts to institute abortion as a civil "right." As pioneer feminist Betty Friedan recalls: "[D]espite the well-laid plans of the male abortion politicos and medicos, the right of woman was spelled out as the basis of the abortion movement. . . . [The] right to sexual privacy and the control of our own bodies in the matter of child-bearing and abortion was more basic than many of the rights spelled out in the Bill of Rights, as it was written of, by and for men."[14]

Thus, in Chicago in 1969, four years before *Roe v. Wade,* at the First National Conference for Repeal of Abortion Laws, Friedan officially proclaimed abortion as a civil right:

> The right of woman to control her reproductive process must be established as a basic, inalienable, civil right, not to be denied or abridged by the state—just as the right of individual and religious conscience is considered an inalienable private right in both American tradition and in the American Constitution.[15]

Although physicians (for professional reasons) and women (as a matter of civil "rights") were largely responsible for the legal efforts to decriminalize abortion and to establish it as a right, Tribe explains that

> there were many other forces underlying popular support of abortion reform in general during the 1960s. Greater sensitivity to issues of poverty and race heightened awareness of the unequal quality and availability of abortion services to women according to social class and skin color. By the late 1960s as many as 1,200,000 women were undergoing illegal abortions each year: more than one criminal abortion a minute. . . .

> The movement toward relaxation of restrictions on abortion also took place in a context of growing concern in America about worldwide overpopulation. Between the two World Wars the focus of population theory underwent radical change. Economists now argued that the key to economic prosperity and equality was a low birthrate. . . . Indeed, in what must be regarded as a measure of the consensus on this issue and of its importance, former Presidents Harry Truman and Dwight Eisenhower became cochairmen of Planned Parenthood/World Population in 1965.[16]

For these reasons, support continued to widen for the repeal of laws criminalizing abortion in cases where the unborn child had a serious physical or mental defect, and where abortion was determined by a physician to be necessary to protect the mental or physical health of the pregnant woman, as well as in cases of rape or incest.

The discrete support for decriminalized abortion evolved into the view that, as Tribe notes, "women had a *right* to a legal and safe abortion. For many women, more reform of abortion laws was not enough, for it would simply mean that (primarily male) physicians would have wider latitude to make a decision that these women believed was the business only of the pregnant woman."[17] "While the belief that elective abortion was every woman's right originated with radical feminists, by the late 1960s it had become dominant within the movement against restrictive abortion laws."[18]

After having kept its distance for several decades, the population control movement also openly acknowledged abortion as a significant factor in controlling fertility. In 1969 Planned Parenthood publicly supported the repeal of criminal abortion statutes, and in 1972 the Commission on Population Growth issued a favorable report on abortion reform.[19]

ROE V. WADE AND ITS PROGENY

It was in this climate of cultural ferment that a twenty-five-year-old unmarried woman, claiming to have become pregnant as the result of a gang rape, asked the Supreme Court to overturn the Texas ban on abortion so that other women would not have to suffer such an unwanted pregnancy. The Supreme Court listened, and its answer in *Roe v. Wade* was a compromise that forever changed America's beliefs about life:

[N]o judicial ruling since segregated public schools were held unconstitutional . . . has generated anything resembling the degree of criticism and even outright violence triggered by *Roe v. Wade.* Criticism of the decision, and particularly of its result, has led to a revolution in constitutional law that may have profound consequences for all Americans, a revolution touching the full range of our rights. It has already led to a radical transformation in the role of the American judiciary.[20]

But was the Court's answer in *Roe* what 1970s America really wanted, as some have argued?[21] Professor Tribe, who supports the "right" to abortion, answers the question from his perspective:

In 1973 only four states, two of them (Alaska and Hawaii) geographically remote from the rest of the nation, guaranteed a woman by law the right to choose for herself whether to terminate her pregnancy. There is little evidence that the United States was on the verge of emerging, in the early 1970s, from the long shadow of shame that had branded women as blameworthy for extramarital sex and nonprocreative sex and that condemned them for choosing abortion even when the choice was a painful and profoundly reluctant one.[22]

101

The "long shadow of shame" Tribe refers to is the shadow cast by the Judeo-Christian value of the sanctity of human life. Thus, the Supreme Court's decision, "perhaps . . . for no good reason[,] said to a large and politically active group, 'Your metaphysics are not part of our Constitution.'"[23]

As a result, some 1.5 to 1.6 million unborn babies have been aborted each year in America since 1975—cumulatively, some 30 million deaths by abortion up to 1993.

Many religious and conservative people hoped that Ronald Reagan's new federal judges and Supreme Court justices would end this tragedy since President Reagan espoused both pro-life and conservative views. Many pro-life activists believed *Roe v. Wade* would soon be overturned and would no longer be the law of the land.

They were wrong: Reagan's Justices Sandra Day O'Connor and Anthony Kennedy, in the *Planned Parenthood v. Casey*[24] decision, held that *Roe v. Wade* was, in their words, "reaffirmed" and "retained" as good law.[25]

*O*nce society's declared a fetus dead, and abrogated its rights, I don't see any ethical problem [in carrying out extraordinarily gruesome research on unborn babies]."

Though she upheld some regulations on abortion, Justice O'Connor decided that it was unconstitutional to require wives even to notify their husbands, let alone obtain their consent, before they aborted babies that would otherwise be born to the marriage. Justice O'Connor asserted that such a requirement is based on a traditional view of marriage that, in her word, is "repugnant" to the Court.[26] Justice O'Connor also declared that no state regulation of abortion could impose what she called an "undue burden" on any woman's decision regarding the life or death of her unborn child.[27]

The election of President Bill Clinton further polarized the issue. For example:

On January 22, 1993, the twentieth anniversary of *Roe v. Wade* and *Doe v. Bolton,* as tens of thousands of pro-life demonstrators marched peacefully from the White House to the Capitol, President Clinton reversed twelve years of pro-life federal policy with the stroke of his pen. At 3:00 P.M. that day he signed five executive orders lifting federal restrictions on abortion. As Philadelphia's Cardinal Anthony Bevilacqua said: "Explanations notwithstanding, Mr. Clinton called once again on the power of symbolism and sent a clear and unmistakable message to the nation—the Clinton administration is solidly committed to a policy of abortion-on-demand."[28]

The Supreme Court's *Roe* redefinition of human life has permeated and forever changed America. *Roe v. Wade*, therefore, is no longer merely a Supreme Court decision—*it is a philosophy*, part of the new American cultural worldview:

> Under *Roe's* protection, abortion rights appear to have taken root and flourished. The pro-choice political movement is in this sense among *Roe's* progeny. . . .

> Affluent professional women who would probably be able to obtain safe abortions even if the procedure were criminalized now see access to abortion not merely as a question of a *service* that can be bought elsewhere if it is unavailable in the current manner but as a *right* women must have if they are to achieve equal respect and an equal capacity to control their own destinies. These were not widely held views in the United States at the beginning of 1973.[29]

INCENTIVES TO KILL

The implications of a *Roe* culture are terrifying: If human beings (for example, the unborn, elderly, handicapped, poor), whether through legislation or Supreme Court cases, may be defined as no longer part of humanity, then they have no rights and may lawfully be disposed of or treated in any manner that serves the purpose of the day.

These are not merely theoretical implications. Indeed, the economic and professional incentives for experimentation based upon abortion have greatly increased, and new incentives are being discovered rapidly.

The *Roe* redefinition of human life has been readily accepted by the medical profession. For example, only six months after the decision in *Roe v. Wade*, Peter A. J. Adam, an associate professor of pediatrics at Case Western Reserve University in Ohio, reported to the American Pediatric Research Society on research he and his associates had conducted on twelve pre-born babies up to twenty weeks old who had survived hysterotomy abortions. These men cut the heads off these tiny babies and placed tubes in the main arteries feeding their brains. The researchers kept the heads of these babies alive, much as the Russians kept dogs' heads alive in the 1950s. In response to concerns raised about this "research," Dr. Adams said, "Once society's declared a fetus dead, and abrogated its rights, I don't see any ethical problem. . . . Whose rights are we going to protect, once we've decided the fetus won't live?"[30]

President Bill Clinton has now brought this philosophy into full force. This is illustrated by the first pro-abortion order signed by President Clinton on January 22, 1993. There he lifted the ban on federal funding of fetal tissue research, meaning that tax monies can now be used to fund research using tissue collected from unborn babies: "With the stroke of the presidential pen the Federal government and taxpayers were forced into a relationship with abortion clinics retrieving fetal tissue to be used in experiments."[31]

Previously, most fetal tissue used in medical experimentation had come from first-trimester abortions.[32] However, now "pancreatic tissues taken from second-trimester babies already is [sic] being used to try to reduce the diabetic's reliance on insulin. And there are other proposals for other diseases which also required second-trimester abortions. Can't you just hear the whiny protest, 'You're not going to let all that life-giving tissue go to waste, are you?'"[33]

Various state and federal provisions have regulated government research involving aborted fetuses since *Roe,* and the Uniform Anatomical Gift Act (adopted in all fifty states between 1969 and 1973) permits the donation of a dead fetus for research or therapeutic purposes.[34] The matter of fetal tissue experimentation, however, has renewed urgency inasmuch as new abortion techniques render it possible to "harvest" tissue and/or organs from a baby who is not yet "born" but who is not yet dead. As one writer notes, under the new late-term abortion technique dubbed "D & X" (dilation and extraction):

> [W]hat's to prevent the abortionist from taking organs directly from the hapless victim? The child is not "born," since her head is still in her mother's uterus. Much "better" to take the organs of babies without flaw than to try to harvest them from, say, babies born with anencephaly, which virtually never works.[35]

The "D & X" procedure that will facilitate such harvesting is horrifying. Dr. Richard Glasow explains the technique:

> A gruesome, relatively new abortion technique is now being used to kill second- and third-trimester unborn babies. . . . The ghastly new technique, dubbed "D & X," was described in detail by Dr. Martin Haskell at a September 13, 1992, "Risk Management Seminar" sponsored by the National Abortion Federation, the trade association of the largest abortion facilities in the country.

Haskell said that he "routinely performs this procedure on all patients 20 to 24 weeks LMP," with certain rather narrow exceptions. He also said he performs D & X abortions on "selected patients 25 through 26 weeks LMP," which is certainly at, or even past, viability in most cases. According to Haskell, Dr. James McMahon performs such abortions up to 32 weeks. . . .

During the abortion procedure itself, Haskell initially uses ultrasound to identify how the unborn child is oriented[,] [then pulls the child's legs and torso out of the uterus]. . . .

. . . Haskell hooks his index and ring fingers over the [baby's] shoulders and uses his middle finger to hold the woman's cervix away from the baby's neck. He then takes a pair of blunt-tipped surgical scissors and, after locating the base of the baby's skull, [removes the contents].[36]

Beyond the fact that a child is being killed through the D & X method, the other mid-trimester abortion techniques are almost as horrible because the abortionist must remove a child through a relatively small cervical opening.

The widely used "D & E" method involves the use of specially designed tools to dismember the baby and crush its skull (all, of course, *without fetal anesthetic*). Other methods involve the injection of a concentrated saline solution that kills the unborn baby from salt-poisoning dehydration and hemorrhages of internal organs. In this case, the mother delivers a dead or dying baby 24 to 48 hours after the injection. Abortionists also use prostaglandins, which induce premature labor.[37]

The new enthusiasm for recycling aborted babies for the treatment of disease has, to date, produced only speculative results. For example, *The New England Journal of Medicine* published a series of articles concluding that, with respect to the highly recommended "cure" for Parkinson's disease using fetal tissue transplantation: "Our experience confirms that the implantation of fetal neural tissue or other cells into the adult brain remains highly investigational and should not yet be considered a clinical treatment for parkinsonism."[38]

It is important to understand that the tissue transplantations in the Parkinson's disease experimentation require what is called "fresh tissue"—it must be taken from the viable brains of newly killed (or alive) babies. Robert J. White, M.D., has written:

In the final analysis, transplanting fetal brain tissue to the brains of patients with terminal neurological disease represents a double violation of medical morality. First, it involves human experimentation without adequate animal-model investigation significantly demonstrating its therapeutic advantage and safety; and, second, the absolute requirement of transplanting living tissue from a viable brain—*a brain that remains a functioning entity until direct surgical dissection removes the deep structures needed for grafting.* At that moment, the fetal brain is immediately and irreversibly destroyed.[39]

Although the federal government may not directly pay for fetal tissue, President Clinton's order provides that the government may reimburse abortion clinics for their time and services in obtaining such fetal tissue. This is a distinction which makes no practical difference.

The National Organ Transplant Act, which prohibits any sale of human organs affecting interstate commerce, does not preclude the sale of fetal tissue.[40]

According to one commentator, "without fetal research, numerous techniques for detecting and preventing complications of birth, treatment of respiratory distress syndrome, amniocentesis to detect hereditary defects, and improved measles and polio vaccines would not have been possible."[41] But the issue is not whether it is desirable to find a cure for diseases and debilitations that extract a very high toll from the afflicted persons, their families, and society as a whole. The issue is that fetal tissue research funded by federal tax monies means that the state coerces taxpayers to support abortion. This is done ignoring the strong moral and religious objection of a large part of the populace. Once again, religion's role is completely separated from public policy discussions affecting life and death of humankind.

CLONING

The landmark experiment that produced forty-eight human embryos from seventeen human microscopic embryos sparked the "fiercest scientific debate about medical ethics since the birth of the first test-tube baby fifteen years ago. A line had been crossed."[42]

Human cloning is apparently viewed, in this experiment, as "simply the next step in the logical progression that started with in-vitro fertilization and is driven by a desire to relieve human suffering—in this case, the suffering of infertile couples."[43] Even this narrow use of human clones is replete with ethical nightmares.

However, perhaps the greatest nightmare is that such experimentation is proceeding in an "ethical vacuum, one created *not by technology but by the politics of abortion.* 'Congress and our state legislatures are fearful of anything that gets them near the abortion debate' . . ."[44]

There is currently no federal body responsible for setting bioethical policies in the U.S. The Biomedical Ethics Advisory Committee, created by Congress to determine such policies, dissolved in 1989 because of the abortion issue. Since that time, the U.S. has had no coherent or coordinated way to manage these issues. It is interesting to note that the country which pioneered bioethical review now has no public debate and no national policy. "Bigger questions relating to medical ethics have been left to the courts, which can respond to crises only after they have occurred and then must rely on the relatively crude tools of common law and contract law to decide issues of deep moral and philosophical significance."[45]

As Arthur Caplan, Director of the Center for Bioethics at the University of Minnesota, observes: "Any discussion of reproductive technology means you have to talk about conception, embryos, and yes, abortion. . . . And that's a 300-pound gorilla that makes government officials take a classical ostrich-like pose."[46]

Yet, in light of *Casey,* are any ethical restrictions on human cloning projects possible? Russell Hittinger has posed the question:

> If the rhetoric of the joint opinion [*Casey*] is taken at face value, the abortion right cannot be denied without destroying the very fabric of the Constitution, the rule of law, and the legitimacy of the Court.
>
> Therefore, the *Casey* decision forces us to ask unsettling questions. What does it mean for citizens to live in a polity in which the fundamental law of the Constitution requires them to cease and desist from conducting any serious business that touches upon killing of the unborn? What does it mean for citizenship once the right to kill the unborn is equated with the franchise itself, and declared to be a more or less permanent feature of the law of the United States? What does it mean for a democratic republic if the people are declared legally incompetent to deal with an action that a large number of them regard as homicide?[47]

THE FEDERAL GOVERNMENT'S ABORTION ADVOCACY

The regulations that prevented anyone other than doctors in federally funded family planning clinics from counseling regarding abortion were suspended by President Clinton's January 1993 executive order. Under such acts as the "Freedom of Choice Act" (FOCA), the federal government will widen its support for abortion and further institutionalize the *Roe* philosophy. Under FOCA, for example, states may not prevent abortions undertaken for reasons of sex selection.

In fact, states may not prevent abortion for any reason before viability, and may only do so after viability when necessary to protect the health of the woman. Once an unborn child has been found not "viable," the state may not prevent the abortion. The term "health" would be construed broadly, as it was in *Roe*. Therefore, any post-viability abortion that is performed for a reason "relevant to the well-being" of the woman would be protected as "necessary to protect the woman's life or health."

FOCA would prevent the states from attempting to improve the survival chances of an unborn child aborted after twenty-four weeks by enacting statutes requiring the use of the abortion method most likely to produce a live child. FOCA does not appear to prohibit a state from banning the use of public facilities or public employees for abortions. However, the statement of the bill's sponsors on this point suggests that such restraints could be unlawful if FOCA were passed:

> [A] state could not enact legislation which would have the effect of denying access to abortion for women. Thus, it could not enact legislation which would preclude all hospitals, public or private, from providing abortion services *or bar the use of a public facility in localities where such a facility is the only available facility for such services.*[48]

Moreover, under FOCA, states may not "deny" access to abortion funding.

Courts have repeatedly upheld state laws that required parental notification before performing an abortion on an unemancipated minor, as long as there was a judicial bypass provision, as described earlier.[49] However, the plain language of FOCA would probably prohibit a parental notification requirement since it applies to every woman and does not distinguish between adults and minors. Although the sponsors' statement evaded this problem by stating that the bill did not specifically address the question of parental notification, an amendment that would have allowed parental notification status was voted down.[50]

Spousal notice requirements would be invalid under the bill, as they would be construed as unduly restricting abortion for reasons not related to the health of the woman.

The same is true of pre-abortion waiting periods. The Court has previously stated that a waiting period has no medical basis.[51] Thus, a waiting period would be an invalid restriction because it was not enacted in order to protect the health of the woman.

FOCA would probably not invalidate state laws that permit medical professionals to refuse to perform abortions for reasons of faith or conscience, since conscience laws would not restrict the right to abortion or conflict with *Roe* or its progeny. Once again, an amendment that would have explicitly upheld the validity of conscience laws was voted down.

Courts could also require medical professionals to perform abortions in spite of religious or conscientious objections if, because of scarce facilities or personnel, their refusal would effectively prevent the woman from obtaining an abortion at all.

State laws requiring first trimester abortions to be performed only by licensed physicians might also be successfully challenged under FOCA. In order to restrict a woman's right to terminate a pregnancy before viability, the state must show that the restriction was "medically necessary to protect the life or health of [the] woman."[52] The outcome would then appear to turn on the factual determination of whether or not non-physicians could perform abortions without endangering the health of the woman.[53] This would decrease medical professionalism and increase various dangers with the abortion procedure.

As evidenced by FOCA, abortion advocates adamantly oppose measures that they consider "undue burdens" on abortion or access to abortion, such as laws requiring parental notification, bans on abortion for gender selection, family life education promoting abstinence,[54] advertising restrictions on crisis pregnancy centers, pregnancy counseling, and waiting periods.[55] And, sad to say, the federal government under the Clinton administration is supporting the abortion advocates and their objectives.

EXPANDED DEVELOPMENT OF PERSONAL ABORTION AIDS

Imagine this:

> If [a]bortion could be a truly private matter. Say, something as easy as visiting a doctor, getting a few pills, returning home to swallow them, then checking back a few days later to make sure that all went as planned.[56]

Another of President Clinton's directives, issued two days after his inauguration, ordered the United States Secretary of Health and Human Services to "promote the testing, licensing and manufacturing" of RU-486, the French personal abortifactant.[57]

As a correspondent for the *Washington Post* notes: "The shooting of David Gunn outside an abortion clinic in Pensacola, Fla., has added a macabre plot twist to the ongoing morality play of abortion in America. Add the doctor's murder to the mounting pressure from advocates and opponents of the abortion pill, RU-486, and the Clinton administration's removal of restrictions on counseling and fetal tissue research, and you have both sides wielding the value of life—unborn vs. in-progress—with equal, perhaps unprecedented vehemence."[58]

In discussing the importance of *convenience* in abortions (the primary attraction of RU-486), a pro-abortion journalist writes:

The fact is, abortion right now is being left undefended by its true champions—by the women who owe not their lives, but their lifestyles to the convenience of legal abortion. Yes, convenience.

The reason you don't hear abortion-rights leaders talking much about this matter is obvious: It's as politically effective as letting Operation Rescue write your direct mail. It's also, of course, oversimplifying, since for many women choosing abortion involves a profound moral and medical dilemma. But for many women—especially young, middle- and upper-middle-class, ambitious ones—it does not. They just know they don't want children.

Admitting that convenience is a common justification for abortion makes some people squeamish. The plain fact is that women would benefit most from the legalization of RU-486 because it would give them more control over their choice of lifestyles. But you could never tell that from the nature of advocates' cries: that the pill can be used to prevent pregnancies, and may also be effective in the treatment of some diseases. Though perfectly respectable, these arguments are beside the point—especially since the other pill, the legal one, already can serve as an effective morning-after pill. The point of RU-486 is to make abortion more convenient. . . .

For many women the regrets and wistful what-ifs they indulge in after an abortion rank slightly below, say, "What if I had chucked economics and majored in art?" Ask around, and you'll find that more than a few women have abortions and get on with their lives—sometimes both in the same day. . . .

The attitude of abortion as convenience has its strength in the generation that had barely reached elementary school when *Roe v. Wade* was decided and was well into its teens when Republican administrations and clinic-storming mobs began to challenge it. We came of age as women in the eye of the abortion storm, a relative calm of acceptance during which millions of women learned to take abortion for granted, as a means to a lifestyle that would allow them to view sex as a pleasure and being single as a way of life—a lifestyle that allowed room for irresponsibility.[59]

According to one writer, the entire landscape will change now that a pill will solve the problem:

These developments could change the nature of abortion and even birth control by eventually permitting the widespread distribution of pills. Though the Supreme Court's *Roe v. Wade* decision of 1973 made abortion legal in the U.S., the ruling was rendered moot in some places by the dearth of doctors willing to perform the procedure and by the fervor of demonstrators who frightened women away from clinics. Now the battleground may shift to the FDA, drug manufacturers and state legislatures.[60]

RU-486 and other drugs will make it easier for women to discount the moral, psychological, and physical toll of abortion. As one account notes: "'Taking a pill seems far less murderous and violent to the child than using a vacuum cleaner,' says a 31-year old woman who has had both types of abortion."[61]

> The lifers will talk about death that hides in the palm of a hand; the choicers about empowerment a woman can hold between two fingers. Although the advent of RU-486 could greatly change the nature of the abortion debate, it is unlikely to make it go away.[62]

President Clinton's new Supreme Court Justice Ruth Bader Ginsburg views it differently: "I expect that more and more science is going to make the problem [abortion] less turbulent than it is now."[63] Justice Ginsburg says that "much-improved versions" of RU-486, known as the morning-after pill, will make abortion less prevalent. "This new pill may not be the grand solution, but more and more I think that science is going to put this decision in women's own hands. . . . The law will become largely irrelevant."[64]

CENSORSHIP OF SPEECH AND DEBATE

The media has silenced the pro-life position in the marketplace of ideas through its pro-abortion coverage. For example, as a pro-life newsletter reports,

> The scenes on television and in the newspapers are graphic, powerful and constant: tangled, dismembered bodies fill a Sarajevo street; a near-dead Somali baby winces meekly as her eyes are covered by flies that she does not have the strength to brush away; a Washington, D.C., murder victim lies in a pool of blood, a portion of his brain by his side. The reactions of the media, the public and interest groups are swift and loud: something must be done to curb or stop these abhorrent scenes from occurring.

> This scene, too, is graphic, powerful and constant: in a trash bin outside an abortion clinic lie aborted babies, some covered with saline burns, others in bloody pieces. There are, however, no pictures on the evening news or in the newspapers. The major media ignore the voices of an outraged public and speak only of the "fundamental right" to an abortion; the right of women to safe and legal "health care."

> Those caught in war or famine or those affected by crime are, rightly, considered human victims. Thus, we see war, famine and crime on television and in the newspapers. Paradoxically, however, the depiction of a woman exercising her "fundamental right" to abort a "tissue mass" which is not deemed human until birth is decried by the media

111

and the pro-abortion community as, among other things, "indecent," "in bad taste" and "psychological terrorism."[65]

During the 1992 election campaigns, a pro-life republican congressional candidate in Indiana, Michael Bailey, aired advertisements featuring photographs of aborted babies, along with a voice-over: "[This advertisement] is not suitable for small children; that is because abortion is so evil it is not suitable for America. . . . When something is so horrifying that we can't stand to look at it, then why are we tolerating it?"[66] A CBS newscaster declared that "Bailey . . . began airing what could be the most tasteless ad ever shown on television. What's more, because he's a candidate protected against censorship, nobody can stop him." This declaration was accompanied by CBS's alteration of the photographs.[67]

Subsequently, in July 1992, Daniel Becker, a Republican pro-life candidate in Georgia, aired a 32-second ad using Bailey's footage during an Atlanta Braves baseball game. The ad was aired, in deference to network understandings of FCC rules barring refusals or censoring of a federal candidate's commercials.[68] Nevertheless, the owner of the television station which aired the Becker ad along with several unnamed television and radio stations sought agreement by the FCC that relegating such advertisements to hours when children were unlikely to be in the audience would be in compliance with the provisions of the Communications Act of 1934.[69] In other words, they sought means of censoring these ads.

The media also sought a ruling that even if the pro-life ads were not indecent, the FCC should permit a station to make a reasonable good-faith judgment that such content is indecent or unsuitable for children and thus could be channeled to "safe harbor" hours. The FCC responded that the broadcasters had to air the material (although a neutral viewer advisory warning on the air would be permissible) and that the station could not channel the pro-life material to the "safe harbor" hours.[70]

Four days before the national election of 1992, the United States Supreme Court, through the sole and unexplained decision of Justice Anthony Kennedy, refused to hear an emergency appeal of the case and thus let stand the rulings of the lower federal courts permitting the broadcaster to "channel" to other than prime-time hours Becker's subsequent "infomercial" entitled "Abortion in America: The Real Story." This was done on the pretext that it was "inappropriate for children and young teens."[71]

The point of this matter is that the truth about abortion faces serious obstacles in the American marketplace of ideas. The "real pictures of real dead babies [were] inappropriate viewing during its 'decent' prime-time programming depicting, for example, murder, rape, torture, sex, child abuse, violence and adultery."[72] Perhaps more importantly, the pro-life movement has gained a clearer understanding of the power of the mass media and the need of the pro-life movement to harness that power for its own use.

Commenting on the matter of censorship of pro-life expression, the *Wall Street Journal* notes:

> American politics is not going to escape the corrosive atmosphere in which it now operates if one side of the argument is going to be routinely read out of the debate, if even its attempts to offer a rationally persuasive case for its views are deemed "offensive." There has to be a civilized way for the parties to these disagreements to get their message out. Otherwise, the most frustrated partisans will be driven into the streets, and worse.[73]

The "and worse" has happened. Violence and killing have been perpetrated by some in the pro-life movement. The reaction to such violence and killing has been federal and state legislation and court action that will further restrict public pro-life expression under the guise of guaranteeing "access" to abortion clinics[74] although the constitutionality of much of the legislation and some of the judicial actions are constitutionally suspect and will undoubtedly spawn years of litigation. For example, in a situation that made it to the U.S. Supreme Court, there was no dispute that law enforcement officials charged with enforcing the "buffer zone" surrounding an abortion clinic in Florida understood that it applied only to those engaging in *pro-life* speech activity.[75]

DEATH

The final manifestation of the *Roe* philosophy is the so-called right-to-die. America now chooses death over life whenever it must make the choice. Yet the power over life—and death—belongs to God. This is the essence of the clash of the *Roe* philosophy and the sanctity of life.

In terms of euthanasia, in contemporary America, the clash is imminent, as James Pogers observes, for "once physicians have a license to kill, they have a duty to kill."[76]

There are fundamental life and death issues that must be resolved as part of the reform of America's health care system. "[It would be social catastrophe] to permit euthanasia in a society that fails to provide universal health care, particularly for the elderly, the poor and minorities," according to Nancy Dubler, director of the Division of Law and

113

Ethics at Montefiore Medical Center in New York City, and a member of the newly formed ABA Coordinating Group on Bioethics and the Law.[77] Dubler and others point to some of the ambiguities:

[1.] [They] express concern that the medical system, despite advances in life-sustaining technology, has still not come to terms with the real needs of the terminally ill. Often, medical-care providers find it too easy to shunt these patients aside and grant them their requests for the end of treatment, and life, "when the real problem is not their desire for death, but their desire for comfort."

[2.] "We must recognize that as long as there is no universal health insurance, families and health care institutions can exert a subtle pressure on patients to terminate their lives because of the costs involved in life-sustaining treatment."

[3.] There is ambivalence over the issue even within the medical profession. Few would suggest that incidents of physician-assisted suicide and even euthanasia don't occur occasionally.

[4.] It is generally accepted procedure to provide palliative treatment to patients, such as gradually increasing doses of morphine, that are intended primarily to make them comfortable but that may foreseeably hasten death (sometimes called "double-effect euthanasia").[78]

The Clinton Administration's health care program, crafted by Hillary Rodham Clinton, will give momentum to the euthanasia movement. As *Time* magazine essayist Michael Kramer writes: "The Clintons' true goal is the most ambitious of all, a change in the culture of dying. 'That's why Hillary's talking up living wills and advance directives,' says an Administration official. 'She hopes to spur others to get comfortable with pulling the plug.'"[79]

Technology will not resolve the dilemma that the *Roe* philosophy has introduced in connection with these issues, whether medications or machines. Moreover, health care reforms instituted without a clear and uncompromising value on the absolute right to life will, in the end, further compromise an American conscience numbed by *Roe* and the countless deaths of convenience it has spawned.

"A KNIFE IN THE GUT"

As Lawrence Tribe acknowledges:

Few people who really permit themselves to feel all of what is at stake in the abortion issue can avoid a profound sense of internal division. Whatever someone's "bottom line"—whether it is that the choice must belong to the woman or that she must be prevented from killing the fetus—it is hard not to feel deeply the tug of the opposing view.

A story told in a recent newspaper interview by Dr. Warren Hern, director of the Boulder Abortion Clinic in Colorado, demonstrates this well. Dr. Hern recounts calling one of his closest friends, a "strongly pro-choice" physician who had "done abortions himself." When Dr. Hern told his friend that he was at work at his office, his friend asked, "Still killing babies this late in the afternoon?" Dr. Hern recalls: "It was like a knife in my gut . . . it really upset me. What this conveys is that no matter how supportive people may be, there is still a horror at what I do."

Something akin to horror must be felt by everyone involved in the question of abortion who has not become anesthetized to the reality of what is at stake. This feeling may be less intense with abortions performed in the very beginning stages of pregnancy, when the embryo is a tiny, visually undifferentiated, multicelled growth without discernibly human features. But certainly by some point in pregnancy, as soon as abortion involves a fetus that is recognizably human in form, or when it involves a fetus that one might imagine feeling pain, few of us can avoid the sense of tragic choice that each abortion entails.[80]

In fact, pro-abortion advocates are aware of this point.

To judge by the life choices we make, then, there are dozens of reasons for women to be pro-abortion. Yet not since the heady early days of the abortion rights movement in the late 1960s have we heard its leadership bandy around the phrase that summarizes the right we want and have come to expect: "abortion on demand." Instead, those who favor abortion rights prefer to argue from the positions of pro-child, pro-woman, pro-family, pro-Parkinson's victims—their lives, after all, may depend on fetal tissue research. . . . In most cities it's far easier to find a non-traumatic abortion of convenience than it is to find an abortion-rights advocate willing to validate that choice. . . . If you don't want your baby, *I* don't want your baby.[81]

Every person alive today is personally facing or will personally face the issue of human redefinition: Will we tolerate the redefinition of persons to suit our political, social, and economic needs and/or personal desires? For example: Are the elderly "useful" enough to deserve an allocation of scarce medical resources such as government funding or organ transplants? Are chronically and seriously ill, but not yet dying, patients enjoying sufficient "quality" in their lives to deserve treatment? Are disabled newborns "strong" enough to merit a chance to live? Is a woman "human" enough to avoid being raped as her date's reward for his spending money on their dinner? Are the homeless politically "powerful" enough to merit shelter? And finally, are the unborn "persons" enough to deserve their lives?

As we ponder these questions, the death toll in the killing fields continues to climb. Furthermore, religious apartheid in the arenas of life and death continues to grow and widen.

7

THE
GAY AGENDA

*T*urning back in time, Chandler Burr describes a film of the 1940s depicting a "young gay man undergoing a transorbital lobotomy. We see a small device like an ice pick inserted through the eye socket, above the eyeball and into the brain. The pick is moved back and forth, reducing the prefrontal lobe to a hemorrhaging pulp." Then we turn to a 1950s U.S. Navy training film where "a gay man lies in a hospital bed. Doctors strap him down and attach electrodes to his head. 'We're going to help you get better,' says a male voice in the background. When the power is turned on, the body of the gay man jerks violently, and he begins to scream."[1]

Contrast the foregoing scene with the comments of a public school teacher of the 1990s:

> Lesbians and gays *are* family. We are your mothers, fathers, brothers, sisters, aunts, uncles and children. There is no legitimate reason why we should not be included in the family life curriculum. Children can understand and respect us. Statistics indicate that three out of 30 chil-

dren in our classes will also grow up to be gay or lesbian. Additionally, 6 million to 14 million children are being raised in gay families.[2]

WHAT ARE GAY RIGHTS?

In the "Gay Nineties" (as television commentator Maria Shriver once termed this decade), "The issue of homosexuality has arrived at the forefront of America's political consciousness."[3] The foregoing are examples of the issue at both extremes. As one writer observes:

> The nation is embroiled in debate over the acceptance of openly gay soldiers in the U.S. military. It confronts a growing number of cases in the courts over the legal rights of gay people with respect to marriage, adoption, insurance, and inheritance. It has seen referenda opposing gay rights reach the ballot in two states and become enacted in one of them—Colorado, where local ordinances banning discrimination against homosexuals were repealed. The issue of homosexuality has always been volatile, and it is sure to continue to inflame political passions.[4]

But questions of whether homosexuality is desirable and healthy or whether it is something society should encourage alongside heterosexuality have largely been answered by homosexuals only with an assertion of "rights" and allegations of bigotry, homophobia, and heterosexism toward those who oppose them.[5] Still, one gay man argues:

> [N]ow, more than ever, the agenda of the lesbian, gay, and bisexual community has the chance to be seen in the mind of America for what it is: a critical part of a powerful movement for civil rights that emerged in the latter part of the 20th century. The dignity, power, and weight of moral justice that have been seized by the African-American community in its leadership role initiating this movement can rightfully be brought to bear on the Lesbian and Gay community of the 90s. We have the opportunity to place our movement solidly within the tradition of the modern day movement for freedom and equality in our nation.[6]

These words ring with the tradition and majesty associated with the efforts of the African-American civil rights movement and the Abolitionists before it.[7] Indeed, most Americans long ago accepted the notion that freedom and equal rights belong to every American, as the homosexual movement now recognizes:

> Instead of framing our discussion on "anti-discrimination," "human rights," or "freedom of choice," we need to state our community's current struggles for what they are: a fight for freedom, justice, and democracy in the purest sense of these words. When we articulate our struggle under the limited category of "gay rights" we play into a strategy that considers this as a movement for "special rights" for our community. Let's not be afraid [to] say that we are fighting very specifically

118

for *civil rights* generally and the civil rights of Lesbians and Gay men specifically. The Christofascists who have targeted our people in Oregon and Colorado are not only homophobes or bigots, they are the enemies of democracy attempting to reign in the "life, liberty, and pursuit of happiness" supposedly promised to the citizens of this nation. We have got to make these connections . . . and we must be unashamed to embrace the history, traditions, and rhetoric of the broad movement for civil rights in this nation.[8]

The homosexual movement asserts: "We are poised on the brink of a powerful shift that will acknowledge our community's agenda as part of this nation's civil rights movement."[9] Indeed, as the deputy chaplain of the United States Marine Corps has written: "American society is experiencing the concurrent phenomena of increasing sensitivity regarding human rights accompanied by growing rejection of sexual morality. The movement to approve homosexual conduct as an acceptable lifestyle is not surprising in today's permissive society."[10]

But there is another perspective on the matter from Thomas Fleming:

Of course homosexuals have rights, the same rights the rest of us have, as guaranteed by federal and state constitutions and by the traditions of the Common Law. But . . . what rights can they possibly have in a society that has always regarded their practices as unwholesome, unnatural, and contrary to divine ordinance? Will there now be thief rights, cannibal rights, child molester rights? . . .

Yes, criminals and perverts do have rights, and where an activity takes place in privacy and between consenting adults, no sensible or well-bred person would want to stick his nose in, especially if one has retained a fine sense of smell. But do these people have a right to intrude their problems into my life, by coming out of the closet or by preaching to my children in school or by flouncing about in military uniforms? The proposed Oregon ordinance . . . was directed not against homosexuals themselves but against "gay rights." The main object, so it seemed to most of us, was to prevent teachers and counselors from indoctrinating schoolchildren into a positive view of a perversion that will not only ruin their lives but will condemn them to an early grave.[11]

What are the goals of the homosexual and lesbian movement? Is it really a struggle for freedom, justice, and democracy? Or is it a struggle for dominance of the rights of homosexuals over nonhomosexuals and the neutralizing of religious and moral objections in terms of having any influence on homosexual conduct?

A national figure in the homosexual movement answers the question this way: "Our voices and presence will focus on the real enemies: any law or any person who stands in the way of us achieving our rights."[12]

Thus, a homosexual newspaper exhorted homosexuals to "AVENGE COLORADO" and "AVENGE TAMPA, FL" (where citizens passed legislation denying homosexual rights legislation) by focusing efforts on enactment of a federal civil rights bill for homosexuals.[13] Supporters of special rights for homosexuals called for a boycott of the state of Colorado until its citizens changed their minds (and votes) regarding homosexual rights legislation.[14] In turn, the Colorado Supreme Court prevented Colorado's referendum forbidding homosexual anti-discrimination laws from taking effect, holding that the new law effectively denied homosexuals equal participation in the political process.[15] This demonstrates the degree to which the courts are beginning to view the rights of homosexuals as equal rights.

CHRISTOFASCISTS

What are those laws and who are the persons who supposedly stand in the way of rights for homosexuals? What rights do homosexuals seek that they do not now possess? How will the homosexual movement impact those who do not consider themselves "homophobes," "heterosexists," or "Christofascists," but who have sincere religious beliefs and/or moral objections concerning homosexual conduct?

Rather than objectively scrutinize the homosexual agenda to find answers to these questions, proponents as well as opponents of "gay rights" tend to polarize positions and inflame emotions. The homosexuals, with ample support of the media[16] and government officials, have taken the "high moral ground" of additional freedom and rights while those who oppose the agenda have been labeled bigots and people who are afraid of homosexuals.

Most Americans do not appear to believe that homosexuals are undeserving of the same individual rights, property rights, workplace rights, and voter rights accorded to all Americans. For example, a *Newsweek* poll revealed that 78 percent of Americans believe homosexuals should have equal rights in job opportunities and that 43 percent said they have a friend or acquaintance who is gay.[17] In fact, some states and municipalities already have legislation that protects homosexuals from discrimination in employment or housing.[18]

Yet what about the right of individuals to rent rooms in their own homes to whom they please, or privacy concerns in a military composed of heterosexuals and "out of the closet" homosexuals,[19] or the long-term effect on children being inculcated from a very young age with "tolerance" (that is, "acceptance") of homosexuality. These demands by homosexuals go far beyond the above list. Perhaps more important, no clear-cut case has been accepted regarding the *constitutional rights of religion* for persons holding sincere religious beliefs opposing homosexual conduct.[20] The rights of religious persons (called "Christofascists" by some) are dismissed as, at best, antiquated and irrelevant and, at worst, antithetical to an all-inclusive democracy.

THE TREATMENT STATE

The essence of the struggle inescapably involves the definition of homosexuality itself. One view of the issue concerns the sexual desire of a person for another person of the same gender (the "orientation" issue). The other side of the issue concerns the activities of persons stemming from or based on such a sexual desire (the "conduct" issue).

The *state* should not involve itself in the orientation issue except, perhaps, for the special concerns of the military.[21] Such involvement has led, in the past, to events such as the ones described at the beginning of this chapter.

Contemporary involvement by the state in the orientation issue has resulted in more or less "affirmative action" programs in government agencies. Schools produce curricula that include information about lesbians and gays in all curricular areas and teach that same-sex parents deserve the same social status as a married mother and father.[22]

State-mandated toleration and state-mandated persecution of homosexual status are but opposite sides of the same coin. If the state has the power to mandate toleration (and, in cases such as the public schools and government employment, promotion) of homosexuality, it also has the power to persecute homosexuality under a different regime.

On the other hand, the state has a *duty* to *regulate* conduct that is harmful to society. The limits of such regulation with respect to homosexuality should be the focus of the debate on the matter. Whereas the state should not concern itself with the innermost sexual desires of a person (whether a matter of choice or birth), the state has a duty to regulate conduct that is harmful to society as a whole.

Thus, for example, whether one is homosexual by way of sexual orientation should be viewed as irrelevant to the state in connection with state (or other) employment.[23] On the other hand, sexual *conduct* during the performance of one's employment duties would be a matter of appropriate government concern. Under this dichotomy, state employers would not be required to inquire as to the matter of the sexual orientation of their employees—homosexual, heterosexual, or bisexual. Employers are already required to prevent harm to their employees —whether from other employees, third parties, or workplace hazards.

Safety and privacy concerns, as well as the rights of the dissenters (whether the majority or a minority) are thus protected, and the view of the state as to the "correct" sexual orientation poses no hazards to freedom and religious liberty despite the prevailing contemporary bias toward toleration or even promotion.

On the other hand, employers who are required to be concerned with sexual *orientation* must invade the privacy of *all* their employees to determine the status quo. If such status quo does not meet the requirements of the prevailing regulations, then the employer must take steps to correct it—through "training" and, perhaps, affirmative action and quotas. Safety, privacy, freedom, and religious liberty are the casualties of this scenario.

> *Militant homosexuals do not seek the "right" to their sexual orientation [but] seek to legitimize their sexual conduct.*

Again, although today's state may wish to "train" heterosexuals to tolerate homosexuality, tomorrow's state may wish to "train" homosexuals into heterosexuals—a return to the Navy's training film of the 1950s and all it symbolizes.

Finally, restricting the state's involvement to matters of sexual conduct negates any legitimate state interest in the *causation* of a homosexual orientation. Whether it is inborn or voluntary should remain a matter of private, non-state concern.[24]

To the extent that homosexuality is viewed as aberrant and inborn, a state involved in the matter will be duty-bound to "cure" the aberration. To the extent that homosexual orientation is viewed as a legitimate lifestyle choice, a state involved in the matter will be duty-bound to compel its citizens to affirm the choice. To the extent that homosexual orientation is viewed as a *right,* a state involved in the matter will be duty-bound to *enforce* the exercise of that right.

The state has always had legitimate authority to regulate conduct deemed to be harmful to society, including sexual conduct. As it has restricted the right to kill, steal, speed, and indulge in pornography, the state has the duty to restrict homosexual *conduct* and its promulgation as a legitimate lifestyle to the extent that such conduct is harmful to society.

THE SECRETARY FOR
HOMOEROTIC CONCERNS

Militant homosexuals have blurred the contours of their real agenda. In truth, militant homosexuals do not seek the "right" to their sexual *orientation* (as distinguished from sexual conduct). Nor do such homosexuals seek the individual rights of citizens such as voting, property, free speech—they already have those rights. Rather, militant homosexuals seek to legitimize their sexual conduct with attendant negative consequences for religious liberty and society itself.

Society may not legitimize such conduct, even in private, without consequences. As Linda Chavez explains,

> The common bias against homosexual behavior, however, is neither irrational nor necessarily mean-spirited but reflects a rational desire to establish limits on sexual behavior necessary to maintain the social order and protect the family.

> Sex is not merely a private matter. No society recognizes the right of individuals to engage in sexually gratifying acts whenever, wherever, and with whomever they want. Intricate codes of behavior and social sanction apply to this most private of activities, and most of these aim at preserving the basic social unit, the family. Historically, virtually all societies have condemned incest, adultery, and homosexuality because such practices, in distinctive ways, threaten the family. What has varied over time and place has been the punishment imposed for violating these bans. In our modern, generally tolerant society, few sanctions apply to those who engage in these practices so long as they occur, as we are fond of repeating, between consenting adults. Indeed, over the last twenty-five years, we have become increasingly tolerant of sexually permissive behavior. But that tolerance has had consequences. We face epidemics in sexually transmitted diseases, teenage pregnancies, abortions, illegitimacy, rape, and sexual abuse. . . .

> In this atmosphere, it is both understandable and prudent to draw the line at approving homosexual behavior.[25]

Perhaps the best way to understand, in practical and nontheoretical terms, what homosexuals really want from society is to examine some of the information published by the movement itself. For example, one publication details the homosexual "agenda." The main demands are said to include the following:

Passage of the federal gay and lesbian civil rights bill

An end to discrimination by state and federal governments, including the military

Repeal of all sodomy laws

Recognition for gay and lesbian families

A huge increase in AIDS funding

The inclusion of queers in public-school curricula[26]

To generate enthusiasm and commitment for these causes, homosexuals are urged to continue in their activism:

> Restart your engines, queers: Now that you're done using every bone in your body to fight for Clinton's election and against the antigay ballot measures, you need to use every bone in your body to make sure a million of us attend the March on Washington.[27]

A public demonstration by homosexuals in Washington, D.C., in April 1993 was held to revitalize and strengthen the movement. As one writer proclaims:

> The March is one of the few topics that is just as urgent for us as Clinton's victory. The last Washington march, in 1987, did more for our movement than 100 Clintons. In fact, Sweet William's embrace of our cause in the presidential election would not have come about if we hadn't hauled our butts to D.C. on that fateful October day. Out of the 1987 event, ACT UP went national; lesbians and gays from umpteen cities saw the original New York chapter and became hungry to follow its example. Many towns that had never had a gay or lesbian organization before suddenly had several. In some places, the local March organizing committee turned into a permanent queer rights group, and in others, lesbians and gay men who'd been galvanized by the March returned home with so much extra energy that they formed new groups.

> All of us, even those who didn't attend, found a new defiance we had hardly known was possible for pervs to feel. As one Alison Bechdel character put it, "Half a million of us! We turned that creepy, imperialist capital into a whole different world! For one weekend we had a glimpse of real freedom. It was like being 100% queer and proud of it, but at the same time not being queer at all anymore . . . y'know?"

> We gained new civil rights laws, sodomy law repeals, and domestic-partner benefit programs all over the country, all because of the 1987 March. We glommed state and city funds for AIDS programs and forced concessions from the Food and Drug Administration and the Centers for Disease Control—because we suddenly had ACT UP chapters and other new groups. Queer Nation, springing out of ACT UP's belly two years later, won fights for us all over the country on employment dis-

crimination, antigay violence, and Hollywood misportrayals. Our political muscle expanded fivefold. We went from being the group Dukakis wanted to ban from foster parenthood to the group that Clinton publicly courted. . . .

It's time to march again. You need to march to make sure Sweet William fulfills his promises and goes beyond them: an end to the military ban, passage of the federal civil rights bill, Roberta Achtenberg on the Supreme Court—now!

I want this march to have such far-reaching effects that the Republican Party never runs Dan Quayle for anything again. This march could inspire so much new queer organizing that Bill Clinton would have to grit his teeth and *create a cabinet position for a Secretary of Homoerotic Concerns*. We have so many needs, and this is by far the best way to fight for them. If not now, when?[28]

What would a Secretary for Homoerotic Concerns do? What *are* "homoerotic concerns"? One could surmise that such a cabinet position would, at a minimum, be charged with ensuring that no voice is raised against homosexual conduct *or* orientation, for whatever reason.

Attention to homoerotic concerns seems already underway. Roberta Achtenberg, mentioned above, is an "outed" lesbian who is an assistant secretary of housing and urban development in the Clinton administration.[29]

Various international corporations, such as Levi Strauss and Wells Fargo & Company, have withdrawn funding from the traditional family and religious-based Boy Scouts because the Scouts will not accept homosexuals as scoutmasters.[30]

Public schools are following their lead. For example, because of the Boy Scouts' ban on homosexuals, the San Francisco School Board[31] and the San Diego Unified School District refused in 1992 and 1993, respectively, to renew the "Learning for Life" in-school program run by the Boy Scouts in eleven high schools and four elementary schools.[32]

Public forums (and private groups legally characterized as "public accommodations") are being subjected to the homosexual agenda of compelled acceptance. For example, the vice president and general manager of a major country-western music station[33] in Washington, D.C., refused to carry an ad sponsored by the Gay and Lesbian Activists Alliance. The station was advised that not running the ad might be discriminatory and, thus, a violation of the Washington, D.C., human rights law. The ad was run.[34]

An invitation to the president of an evangelical lobbying organization in Washington, D.C., to speak at the annual U.S. Coast Guard prayer breakfast was blocked by self-admitted homosexual Representative Gerry Studds.[35] The congressman allegedly protested that someone with the traditional views of the invited speaker should not be permitted to address the Coast Guard.[36] In responding to the matter, the speaker wrote to the congressman that he was "utterly amazed that a member of Congress would abuse his power to suppress free speech rights. You have unethically imposed a discrimination based on [the] viewpoint of Coast Guard headquarters personnel. . . . Can this country survive as a free nation if political leaders deny to Americans their most cherished rights?"[37]

THE MILITARY

The homosexual agenda captured the nation's attention during the first seven months of 1993 when President Bill Clinton promised to lift the ban on gays in the U.S. military. A political compromise in July 1993 provided that gays and lesbians may serve in the military "as long as they abstain from all homosexual activity."[38]

During the nationwide debate on the subject, the media and others depicted opposition to acceptance of homosexuals in the military as *comparable to the racist opposition* to a desegregated military in the 1940s, alleging that it was a matter of *status* rather than *conduct*.[39] General Colin Powell, Chairman of the Joint Chiefs of Staff, responded:

> I am well aware of the attempts to draw parallels between this position and positions used years ago to deny opportunities to African-Americans. I know you [Representative Patricia Schroeder] are a history major, but I can assure you I need no reminders concerning the history of African-Americans in the defense of their Nation and the tribulations they faced. I am a part of that history.

> Skin color is a benign, nonbehavioral characteristic. Sexual orientation is perhaps the most profound of human behavioral characteristics. Comparison of the two is a convenient but invalid argument. I believe the privacy rights of all Americans in uniform have to be considered, especially since those rights are often infringed upon by the conditions of military service.[40]

Others claimed that those supporting elimination of the ban against homosexuals in the military *did not seek approval of homosexual behavior*. This claim was disingenuous, as evidenced by the outcry of gay activists once President Clinton announced his policy. One author observed:

> As *The New Republic* declared in a recent editorial: "No one is urging the approval or promotion of homosexual acts among military personnel; all that is at stake is that homosexuals, if they so wish, should be

able to disclose their sexuality without fear of direct retribution. This minimal level of toleration implies no approval of any activity, merely acquiescence in the free existence of the other." But that assurance rings hollow in light of the increasing pressure to accept homosexuality as relatively common, benign, unalterable, and, most important, deserving of equal treatment with heterosexuality.[41]

The "orientation only" claim is further discredited by a review of the new policies homosexuals planned to extract from the military if the ban on homosexuals had been lifted.[42] For example, the Universal Fellowship of Metropolitan Community Churches issued a statement that the group would renew its efforts to achieve acceptance of its openly homosexual ministers by Pentagon officials.[43] (The Armed Forces Chaplains Board had previously rejected a UFMCC chaplain nominee as being unqualified under military policy.)[44]

A member of ACT-UP (AIDS Coalition to Unleash Power) confirmed another goal of the homosexual agenda regarding the military in a letter to the superintendent of West Point:

> Lifting the ban is not enough. . . . We intend to sue in Federal court as soon as the ban is lifted to insure compensatory representation in the service academies. In particular we intend to get a ruling mandating a set number of places for homosexuals in the Air Force Academy, the Naval Academy and West Point.[45]

These proposed plans expose the nub of the matter regarding the homosexual agenda in America. Those who oppose homosexual conduct on religious and/or moral grounds should wonder precisely what "didactic" and "experiential" training will involve: Role playing? Living with a homosexual for a weekend? Writing essays? It should be noted that the plan *specifically targeted,* among others, *chaplains.* Presumably, if the objections of the religious leaders can be "trained" away, the objections of those following their leadership will dissipate more quickly. These plans did not appear to include training for homosexuals regarding heterosexual lifestyles or the special demands that military life imposes on sexual conduct.[46]

One may speculate why the military issue was so important to the homosexual agenda, especially since the American military is downsizing at an unprecedented rate. For many reasons, the military represents the most serious challenge to integration of homosexuals into the structure of American society. The sole purpose of the military is to protect the United States. The military does not need to "look like America." The military is not the place for social experimentation or equality, and it has never been viewed as such a place. There is no constitutional right either to serve in the military or not to serve in the military. The exclusionary policies of the military are designed so that those who do not have physical, emotional, and mental qualities that further the ends of defending America will not be called to serve.[47]

These military policies are based on *classes* of people, not individuals. Even though a particular individual within an excluded class might be able to overcome the challenges to his or her success, that is not a sufficient reason for the military to abandon the overall exclusionary policy.

Thus, the military is a special society with requirements that naturally bring the issues of the homosexual agenda to a critical point.[48]

For example, those in the military must often live in situations that provide little space, privacy, or convenience. If homosexuals are able to require that the military accept their status as practicing homosexuals and they are housed with heterosexuals, the objections involved with nonmilitary housing (where there is much more space, privacy, and convenience) will be less forceful.

If military personnel are successfully required to attend training classes to desensitize them and overcome their religious and/or moral objections to homosexual conduct, objections to such classes at schools and in the workplace will have already been overruled.

In other words, *the military represented the watershed for the homosexual agenda.* If America would risk degrading its military prowess in order to implement the homosexual agenda, there would exist no substantial rationale for nonmilitary institutions and population, where the collective stakes are much less direct, to successfully resist such an agenda.[49]

THE HOMOSEXUAL "FAMILY"

Although the issue of homosexuals in the military became a matter of national attention, there is perhaps an even more significant struggle underway that has largely escaped the glare of the media, the focus of politicians, and the average American. That is the struggle to redefine the family in nontraditional ways. Children are now procured through courtroom successes and lesbian "artificial insemination" rather than through the traditional structures of marriage and procreative monogamy.

A teacher and author in the New York City public schools has summarized the essence of the matter:

There is no desire on my part to interfere with homosexual cohabitation. And tolerance of a wide diversity of people is being encouraged in our nation of immigrants. It is one thing to tolerate homosexuals; it is something quite different, however, to teach children in the first grade, or any grade, that there be "support for sex education courses, prepared and taught by gay women and men, presenting homosexuality as a valid, healthy preference and lifestyle as a viable alternative to heterosexuality." This quote is from the "1972 Gay Rights Platform," formulated in Chicago. The demand is being met beyond gay expectations, because all teachers are being required to promote homosexuality and homosexual couples as "family." . . .

In no event should children learn in school that "homosexual couples are family." Homosexuals should be tolerated, but they should not be permitted to undermine traditional family values by using the schools as a vehicle for their false expansion of our already diverse family structures.[50]

Acceptability of a gay lifestyle is currently being indoctrinated into the public through the media, especially television:

Television in particular, both in entertainment and news programs, virtually indoctrinates the viewing public with the message that homosexual behavior is—or should be—acceptable. Homosexual characters have appeared on "Roseanne," "L.A. Law," "Coach," "Northern Exposure," "Picket Fences," "Thirtysomething," and dozens of other shows, almost always in portrayals meant to show that, but for the prejudice of homophobes, homosexuals lead ordinary, even exemplary, lives. However, the empirical evidence we have suggests that a great many homosexuals, perhaps a majority, lead lives far different from their idealized TV portrayal.[51]

But the picture depicted by the entertainment media is generally distorted:

According to one of the most extensive studies of the subject, *Homosexualities: A Study of Diversity Among Men and Women* (1978), only about 3 percent of male homosexuals are relatively monogamous, defined in the study as having ten or fewer lifetime partners. Promiscuity among the homosexual population "would boggle the heterosexual mind," says Michael Fumento, author of a book on AIDS, noting studies of early AIDS patients who reported an average of 1,100 sexual partners. The prevalence of sexually transmitted disease among homosexuals far exceeds that in the general population by a factor of as much as twenty, depending on the disease. Disturbing as well are estimates that even though homosexuals make up only 3 to 7 percent of the population (according to most reliable data), about one-third of recorded instances of child molestation involve male sodomy.[52]

Homosexuals in many states may already live with each other in a monogamous relationship that they may view privately as "marriage." Yet, for militant homosexuals, this apparently is not enough. Thus, in describing two men who wish the state to sanction their union, the

National Law Journal reports: "The gay men have been together for 15 years and consider themselves 'life partners.' But they want more than a church ceremony to celebrate their bond. They want a state-issued marriage license because only that can automatically confer upon them hundreds of legal rights, including the right to share each other's health benefits and to visit each other in the hospital if one of them becomes ill." So the two are asking the Hawaii Supreme Court to sanction their union.[53]

No state currently permits same sex marriages.[54] The United States Constitution does not require that homosexuals be allowed to marry,[55] even though the Supreme Court has stated that the right to marry is guaranteed by the Due Process Clause of the Fourteenth Amendment.[56] The primary rationale of the courts that have considered the issue is that it is the *very definition of marriage* which prohibits persons of the same sex from marrying, marriage being defined as the "[l]egal union of one man and one woman as husband and wife."[57] And since it is the very definition of marriage that makes it impossible for persons of the same sex to marry, it therefore is not a discriminatory act of the government that is preventing recognition of such marriages.

However, it seems that such a rationale will only withstand homosexual pressures for so long. For example, the ACLU has published a booklet describing legal arguments that "can be used to challenge a state's refusal to sanction gay marriages"[58] and has documented other countries, such as Denmark, Sweden, and The Netherlands, where same sex marriages are recognized.[59] Although American courts have been unwilling to change this traditional definition of marriage themselves, some have directly stated that it is within the province of the state legislatures.[60] Thus, if a state legislature were to decide to modify the marriage requirements to allow the state to recognize same sex marriages, some courts might allow the modifications to stand.

But marriage is much more than a matter of contract or registration at the local courthouse. If marriage is simply the legal recognition of any configuration of human beings, the force and sanctity represented by the lifelong union of a man and a woman that is designed to produce the next generations and a worthy place for them to grow to adulthood will cease to exist. As one commentator has written:

> [M]arriage and the family will not survive in a society that recognizes no limits to personal sexual gratification. A great many people will decide that fidelity and child-rearing require too much sacrifice and denial and will simply abandon both duties when they have been stripped of the special honor with which our traditional moral code invests them. It is this fear—that ultimately we may be forfeiting our basic so-

cial institutions—that makes so many of us indisposed to eliminate yet another sexual taboo.[61]

Moreover, the decline of marriage, as conceived by Judeo-Christian theology, is also the demise of a powerful force for limiting the power of the state, for such a union is based on authority not derived from the state and thus is not subject to it. This provides a basis for citizenship that is outside the control of the state.

THE HOMOSEXUAL "PARENT"

The concept of "parent" is being revolutionized by the homosexual agenda. Traditional concepts such as "mommy," "daddy," and "family" have, in some cases, given way to "egg donor," "sperm donor," "alternative inseminator," and a "private ordering relationship."[62] A 1992 workshop in Washington, D.C., covered methods of "alternative insemination" (a term preferred by lesbians to "artificial insemination").[63] Using "straws" of donated or purchased semen, lesbians inseminate each other. As one lesbian puts it, "I want to do it at home in our bed, and I want Elena to do it. It's important to me to have her involved."[64]

The status and rights of a "parent" are now often dependent upon only the legal relationship between the adult and the child. Adults assert claims to children that until recently were not even conceptualized, much less addressed by law or theology.

Thus, Paula Ettlebrick, staff attorney at gay rights organization LAMBDA, asserts: "It's an 'ethical breach' for a biological, lesbian mother to secure a slam-dunk win in the 'patriarchal' courts where biology is held preeminent over any other consideration of the child's interest."[65]

The courts' view that biology remains an important factor in determining these relationships[66] may account for the fact that "[h]omosexuals' greatest gains in family law seem to have been with adoptions by individuals and in 'second-parent' adoptions: those in which homosexuals become the legal guardians of their lovers' children."[67] According to a family law professor at American University Washington College of Law, "In the area we call second-parent adoption, there has been extraordinary success. . . . But . . . such actions have been brought [only] in the District of Columbia and seven states: Alaska, California, Minnesota, New York, Oregon, Vermont and Washington."[68]

Thus, the opposition to gay and lesbian custody has forced homosexuals to seek alternative forums for their claims. It is indeed difficult to mediate disputes or even agreements within homosexual relationships.

> [W]hile gays slowly chip away at courts' reluctance to recognize their relationships as familial, advocates are creating a parallel justice system for such matters: contracts between "spouses" and mediation for child custody disputes.[69]

For this reason, among others:

> It is harder to quantify homosexuals' success as single, adoptive parents.

> A few jurisdictions, such as the District of Columbia, have non-discrimination laws. Others, such as Florida and New Hampshire, legally bar gay men and lesbians from adopting. But a trial court declared Florida's prohibition unconstitutional.

> In many states that have no laws addressing the issue, policy varies from agency to agency. An adoption service's stated policy sometimes has little effect on actual practice. . . . And, oftentimes, judges simply will not ask about the adopting parent's sexual orientation.[70]

For example, the New Mexico Supreme Court refused to overturn a lower court's decision that a nonbiological, nonadoptive co-parent may seek custody or visitation of a child conceived and raised with her partner.[71] Many "states have rejected any *per se* rule forbidding custody by lesbian and gay parents and require the party opposing custody to prove the lesbian or gay parents' sexual orientation will harm the child."[72] And several states now have statutes or court decisions which provide that sexual orientation is *irrelevant* in custody disputes.[73]

In addition to the courts, the media is contributing to popular acceptance of the notion that homosexual families are as acceptable as traditional families.[74] For example, *Parents* magazine specially featured five "happy" families in early 1993.[75] Among the secrets to being a happy family, according to the article, were the abilities to "accommodate their own needs and meet their own goals" and to be "like any other organism that grows and changes through time."[76] One of the five featured families was a "two-mom household" composed of two women who "have been together for more than thirteen years" along with their two daughters who "have the same father . . . a friend of the family."[77]

Yet, some still maintain that it is not in the children's best interests to be raised by gays and lesbians if homosexuality is unhealthy psychologically and medically, which they believe can be shown.[78] The "best interests of the child" is the general maxim followed in custody and visitation determinations.[79] In custody disputes where one of the parties is a homosexual, some courts are now unwilling to denote the homosexual party unfit as a matter of law, and instead are requiring a showing of concrete harm before custody/visitation rights will be infringed upon.[80] One court has held that a lesbian may adopt the children of her lesbian partner, such being in the best interests of the child.[81]

Yet, other courts, primarily located in the midwestern or southern portions of the United States, hold that the very possibility of an adverse effect on the child is a sufficient reason to restrict or prohibit custody or visitation by the homosexual parent.[82]

Two New York courts have dealt with attempts by homosexuals to adopt their adult partners in order to gain similar benefits enjoyed by married heterosexual couples, since same sex marriage remains illegal.[83] A New York Family Court decision in 1981[84] *permitted* the adoption on the rationale that since sodomy is no longer a crime in the state, there are no public policy or public morality considerations to prohibit it,[85] and that the cause of public morality would not be advanced by discriminating on the basis of sexual orientation in the adoption proceeding.[86] The incest statute was not invoked, since the two homosexuals had no blood ties.[87]

The second decision, this one in 1984 by New York's highest court, *would not allow* the adoption, however, holding that adoption "is plainly not a quasi-matrimonial vehicle to provide nonmarried partners with a legal imprimatur for their sexual relationship, be it heterosexual or homosexual."[88] Additionally, adoptions are meant to constitute a parent-child relationship, to which "any such sexual intimacy is utterly repugnant."[89] The Court refused to modify the rules of adoption in the state, and stated that such changes must be made by the legislature as a matter of state public policy.[90]

Courts have apparently been more willing to grant certain family *benefits* to individual homosexuals than they have been to grant family *status* to a homosexual arrangement. For example, in one New York Court of Appeals case, it was held that a homosexual couple fit the legal definition of a family in terms of inheriting the deceased lover's rent-controlled apartment.[91]

SEX WITH CHILDREN

An issue that has been relatively obscure until recently concerns pedophilia, or sex with children. Most pedophiles are attracted to their own sex, but some adult men are attracted to girls, and some adult women are attracted to boys.

John Money, Ph.D., a retired professor of medical psychology and pediatrics at Johns Hopkins University and Hospital in Baltimore, has attempted to distinguish between child sexual abuse or molestation and "affectional pedophilia" by claiming: "First of all it's extremely important to make a clear difference between all forms of the paraphilias. And that means making a difference between the straight-forward affectional attraction to children as compared with the attraction to children which is combined with sadism and cruelty. I would prefer to say that there are some people who have a pedophilic attraction to children which is an affectionate and loving attraction."[92]

According to Money, pedophilia should be viewed as a "sexual orientation," not a disease or disorder.[93]

The North American Man/Boy Love Association ("NAMBLA") is a "regular participant in homosexual marches" and "is the leading United States organization pushing for acceptance of man-boy sexual relationships."[94] According to the "Statement of Purpose" of *Paidika: The Journal of Paedophilia,* published in The Netherlands, the organization wishes to "demonstrate that pedophilia has been, and remains, a legitimate and productive part of the totality of human experience."[95]

Thus, the logical implication of American acceptance of homosexuality is the acceptance of pedophilia as simply another form of "sexual orientation": "You cannot have a society accept men having sex with boys unless you have them accept homosexuality first."[96] Lowering the age of consent and abolishing of state anti-sodomy statutes would do a lot toward making pedophilia a legal part of America's "lovemaps." As it was hard to imagine these homosexual "rights" twenty years ago, so relaxation of laws against pedophilia are possible without a Judeo-Christian consensus.

Lest one be tempted to believe this issue will not confront one's own family, consider the present controversy about pedophiles in the New York public school system. The New York City Board of Education has known since 1984 that Peter Melzer, a public school teacher, is a pedophile, but no action was taken—even to inform children being taught by Mr. Melzer.[97] Melzer, a regular delegate to an annual conference of pedophiles and pederasts, is part of NAMBLA, a group whose goal is to legitimize sex with children. As John Leo notes, "Leaving a known pedophile in the classroom would be quite a statement about the values of public education."[98] Mr. Melzer, as editor of the NAMBLA *Bulletin,* ran narrative letters such as "In Praise of Penises," which "compared pre- and post-pubescent male organs and a graphically descriptive piece on 'how to make that special boy feel good.'"[99] Mr. Melzer has, of course, threatened to sue if he is discharged from the school system, and the American Civil Liberties Union is standing by to defend him.[100]

THE WORKPLACE

Homosexual issues in the workplace do not yet threaten the very existence of society as do these issues with respect to the family and children, and perhaps the military. But the homosexual agenda in the workplace is radically altering the way men and women do their jobs. More importantly, basic constitutional rights, such as religious liberty, are being subordinated to the homosexual agenda of legitimization.

As noted above, a large majority of Americans believe homosexuals should have equal rights in job opportunities. Yet, the homosexual movement seeks more than equal opportunity in the workplace. The movement seeks validation in the workplace.

Under the rhetoric of creating a "nonhostile" work environment for all of its employees, the federal government . . . is further institutionalizing the homosexual agenda of legitimization and preference.

For example, it has been reported that American corporations such as Xerox and AT&T are using a gay-produced video, "On Being Gay: A Conversation with Brian McNaught," to "train" employees about the "facts" of homosexuality.[101] Some of the largest corporations employ Mr. McNaught as a consultant.[102] Other employers currently require their employees to sign a 1990s version of the 1950s loyalty oath that includes nondiscrimination provisions regarding sexual orientation. Prominent companies such as AT&T, IBM, and General Motors are instituting formal nondiscrimination policies.[103]

Employees who have no ability or intention to discriminate against persons because of their sexual orientation are being censored from even expressing their beliefs regarding sexual orientation issues—even when others are permitted to express their contrary beliefs or viewpoints.

Employees with the "wrong" views, including those based upon sincerely-held religious beliefs, are censored, discriminated against, and ridiculed. Employees who seek exemption from employer "training" sessions that involve sexual orientation are increasingly terminated, censored, or punished in less tangible ways, such as the losing of preferred job assignments, work schedules, or even being subjected to social "freezing out."[104]

Asserting that it is committed to creating a work environment where all employees are supported, Eastman Kodak, for example, permitted a homosexual newsletter on the company's electronic mail system.[105] On the other hand, many employers ban Christian newsletters or information on company electronic mail systems. AT&T sponsored the first AT&T Lesbian and Gay United Employees ("LeAGUE") Conference in 1993.[106]

According to a LeAGUE newsletter at NCR Corporation, "LeAGUE groups have existed in many AT&T organizations for several years and are beginning to be formed at NCR."[107] According to this newsletter, one of the purposes of LeAGUE is to "serve as a liaison between the lesbian, gay and bisexual communities and NCR to educate management and employees to eliminate heterosexist bias."[108]

Employees at various companies who hold sincere religious beliefs and oppose homosexuality have reported adverse employment decisions and other discrimination against them based upon those views. As a result of ignorance, popular misunderstanding, apathy, and political or social expediency, employers and others increasingly elevate the rights of the homosexual employee over religious employees.

Under the rhetoric of creating a "nonhostile" work environment for all of its employees, the federal government, as employer, is further institutionalizing the homosexual agenda of legitimization and preference. For example, one United States Forest Service region (part of the United States Department of Agriculture) has published a report entitled "Sexual Orientation: An Issue of Workforce Diversity" which, among other things, calls for that organization to "develop, issue and implement a policy that specifically prohibits discrimination and harassment on the basis of sexual *orientation*, in hiring, promotions, and other employment practices."[109] The policy requires that the regional forester institute "prompt and decisive disciplinary actions to violators of the policy."[110] The purpose of the policy is to:

> [I]ncorporate sexual orientation awareness into the various training programs such as non-hostile work environment, civil rights, and new employee orientation. This could be accomplished by presentations and programs developed by the cadre [of gay, lesbian, and bisexual employees] and/or consultants from the gay, lesbian, bisexual communities. Training to begin with top management and on through to all employees in order to promote better understanding. Include gay, lesbian, bisexual resources and information in local New Employee Ori-

entation package/welcome booklet, Sponsorship Program and transfer of station packets.[111]

The program continues with directives for "local multicultural awareness celebrations that include gay, lesbian, and bisexual issues, for example Gay Pride Month in June" and the incorporation "into existing awards system, awards for non-hostile work environments based on sexual orientation."[112]

The policy also directs "supervisors to consider an employee's domestic partner or nontraditional family member when assigning weekly and daily schedules, or approving annual leave vacations, just as married spouses are considered. Also allowed would be paternity leave to care for an employee's domestic partner or nontraditional family member."[113]

And, among many other provisions, the policy directs "units to consider gay and lesbian owned businesses when arranging local purchase agreements or BPA's and when mailing Bids for Solicitations for contracts."[114] This is not even an issue of discrimination but of preferential treatment.

Aside from the legitimacy of any of these proposals and their effect on the religious liberties of Forest Service employees, it must be remembered that all of the foregoing policies will be implemented through the use of *federal tax dollars*.

EFFECT ON RELIGIOUS EMPLOYERS

Individual states[115] have been quickly moving to add homosexuals to their lists of protected minorities, and as the federal judiciary changes in both composition and judicial philosophy over the coming years, there is a strong possibility that judges will begin to accord more weight to psychological and medical research that purports to prove that homosexuality is indeed immutable,[116] in which case it is more likely that homosexuals will begin to achieve "suspect class" status. To date, the U.S. Supreme Court has labeled only race, alienage, and national origin as suspect classes.[117] Gender and nonmarital children (illegitimacy) are, according to the Court, quasi-suspect classes.[118]

Many of the courts that have declined to accord homosexuals suspect/quasi-suspect status have analogized to the Supreme Court's influential decision in *Bowers v. Hardwick*.[119] The *Hardwick* Court held that there exists no fundamental right protected by the Fourteenth Amendment due process clause to engage in homosexual activity, and that it is thus permissible for states to enact sodomy statutes making the sexual practices of homosexuals illegal.[120]

137

From this holding, however, other courts have reasoned that it would be anomalous to hold that the very practices that identify and define the group seeking suspect/quasi-suspect classification could be criminalized and prohibited.[121]

In any case, although it may not be a violation of federal law to refuse to hire a homosexual, depending upon the jurisdiction, discriminating against an individual solely because he or she is a homosexual may now violate state or local law.[122] For example, Colorado revised its state personnel board regulations when "sexual preference" was added as a separately stated nonmerit factor, in effect prohibiting all discrimination against personnel because of their sexual preference.[123] Similarly, California's Labor Code proscribes "discrimination or different treatment in any aspect of employment or opportunity for employment based on actual or perceived sexual orientation."[124]

The District of Columbia has enacted comprehensive anti-discrimination provisions.[125] Not only does the District prohibit discrimination on the basis of sexual orientation, as some other states do, but it also explicitly *refuses to grant exemptions from the law to religious organizations/churches, even if hiring a homosexual would be directly contrary to the teachings of that organization/church.*[126] This is "religious apartheid" clearly demonstrated.

Under this provision, one could be in violation of the law for refusing to provide services to a homosexual where the sexual orientation of the individual seeking services was a substantial factor in the refusal to meet the need.[127]

More and more states are proposing and debating homosexual anti-discrimination provisions in their legislatures.[128]

PRIVATE HOUSING CONCERNS

While generally individuals are free to contract with whomever they wish, and thus are free to refuse to deal with certain persons (within rather broad legal parameters, of course), some states are currently expanding the coverage of their housing antidiscrimination statutes to prohibit landlords from refusing to rent or sell to homosexuals, even from advertising a preference for heterosexuals. In 1991, for example, Vermont added "sexual orientation" language to its "Unfair Housing Practices" statute.[129] Under this provision, it is illegal to refuse to rent or sell, or to refuse to negotiate for the sale or rental of housing, on the basis of the other individual's sexual orientation.[130] Likewise, the terms, conditions, or privileges of such rental or sale may not be adjusted according to the sexual preference of the renter/buyer.[131] Neither may a landowner in Vermont include in his or her advertising for rental or sale statements that a heterosexual is preferred, or that homosexuals may not rent or buy,[132] or represent to a homosexual that there are no units available when in actuality there are available units.[133] Finally, it is illegal under this Vermont statute to engage in "blockbusting" practices, in which harassment is used to attempt to induce the targeted party (here homosexuals) to leave the neighborhood or housing complex.[134]

The Vermont legislature amended the statute in 1987 to include exemptions for religious organizations, although it does not appear that exemptions are afforded *individual* landowners who may object to rental or sale to homosexuals on grounds of conscience.[135] Churches and religious organizations may limit the sale, rental, or occupancy of their noncommercial units to those of the same religion,[136] although the "religious restriction or preference must be stated written policies and procedures of the religious organization, association or society."[137]

A Massachusetts antidiscrimination statute prohibits housing discrimination on the basis of the sexual orientation of the person seeking to rent or buy.[138] Landowners are not permitted to inquire as to the sexual orientation of any applicant for housing.[139] The section does not apply, however, to the leasing of a "single dwelling unit in a two family dwelling, the other occupancy unit of which is occupied by the owner as his residence."[140]

SCHOOLS AND UNIVERSITIES

As noted in chapter 4, the political correctness regime has changed the vocabulary regarding gender, race, ethnicity, and sexual orientation. In America's public schools and university campuses, the homosexual agenda is being implemented within the PC context.

For example, in mid-1993, the Massachusetts Board of Education reportedly "endorsed a four-point plan suggesting that schools adopt policies to promote sensitivity to gay and lesbian students and provide counseling for the youths and their families."[141] It plans to hold "sensitivity training workshops for teachers and is encouraging schools to cover sexual orientation in their anti-harassment policies." It is reported that "110 of the state's 300 high schools have signed up" for the program.[142]

In May 1993, a high school in Bremerton, Washington, made national news as the homosexual debate resounded in the school's corridors. At issue was a policy proposed by a student that would have prevented openly gay students from serving as student leaders. The principal of the school vowed to veto the policy because it would violate the school's civil rights policy.[143]

It is interesting to note that the ACLU, which has vigorously opposed Bible clubs on campus, is promoting the federal Equal Access Act as a vehicle for gay student organizations to use in requiring access to school facilities for their meetings.[144] In this respect, a federal court has held that a gay male high school student in Rhode Island was entitled to take another male student to the school prom as his date, thus upholding the claim that lesbian and gay students are entitled to the same benefits and access to student activities as other students.[145]

Many American colleges and universities are implementing policies and programs that compel students and professors to accept the homosexual and lesbian lifestyle as legitimate.

For example, Jerry Muller gives us a broad view of homosexual inroads on college campuses:

[E]specially within the last year, homosexual ideology has made a great leap forward in its institutionalization in the American academy. At many colleges, gay/lesbian/bisexual student associations are among the most active organizations on campus, funded by student fees and by institutional funds from the university's Office of Multiculturalism. Frequently, the program of extraacademic orientation for freshmen includes sessions in which students are presented with "homosexual perspectives" alongside what are alleged to be those of blacks, Asians, and other minorities; students are repeatedly reminded that antipathy to homosexuality is on a par with racism. At Harvard, each dorm has a designated gay tutor. Columbia University recently accepted a gift of $200,000 to establish a scholarship that will be given each year to a student who is active in gay matters on campus, and the chairman of Columbia's English Department has let it be known that he is "committed to hiring, tenuring, and working with" gay and lesbian scholars. Universities including Stanford, Chicago, Iowa, and Pitzer College have recently begun to offer spousal benefits including health insurance and tuition remission to homosexual partners of faculty members. Columbia University Press publishes a series, "Between Men-Between Women: Lesbian and Gay Studies," including most recently Allen Ellenzweig, *The Homoerotic Photograph: Male Images from Durieu/Delacroix to Mapplethorpe* (1992). Commercial publishers with similar series include NAL Books and St. Martin's.

There have been several annual national academic conferences devoted to gay studies, three at Yale and one each at Harvard and Rutgers, with plans for others at CUNY and in San Francisco. The national Lesbian and Gay Studies Association was founded in 1991. There are academic journals focused on homosexuality, such as the *Journal of Homosexuality,* which published its twenty-third volume in 1992. The spread of gay studies has led to a proliferation of works on the history, incidence, and culture of homosexuality. This has certainly marked an increase in knowledge. Often, however, this new scholarship has reinterpreted Western cultural history in a manner that underplays the cultural condemnation of homosexual activity or overstates the incidence of homosexuality.[146]

Three of the colleges that make up the University of California at Santa Cruz require all freshmen to go through "homophobia" workshops.[147]

At Penn State, roommates who do not wish to live together (even on the basis of religious objections to homosexuality) must go through counseling sessions designed to "resolve" the problem. Transfers that are requested because of "group membership" are not guaranteed.[148]

The University of Oregon is providing family housing units on the same basis to traditional families and homosexual couples with physical custody of children.[149]

In 1990, a training workshop for resident advisors at Cornell University included a "surprise" film on homosexual behavior that was very graphic. According to a university spokesman, "The facilitators did call some of the resulting outrage 'homophobic' in its origins."[150]

In 1993, East Carolina University introduced a program called "Purple Pride."[151] The announced purpose of the program is to eliminate, among other things, acts of "homophobia" and "religious intolerance" for the university community and "ultimately from the larger society."[152]

Students who express moral objection to homosexuality are often subject to disciplinary sanctions. For example, a graduating college senior at a respected private Christian university in Texas was denied his diploma due to his politically incorrect speech about homosexuals on campus. The student's case was especially poignant because he would have been the first in his family to graduate from college and his entire family had come to his graduation ceremony—only to learn that he would not be permitted to participate because he had not properly repented.

Many states and cities have statutes, ordinances, and executive orders that prohibit discrimination against homosexuals by private as well as public entities.[153] Presumably, these enactments will be increasingly used to silence religious opposition to the homosexual agenda in America's schools.

BRINGING PEOPLE ALONG

Linda Chavez contemplates these issues and writes:

While we ought to treat such persons humanely and compassionately and respect their right to privacy—so long as their sexual behavior occurs in private—that should be the limit of our tolerance. To do more, for example to confer spousal or adoption rights to homosexual partners or even to forbid all forms of discrimination against those who engage in homosexual behavior, is to legitimate that behavior.

That is not, however, meant to imply that homosexuals may be mistreated with impunity. They have a right to be safe and secure in their persons and property, to earn a living, to participate in civic life, to express their views—in short, the rights that all other individuals enjoy in a free society. But because homosexuality is—or should properly be—defined by behavior, homosexuals enjoy no special rights to be protected in an area where behavior routinely determines disparate treatment. . . .

Most homosexual activists are not content simply to be left alone or to be accorded only individual rights. Instead, they crave affirmation.[154]

A recent letter to the editor in the homosexual publication, "This Week in Texas," begins:

Recently, our household received mail from The Rutherford Institute, an organization that helps stop religious persecution. Normally, I would have no problem with this, but now they have pushed their limits too far.

The subject of the mailing was about gay activist groups and gay rights bills interfering with religious freedoms. Anyone with minimal intelligence knows that this just cannot happen.[155]

The last statement could not be further from the truth. The agenda of radical homosexuals is targeted straight at religious freedoms. The militant homosexuals do not seek toleration but the power to *compel* everyone to accept them and give them special rights based on their conduct. If one is a religious person with sincerely held beliefs that such conduct is wrong, then one's very right to *believe* and act upon those beliefs is being subordinated to the special treatment of homosexuals. Religious people are being coerced into accepting homosexual behavior as morally equal to heterosexual mores.

Senator John Kerry said on a session of the "McNeil-Lehrer News Hour" in early 1993 that, of course, this issue will require a lot of education—we'll have to spend a lot of effort, he said, "bringing people along." It's the "bringing people along" that is the problem. For Christians, homosexual conduct is simply against the laws of nature and God—in other words, morally wrong.

In this period of history, militant homosexuals not only reveal and exploit their liaisons and lifestyles but also fiercely promote the homosexual relationship as a morally acceptable alternative to marriage. Governmental coercion that would require the validation and compelled personal acceptance of homosexual conduct by all citizens would grossly violate the rights of most religious persons in America.

C. S. Lewis once observed that, in punishing wrongdoing, there are limits to which most would agree. However, if one is *helping* someone, it's not punishment, so ironically, there are no limits. Thus the issue arises: If religious persons are being "helped" or "brought along" to accept homosexual conduct as a valid moral choice, where are the limits—especially if those who resist homosexual invasion into all areas of life are themselves considered immoral?

Cal Thomas offers this commentary:

The open celebration of homosexuality represents the final disconnection from a personal God. If the barrier against societal acceptance of homosexuality falls, there will be no other that can stand. How can the pedophile be kept at bay if their "brothers" and "sisters" are liberated? . . .

. . . [I]t is necessary to oppose behavior one believes is objectively wrong and counterproductive to the society that tolerates it and to the person who practices it.

The shameless promotion of sexual immorality in the streets of our nation's capital, and the public blessing bestowed on it by the president, are the latest in a mountain of evidence that proves this nation has forgotten God and is exposing itself to the grave consequences that historically have followed spiritual amnesia. A common malady of many nations that have collapsed internally before being conquered externally was a melting of the moral resolve.

Homosexual practice cannot be seen in isolation from other unraveling societal threads. 30 million abortions and counting, broken families, drive-by shootings, riots, drug abuse, a pornography explosion, overflowing prisons, teen suicides—the list goes on. These are reflections, not causes, of a descent into decadence.

Communists outlawed pornography, homosexuality and other forms of sexual looseness. They knew that sex is a powerful force that, if misused, can bring down a nation faster than any invader.

Theologian Carl Henry, who has lived through eight of this century's decades, has written: "No society that disregards ethical finalities can long postpone ignominious collapse." . . .

When a nation loses its power to resist immorality, it is headed for serious trouble. If the United States continues to decline, it won't be because of a faltering economy—it will be for the same reason Solzhenitsyn observed in his land: "Men have forgotten God; that's why all these things happened."[156]

8

THE END
OF PUBLIC
RELIGION

Every vestige of Christianity is being removed from American public life. Christian expression is being hounded into the private sphere—where no one can see religion or hear religious utterances.

In the past, much of the public expression of Christianity in America has been manifested as America's "civil religion":

> If you take the faith out of Religion, you have a wasted Sunday morning. If you take the belief out of Law, all you have is litigation. And if you take the Ritual out of celebration, all you have is Presidents' Day.[1]

Therefore, in contemporary America, the last traces of Christianity in public represent mere religion without faith, law without belief, and celebration without ritual. Only these may now be practiced in public.

Thus, it is little wonder that Illinois schoolteachers may lead their students in the Pledge of Allegiance that still contains the phrase "under God" only because a federal court said that the phrase has lost *any* religious significance through rote repetition and now amounts to "ceremonial deism."[2]

In line with this reasoning, Mark Twain once commented on the national motto "In God We Trust" that appears on America's money: "It is simple, direct, gracefully phrased. It always sounds well—In God We Trust. I don't believe it would sound any better if it were true."[3]

While debating the theoretical small points between "civil liberties" and "civil rights,"[4] the American Civil Liberties Union and other organizations are using the courts and threats of litigation to cleanse all Christian religious expression from American public life. Their subterfuge is the so-called wall of separation between church and state—a phrase that is not even found in the United States Constitution. The wall of separation is, therefore, fast becoming the wall of religious apartheid.

Religious apartheid is becoming a fact of American life for many reasons. Some of these reasons, as discussed in chapter 9, have to do with theology. Some are cultural.

CYBERSPACE AMERICA

The *culture* of late eighteenth century and early nineteenth century America was radically different than today's America. Early America, of course, was agrarian, and black slavery flourished.[5] The center of American life was church and family, generally in that order. Entertainment was mostly limited to religious expression for worship and honor of God.

But the present is much different. A growing number of communities in the America of the 1990s sounds like this:

> Every night on Prodigy, CompuServe, Genie and thousands of smaller computer bulletin boards, people by the hundreds of thousands are logging on to a great computer-mediated gabfest, an interactive debate that allows them to leap over barriers of time, place, sex and social status. Computer networks make it easy to reach out and touch strangers who share a particular obsession or concern. "We're replacing the old drugstore soda fountain and town square, where community used to happen in the physical world."[6]

These "virtual communities" are groups of "like-minded people who meet on-line and share ideas on everything from politics to punk rock. The global village is full of tiny electronic subdivisions made up of cold-fusion physicists, white supremacists, gerontologists and Grateful Deadheads. Like any other community, each has its own in-jokes, cliques, bozos and bores."[7] Citizens of these virtual communities share information without ever sharing themselves. Value systems are replaced with the parameters of interest and need. Indeed, "values" are irrelevant except insofar as they relate to the quality of information and its source.

Much of the America that has not moved to cyberspace (the "globe-circling, interconnected telephone network that is the conduit for billions of voice, fax and computer-to-computer communications")[8] is isolated, disconnected, and drowning in poverty, drugs, abortion, non-marital sex, and desperation.

Many of the remainder are returning to a religion based on their social needs:

> Some successful boomer churches are shrines to secular movements, particularly the 12-step program modeled on Alcoholics Anonymous. "We refer to ourselves as wounded healers," says Minister Mike Matoin of Unity in Chicago, himself a former bellhop, bouncer, cabdriver, and child of an alcoholic. "A lot of baby boomers can relate to us. We've been through our own recovery, and we're not on a pedestal." If a spiritual search is going on, it is for an inner child. In a room remarkably empty of religious paraphernalia, on a riser, behind the pulpit, an enormous teddy bear sits in the background. "The twentysomethings," observes Matoin, "are searching achievers. Working hard. 'I've got a condo, Rollerblades, but something's missing.' They've got prosperity but not peace of mind. The person in his 40s or 50s, it's the life experience. Busted relationships. They're alcoholics, married to alcoholics, bumped around, lost jobs, and they find a safe harbor."[9]

In the America of the 1990s, Americans watch an average of 7.04 hours of television daily, 28 percent of the total births in the country are to unwed mothers, 11.3 of each 100,000 teenagers ages 15 to 24 commit suicide, and there are 75.8 violent crimes committed per 10,000 people.[10]

It is easy to see that Americans no longer share a common cultural heritage, let alone a heritage that might be called "American." As one writer has noted: "Today increasing numbers of nominal Americans refuse to see America as anything more than a collection of ZIP codes. Their ideal is Yugoslavia, without machine guns."[11]

ONCE UPON A TIME

Early America was also a much different place *politically* than cyberspace America. There was no national bureaucracy; the preservation of a decentralized government was an important goal of colonial government. American federalism—the unique system created by a written agreement between nation-states and an overarching government with only specified powers—ensured that the federal government of colonial America remained limited.[12]

Many Americans today *demand* that the government, at some level, provide them with benefits—and rules—that affect every aspect of their lives. Indeed, in the 1990s, when the national debt is shrinking financial support for the benefit state, various groups of Americans, banded together by their common demands, are even attacking each other to preserve their benefits. Thus, the young are picketing against Social Security, and homosexuals are seeking ever increasing federal support of AIDS research at the expense of research for cancer and other serious illnesses.

Therefore, the very size and power of the federal government and the very nature of the contemporary state are wholly different from the government of colonial America. This, in turn, makes church-state relations very different as well.

FROM A STATE CHURCH TO RELIGIOUS APARTHEID

Early America was an era of *established state religions*.[13] As one historian writes: "To the colonists, religion, but of their kind, was not only a way of life but was life itself, here and in the hereafter."[14] Although the state churches were of different denominations, they shared the common heritage of Protestant Christianity. As one commentator who disagrees with this religious configuration notes: "Despite the breath of fresh air which blew over the newly-created United States and states in 1787 [through] 1789, [religious] repression and conformity were still the rule."[15] For those who were or seemed different, colonial Americans "obliterate[d] the differences."[16] In other words, "established" religion persecuted those who did not agree with the main Protestant consensus.

Americans today obviously no longer share a common religion. New secular thought from Europe and the increased immigration of the 1800s began the erosion of the dominance of the Protestant religion in American society.[17]

For example, between 1865 and 1900, at least 13.5 million immigrants arrived in America. During the first decade of the twentieth century, another 9 million emigrated.[18] These immigrants represented a wide variety of ethnic groups, and many of them professed religious beliefs different from those that were prominent in America at the time.[19] During the same period, the rising presence and influence of American Judaism, Catholicism, and lesser known religions, such as the Mormons, further diminished the Protestant role as the nation's religious yardstick.[20]

148

More recently, mainline Protestantism and Judaism in America have declined, while, as *Time* magazine's Richard Ostling reports, "churches on either side of the spiritual spectrum are growing fast: the conservative evangelical Protestantism on one hand and an assortment of Eastern, New Age and unconventional religions on the other."[21]

CHRISTIAN AMERICA

Even though the cultural, political, and religious milieu of America has changed dramatically since the early 1900s, America is still sometimes referred to as a "Christian nation."[22] In connection with contemporary America, this term is now generally used to mean only that a majority of Americans are churchgoers who profess some belief in God.

But the use of even such a generalized historic reference can inflame passions today. Some of these passions reflect concerns for the protection of religious *diversity* in America, as can be seen in one writer's recounting of a political event in late 1992:

Mississippi Gov. Kirk Fordice was soundly criticized for his remark at a Nov. 17 [1992] meeting of Republican governors that "The United States of America is a Christian nation."

After his remark, South Carolina's Gov. Carroll Campbell said, "The value base of this country comes from the Judeo-Christian heritage and that is something we need to realize. I just wanted to add the 'Judeo' part." Fordice replied, "If I wanted to do that, I would have done it."

Fordice defended his remark later on CNN, saying: "It is still a simple fact that the United States is a Christian nation."

He explained, "Christianity is the predominant religion in America. We all know that's an incontrovertible fact. The media always refer to the Jewish state of Israel. They talk about the Muslim country of Saudi Arabia, of Iran, of Iraq. We all talk about the Hindu nation of India. America is not a nothing country. It's a Christian country."

Fordice cited surveys noting that 86 percent of Americans consider themselves Christian, but praised America's ethnic diversity. "It's the true melting pot of the world," he said. "That's the strength of our country, and the strength certainly is not enhanced by denying simple facts that Christianity is the predominant religion. That can't possibly be construed as denigrating the Jewish faith."

Fordice may need to look up "possibly." Denunciations from Jewish organizations were fast and furious. Anti-Defamation League leaders called his remarks "unworthy of any governor elected to represent a diverse and pluralistic constituency." And Rabbi Steven Engel, who leads Mississippi's largest Jewish congregation, added, "There is a fine line between anti-Semitism and ignorance. But we all know what happens where there is a great intolerance for people that are different in any way."[23]

The term "Christian nation" also stirs strong emotions on the part of *religious separationists,* as may be seen in an article in a separationist magazine:

Generally speaking, when Religious Right leaders use the term "Christian nation," they are referring to their desire to see the nation's laws reflect the narrow sectarian principles they themselves hold—not simply saying that most Americans identify with Christian denominations. These misguided activists want to send a signal that only those individuals with the "correct" religious views are real Americans.

Mainstream American religious denominations do not use the term "Christian nation" or speak of such a concept as desirable, recognizing that it offends and excludes those Americans who are not affiliated with the Christian faith. Thus, the term is closely tied to the Religious Right and its extreme religion-political goals. Today, as in previous eras of American life, it is unmistakably a term of exclusion, not inclusion.[24]

EXCLUSION OR INCLUSION?

The foregoing examples summarize the nature of much of the religious apartheid problem in America today: Many who are leading the effort to rid American public life of Christian influence are concerned that Christians are trying to re-Christianize America through the political process—at the expense of the religious views of other Americans.[25] These separationist groups apparently intend to fight such a perceived re-Christianizing at every opportunity,[26] because of their extreme view of the separation of church and state.

Some individuals and organizations do, in fact, seek a Christian Reconstruction of America. "Christian Reconstruction" means rebuilding a strictly Christian consensus, that is, in the ethics, behavior, and beliefs of all sectors of society. This has raised among separationists concerns such as those expressed in *Liberty* magazine:

Of course evangelicals can be involved in the democratic process. But so can I. And part of my involvement, for now at least (I haven't received word from the Lord to run for public office—yet), is to point out dangers to religious liberty.

The problem with the evangelicals (I mean the New Right politicized brand) is not so much their methods—though they have been at times, shall we say, hardly Christlike—but their overt hostility to the wall of separation of church and state. They show no understanding of the principles of the nonestablishment of religion. They continually misla-bel every attempt to keep church and state separate as "hostility" to-ward religion. And what's even worse, is that they do all this in the name of Christ, which, however egregious, is their First Amendment right (guaranteed and protected by the perfidious wall of separation).

I agree, too, that not all evangelicals "march in lockstep" to Robertson and Falwell, at least not now. But Robertson doesn't need them all. He needs just enough to vote in his agenda, which—despite whatever good it possesses—is ruined by the unrepentant hostility to the church-state separation. And that *is* dangerous.[27]

These concerns are often heightened by televangelists and religious television broadcasters who use their "fiber-optic pulpits" to further an agenda that sometimes seems directed to matters other than saving souls or exercising their own religious liberties.[28] Such concerns give rise to the negative image of televangelists. For example, consider the following remarks by a *Time* magazine journalist reacting to the presen-tations of Pat Buchanan and Pat Robertson at the Republican National Convention in August 1992:

Family values, for example, is a perfectly legitimate issue and by any measure a winning one. Yet in 1992 it was driven into the ground by the aggressive, intolerant way it was presented at the Houston con-vention.

Americans are desperately concerned about the corrupting effects of the mass culture on their children. They are rightly aroused by grade school curriculums that present homosexuality as just another life-style choice. They know instinctively that single parenthood, for all the heroism it summons from women, is the surest path to childhood pov-erty. They want to rebuild "family values"—but they refuse to see the rebuilding as an act of religious war.[29]

The term "religious war" connotes a struggle between the state and those who would overrule it. Money and power would be prerequisites for such a struggle. Thus, the growth of televangelism, with its appear-ance of unlimited money and power, has actually made it *seem* more probable that Christians could "re-Christianize America" and wage such a "religious war" at the expense of the religious views of other Americans.

For example, some television evangelism empires, perhaps funded by massive direct mail campaigns and multilevel marketing programs, provide visibility sufficient to produce an aura of influence and sub-stance out of proportion to reality. This, in turn, can foster religious apartheid in three ways.

First, as noted above, the high profile of television evangelism creates an illusion of power and importance that fosters fears of Christian reconstruction, a theocracy, or at a minimum the imposition of religious views upon a people accustomed to significant freedom in the matter of religious beliefs.

Moreover, the political slogans of some groups associated with a television evangelist or a televangelist organization may even raise concern among religious as well as nonreligious persons about the nature of religious freedom in America should such groups actually achieve their asserted (or perceived) agenda.

> *Indeed, [because of] the changed nature of American culture, politics, and religion . . . individual religious liberties are now at risk.*

Second, television evangelism is, by its very nature, a medium that to some degree hastens the privatization of religion by creating the illusion of "community." As Robert Wuthnow writes,

> If anything should draw people out of the secret recesses of their homes and force them to live "in community," it was the church. The Bible itself commanded believers not to forsake the assembling of themselves together. It was in the midst of the assembled faithful that the miracle of *kerygma* happened. Now television was replacing this community with a miracle of its own—the miracle of sitting motionless and alone before a preacher thousands of miles away who could not listen, who could not love, but could only speak.[30]

Perhaps even more importantly, members of the local church may feel relieved of their obligations to visit the shut-ins, the ill, the elderly because, after all, they can hear "the Word" on television. Originally a baby-sitter for America's children, television is now all too often the electronic missionary for a community.

Third, because televangelism by its nature is a product of the entertainment medium, it must, as discussed in detail in chapter 9, entertain. Thus, presentations that deal with the objective facts of Christianity must be replaced with presentations that leave the viewers—sitting alone in front of their television—subjectively "feeling something."

America has become addicted to messages that manipulate—horror shows that horrify, so-called docu-dramas that titillate, news shows that reproduce manufactured "news." Therefore, religious television fare often must present its message in exaggerated forms.

In turn, for those who see no other religious message, religion (Christianity in particular) seems weird, extremist, and manipulative. The effect is twofold: nonreligious persons are motivated to put even more distance between themselves and religious persons, and many religious persons feel led to do the same.

Nonetheless, in the context of religious liberty, the massive growth and power of the modern American state makes it highly improbable that any church or religious organization could ever gain control of the whole state government.

Indeed, taken together, the changed nature of American culture, politics, and religion have *reversed* the concerns of a religious takeover of the state, in the sense that *individual religious liberties are now at risk.*[31] Consequently, "[g]iven the reality of [the] modern administrative state, as government increases the scope of its activities, it must increasingly be sensitive to the interests of religious people in order to merely remain neutral."[32]

Supreme Court Justice Anthony Kennedy acknowledges this point in a 1989 Supreme Court case, where he writes:

> In this century, as the modern administrative state expands to touch the lives of its citizens in such diverse ways and redirects their financial choices through programs of its own, it is difficult to maintain the fiction that requiring government to avoid all assistance to religion can in fairness be viewed as serving the goal of neutrality.[33]

THE NEW MINORITIES

Modern America is too culturally and religiously diverse, and the nonreligious state is too strong and pervasive for any type of religious takeover. The norm of the present is pluralism.

Traditionally-defined pluralism is the concept that cultures and races are different and that they should be respected for what they are. The new pluralism, which fuses quite easily with political correctness, says that certain forms of speech and actions are prohibited in the name of tolerance for groups in the minority.

Thus, one hears it said, for example, that a Christian should not seek to force his or her beliefs on another. Yet by definition free speech in the marketplace is a series of attempts to persuade (or impose) a viewpoint on another. Unfortunately, contemporary pluralism says just the opposite: All views are free and open unless they happen to be overtly Christian. This is modern American diversity.

America's response to diversity has historically been based on the "Melting Pot" theory, basically the "obliteration" of differences. However, with global technology, increased personal mobility, international employers and churches, and the recognition of the sometimes shameful treatment of America's ethnic and racial minorities, the Melting Pot Theory has been discarded in the United States.[34]

Modern America, as historian Arthur Schlesinger has suggested, is moving toward "an open society founded on tolerance of differences."[35] Indeed, the toleration theory is reflected in a proliferation, especially since the early 1960s, of laws, government policies, and court decisions that preserve and protect the civil rights of those who are different.

> *In Illinois, a kindergartner . . . was chastised for writing "I love you God" on her tiny palm.*

Unlike the other classes of persons, however, religious persons are often not included under the toleration theory. The maturing sensitivities of Americans for the rights and differences of others often do not include the rights of truly religious people; their views are supposedly too "limiting" and "judgmental" of others.

Christians who live by and practice a traditional moral code, although an easily recognizable and distinct minority, for example, are generally not recognized as such. One definition of a minority is that "part of a population differing from others in some characteristics and often subjected to differential treatment."[36] In other words, a minority is a class of people that is treated differently than the majority.

Some Christians, often labeled "fundamentalists," reject as theological error the mere superficial acknowledgment of God. These Christians take their religion seriously enough to face social penalties and, thereby, discrimination for their religious viewpoints. And discrimination they do face:

> It is not enough that the murderous ravings of David Koresh and his apocalyptic religious cult have turned into a terrible human tragedy. There seems to be a great desire to turn it into a cultural statement. The

siege at Waco has occasioned a worldwide festival of commentary—and condescension—on the subject of American primitivism. . . . Tut-tutting about American primitivism mixes easily with that other sport, eye rolling about religious primitivism. You know: *There go those religious nuts again.* In keeping with a popular culture that gives serious religion no attention but devotes endless prime time to crooked, hypocritical and otherwise deformed religiosity, the Waco wackos are getting more coverage in a week than religion does in a year.[37]

As another writer notes: "Religion in the popular mind has become virtually synonymous with fanaticism. Preachers are drawn as Elmer Gantry-like caricatures, and their followers are, in the words of the *Washington Post,* 'poor, uneducated and easy to command.' When religion does find its way into the national debate, it is invariably in the context of bombings, terror, murder and cultic violence."[38]

Thus, while members of non-Christian religious organizations, such as Orthodox Jews or Muslims, who face discrimination based upon their religious views, generally find redress under the law, such redress for the fundamentalist Christian or "Christian minority" is often more difficult because employers, lawmakers, and the courts fail to recognize this class as a "minority" deserving of accommodation and non-hostile neutrality by the state.

As often as not, the cultural Christian fails to defend the rights of such Christian minorities with an intensity that matches that of those who oppose Christianity in American public life. Certainly, if all who claimed to be Christians defended religious liberty, the effects of religious apartheid would be more limited.

BELIEVER VERSUS THE STATE

Though the occasions are rare, the Christian believer who may have to face a penalty (even jail) for his or her beliefs is a true minority in America. And these people are finding themselves increasingly at odds with the goals of modern culture and the state.

Thus, the issue today is not church versus the state. It is, instead, *religious believer versus the state*.

For example, in cases where a lone child writes "I Love Jesus" on her valentine and her public school teacher says the valentine must be censored because of "separation of church and state," the question is: Where is the church? There is no church involved but simply a lone religious child versus the state.

Therefore, when using the phrase "separation of church and state," certain people and interest groups are not, in reality, speaking of a separation of church and state. Indeed, they use the phrase as a euphemism to mean the separation of *all* religious expression and symbols from American public life. The phrase then is a propaganda tool to suppress an entire segment of the population—that is, religious people.

Unfortunately, it is the *individual*, the solitary person deeply committed to his or her religious views, who is suffering the loss of religious liberty in America. This fact is more or less acknowledged even by organizations that sometimes tout the "separation of church and state." Thus, according to Nadine Strossen, professor at New York Law School and president of the ACLU: "I think we have a secular society in which people who have deeply held religious beliefs of any kind are looked at with some suspicion. For example, if somebody had a religious view against abortion, I think it's the religion that's looked at with special suspicion rather than the same belief but based on a secular reason."[39]

Yet, the "wall of separation" is being erected around even the smallest public expression of religion. The examples are legion.

> In Idaho, the ACLU has sued to remove religious references from public monuments and memorials.

> In California, crosses erected as memorials in public areas are under legal attack.

> In Virginia, a memorial for former University of Virginia law students who were killed in the Civil War was removed from a wall because of the "overtly Christian message" it contained.

> In Florida, a pastor received a Notice of Violation from the County Enforcement Office where he lived because he had placed a small Latin cross in the front yard of his own private residence—even though the county permitted real estate signs and temporary political signs on residential property.

> In New York, a prison guard was fired because he wore the cross he had inherited from his father under his shirt while he was on duty.

> In Missouri, an elementary school student was placed in detention for praying before eating his lunch.

> In North Carolina, hundreds of people were arrested for praying silently on the public sidewalks.

> In Michigan, a painting of Jesus Christ that had hung in the hallway of a high school for thirty years was removed because it was too offensive to a high school senior.

In Utah, homeowners conducting private Bible studies in their own homes were accused of violating zoning ordinances.

In Illinois, a kindergartner who was grieved about having to cross out the word "God" in her spelling book was chastised for writing "I love you God" on her tiny palm to show her remorse.

In Texas, an uneaten cake was sent home from school by a teacher because the student's mother had baked it in the shape of a cross and sent it to the school for an Easter celebration.

In Colorado, a fifth grade teacher was prohibited from keeping his Bible on his desk throughout the school day. The United States Supreme Court refused to hear the teacher's appeal.[40]

In Texas, teachers have been enjoined from participating in any prayers at their high school or at its extra-curricular events.

In Michigan, a second-grader was prevented from playing a videotape of herself singing a religious song in class as part of her VIP celebration because of the tape's religious content.

In Illinois, the valentines of elementary school children were censored when the public school teacher discovered Christian tracts included in some of the sealed envelopes.

These cases do not represent true church-state concerns. In none of these examples is the "state" trying to "establish" a church.

Rather, these cases represent the *privatization* of religion in America. There is increasing social, cultural, and legal pressure for religion to be merely a "private" matter. Although most Americans will not yet challenge the right to be religious, increasing numbers of Americans appear to believe that religion should be *exercised* only in private. As Supreme Court Justice Antonin Scalia noted in his dissent in the graduation prayer decision of the United States Supreme Court: "Church and state would not be such a difficult subject if religion were, as the Court apparently thinks it to be, some purely personal avocation that can be indulged entirely in secret, *like pornography, in the privacy of one's room.*"[41]

Justice Scalia's comments were based on the majority opinion in that case, which included this statement by Justice Anthony Kennedy: "The design of the Constitution is that preservation and transmission of religious beliefs and worship is a responsibility and a choice committed to the private sphere, which itself is promised freedom to pursue that mission."[42]

THE SWOON

Christians, of course, hold a major responsibility for the removal of religion from public life. A significant factor in this state of affairs has been the dwindling influence of Christianity, which has, in turn, permitted secular thought to progress and dominate the culture. The pronounced effect this has had on our world is illustrated by the evident moral decadence of the West. The noted British theologian H. G. Wood candidly observes: "Somehow the whole bottom has fallen out of our civilization, and a change came over the world, which if unchecked will transform it for generations. It is the death, or deathlike swoon, of Christianity."[43]

Likewise, Professor Harold Berman is concerned that the "whole culture seems to be facing the possibility of a kind of nervous breakdown."[44]

To prevent this nervous breakdown, it is going to take a refocusing of the Christian faith. Call it "old time religion" or whatever you may choose. If those who call themselves Christian believers do not once again begin to meet the real human needs of people in speaking God's truth, the future looks dim indeed.

PART THREE
A TRUE CHRISTIANITY

If I profess with the loudest voice and the clearest exposition every portion of the truth of God, except precisely that little point which the world and the devil are at the moment attacking, I am not confessing Christ, however boldly I may be professing Christ. Where the battle rages, there the loyalty of the soldier is proved, and to be steady on all the battlefield besides is mere flight and disgrace if he flinches at that point.

MARTIN LUTHER

9

THE STATE
OF MODERN
CHRISTIANITY

It has been asserted that there are fifty million evangelicals in the United States. However, in light of the minuscule effect these alleged millions have had on contemporary American culture, how could this possibly be true? Assuming for the moment that the assertion is true, it then appears that a massive number of evangelicals is not enough to carry the day. It is apparent that the faith practiced by most American evangelicals, whatever their number, is not up to the task of being salt and light to their fellow Americans. This may be due to what could be called a misguided, or at least an inadequate, Christianity.

ACCOMMODATION

In view of the pervasive secularism of most contemporary Western cultures, it is hard to deny that, to a large degree, Christianity has made truce with it. Christianity has largely accommodated itself to a secular age, which is a losing proposition since secularism considers itself the sole authentic belief system and seldom makes similar accommodations.

Compromise also has a negative effect on the Christian psyche and morale. Seeking approval from the world and attempting to blend with secularism create a second-class mentality among believers. Christians of this mentality are ineffective and will shirk their duty to stand for the truth. They are schizophrenic in their approach to life—attempting to adhere to a set of beliefs and living an alternate reality.

THE QUESTION OF BELIEF

A 1981 survey of 112 American Protestant and Catholic theology professors found that 99 percent said they believed in God. Moreover, 88 percent believed in eternal life and 83 percent in a final judgment. Yet, as one observer notes, it is quite probable that for a "significant number of these people, God, [eternal] life and final judgment were defined in a way that nineteenth-century Christians would have regarded as blasphemous."[1] In this vein, Michael Harrington writes:

> So when the same percentage confess belief in God in 1981 as did in 1881, that may conceal a transition from the God who spoke to Moses from the burning bush to Paul Tillich's "ground of being." Moreover, even though 83 percent of those respondents said they believed in final judgement, only 50 percent accepted the doctrine of hell. . . . [W]hat is revealing is the way theologians privately and consistently decide which church truths they will accept. And it is of some moment that only 56 percent of the respondents had, over a decade, tried to convert someone.[2]

There is some irony in the fact that the one pointing out this crisis of belief among Christians is an atheist. The problem is doubtless even more serious than Michael Harrington imagines. For example, many major "Christian" universities and seminaries have long abandoned the concept that the Bible is true in all that it says.

It may well be that the claims of large numbers of religious persons in America include those who merely identify with the American civil religion that is no more than theism, includes references to God in public ceremonies and on American money, but which is far from being truly Christian. Pollster George Gallup discovered that, when he probed just how important religion is in the individual lives of various people, he found a pronounced "lack of substance behind the basic belief in God."[3] He adds: "[A]s a people, we lack deep levels of individual spiritual commitment. One sign of this is that the level of ethics in this country seems to be declining—at least in terms of public perceptions of ethical behavior. . . . [W]e found there's very little difference between the churched and the unchurched in terms of their general view on ethical matters, and also their practical ethical responses in various situations."[4]

Another observer has pointed out that there is a tendency, even among evangelical Christians, to withhold the care of their souls from pastors and other believers and relegate it to psychotherapists.[5] This shift is hardly indicative of a robust faith. For their part, some pastors are too often prone to dispense cheap psychological bromides in their counseling rather than the tough ethical standards of the New Testament. Too many "Christian" seminaries have sold their spiritual birthright for a bowl of psychological porridge.

Alexander Solzhenitsyn has noted that "one word of truth outweighs the world,"[6] but Christians in the Western world do not seem to be using the powerful words of truth to combat secular ideas. With some notable exceptions, timidity is the rule. C. S. Lewis noted that Christians were often "tempted to make unnecessary concessions to those outside the Faith." They "gave in" too much, remained silent, and tended to "concede everything away."[7] And when Christians are not accommodating themselves to the world, many are attempting to hide from it.

PHARISEEISM

The Gospels take note of the fact that the Jewish religious leaders of the day resented Jesus Christ's practice of taking His meals with tax collectors and "sinners."[8] It was the Pharisees' practice to maintain a policy of strict separation from such hated and disreputable types. One spokesman for the Pharisees indicated his motivation when he prayed: "God, I thank You that I am not like other men—robbers, evil-doers, adulterers—or even like this tax collector." He went on to tell God what a wonderful fellow he was—in his own eyes, of course—while the tax collector, in his prayer, fully recognized his sin and pleaded for mercy.[9]

Although the Pharisees were part of the social structure, they so restricted their social contacts that they created a kind of isolated enclave. Individually, they were self-righteous, following a complicated set of external rules, which were often easy to circumvent in the difficult parts. Collectively, their lives centered around what amounted to a "holy club." The result was that the Pharisees were harsh and censorious to those outside their immediate circle. They were a kind of Brahmin class that considered everyone else lower-caste or even untouchable. Jesus Christ, however, willingly embraced the outcasts, saying that He had come to save those who were lost.

In similar style, many contemporary evangelicals often practice a legalistic form of separation. Legalism is the establishment of external

165

rules or taboos by which Christians are to live. These rules are usually extrabiblical or rely on certain biblical verses conveniently removed from their contexts. Legalism posits an external code not based on what one does, but on what one does *not* do: no dancing, smoking, drinking, movies, music (other than "Christian"), or card-playing.

These rules and taboos serve as convenient external checkpoints that indicate a supposed spirituality but which often amount only to a facade of holiness, just as they did for the Pharisees. This legalism makes it easy to judge others. The separatist finds it easy to thank God that he is not like other people. There is a sense in which this preoccupation with one's spiritual facade might be called humanism, improving ourselves by our own efforts, because this is not the morality that comes from God.

Many modern Christians emulate the Pharisees by retreating into a private enclave with similar results. This "club" atmosphere may explain the sharp racial divisions that are still to a great degree characteristic of American evangelicalism, even though the Bible is clear that this is not to be. As the apostle Paul recognized: "There is neither Jew nor Greek, slave nor free, male nor female, for you are all one in Christ Jesus."[10]

There is no record of Jesus requesting His followers to withdraw from the world, even though there was ample reason to do so, along with ample opportunity. In those days, there were a number of reclusive sects. Indeed, Jesus did not ask the Father to take His disciples out of the world, only that He "protect them from the evil one."[11]

Withdrawal from the world is monasticism. Throughout history, monasteries, especially during the Middle Ages, served valuable purposes. However, as British evangelical John R. W. Stott notes, monasticism "in whatever form is not a truly Christian ideal,"[12] precisely because it promotes such withdrawal. Stott has also noted that outsiders can easily sense when a church is a refuge *from* them rather than a ministry *for* them. "To the outsider the church is often not inviting but forbidding, smugly satisfied with itself and harshly condemning of others. Non-Christians sometimes say that they find more acceptable, more compassionate understanding of human foibles in the world than in the church. To them the church is lacking in warmth, even positively inhuman."[13]

Evangelical monasticism may well be the result of problems of belief. It is likely that many believers are unsure whether their beliefs will stand up to what the world has to offer. Local churches often attempt to shield their flock from anything the leaders consider "harmful." This can only produce a nonthinking faith, capable only of retreat. For example, a Christian attorney once told me that he would only view home videos with a group of his fellow church members, lest his standards of viewing slip into sin. To me, this betrays a belief system whose adherent does not trust himself enough even in matters entirely within his control. By this, however, I am not saying we do not need accountability or that there is no value in the wisdom of others.

SECTARIANISM

Contemporary Christians not only retreat from the world, they often also isolate themselves from each other. Even while rejecting the grandiose institutional designs of the ecumenical movement, one must admit that Christendom is overly divided, factionalized, and often more characterized by infighting and jealousy than by a true spirit of love and cooperation. To the world, Christendom seems a many-splintered thing, bound together by few, if any, underlying truths.

From another perspective, if Christians are continually fighting each other, or feeling separate from each other, their energies can hardly be marshaled to confront secularism. It may well be that sectarian strife results largely from a reluctance to undertake the hard battle against the real enemy. A soldier who attacks his comrade instead of the enemy is of little use on the battlefield; indeed, he or she is a positive hindrance. A house divided cannot stand.

FATALISM

Christian withdrawal may also be due to prophetic and apolocalyptic fatalism, the idea that the world will soon end. Here we see the sad scenario of Christians storing guns and food and other survival items and homes outfitted like bunkers. Many try to interpret every catastrophic event in terms of end-times prophecy. Not only does this increase the paranoia about the way things are, but any effort to "save" or salvage society seems to be a waste of time and amounts to "polishing brass on a sinking ship." And this paranoia can lead to disaster, as was illustrated by the 1993 tragedy with the Branch Davidians in Waco, Texas.

The early apostles expected the consummation of the ages in their time, but that did not cause them to congregate in holy clubs or survival camps. Rather, they went *into* all the world defenseless and trusting God for all their needs.

As a matter of fact, the "signs" for the Second Coming have been present for ages, but Jesus Christ said only the Father knew the day and the hour.[14] One must be prepared to leave this present world any time, but Christians must also be ready for a long stay, being fully aware in either case that God alone is in control.

EVANGELISM AND SOCIAL CONCERN

An attitude of withdrawal from the world may also be due to a confused view about the relationship between evangelism and "social concern." In its most extreme form, the thesis of this confused view is that God's only concern is the salvation of individual souls and that anything else is a heretical, watered-down "social gospel" that must be rejected by the faithful. Though adherents claim biblical validity, this view is far from the truth. As John Stott explains:

> This kind of evangelicalism which concentrates exclusively on saving individual souls is not true evangelicalism. It is not evangelical because it is not biblical. It forgets that God did not create souls but body-souls called human beings, who are also social beings, and that He cares about their bodies and their society as well as about their relationship with Himself and their eternal destiny. So true Christian love will care for people as people, and will seek to serve them, neglecting neither the soul for the body nor the body for the soul. As a matter of fact, it has not been characteristic of evangelicals in the past to be shy of social action, or even, when necessary, of political action.[15]

The involvement of Christians in the abolition of slavery is only one example of past "social action" by Christians. Slave owners of the time considered such activism to be religious meddling and a humanistic "social gospel." George Mueller's work with orphans is another of many examples. The involvement of Christians in AIDS ministries is a contemporary example of a truly biblical integration of evangelism and social concern.

Whatever the reasons for it, and whatever one chooses to call it, contemporary Christian "monasticism" is an inadequate response to the challenges of this age. In addition, just as it is impossible to "stay out of politics," it is impossible to withdraw completely from the world. Modern Phariseeism, feeling above and apart from the "unwashed," is not only wrong, but guaranteed to fail.

CHRISTIAN UTOPIA?

While some Christians are busy avoiding the world around them, others go to the opposite extreme. They believe Christians are destined to take over and rule the world, specifically by "taking dominion" over the political process until the "righteous," namely themselves, hold the reigns of power and reinstitute Old Testament law. As those who would rule like to put it, it is not they who are actually in charge, but God, although He would rule only through His chosen intermediaries.

This is, in short, a theocratic position. At best, it is a minority movement, though like those of the Christian Left, its influence is often out of proportion to its numbers.

In the past, such views have been associated with post-millennialism, the idea that Christians, not the return of Jesus Christ, will bring in the kingdom of God on earth, and then Christ will return to a triumphant church. Today, this movement is often referred to as "reconstructionism." But what might be called the dominion perspective, taking over our society for Christ, has more to do with utopianism than solid biblical theology.

Psychologists such as Erik Erikson have pointed out that humans have a strong, inbred tendency toward utopianism, a "universal nostalgia for a lost paradise."[16] Utopianism is part of our nature and even fits in with humanism. However, history is littered with the wreckage of failed utopian experiments, many undertaken by Christians, most well-meaning. This latest utopian concept will fail as well and will only confirm the fears of the secularist.

In the first place, the Bible is clear that no person possesses righteousness and that true Christians are only repentant sinners. The dominion impulse to subdue the earth, spoken of in the first chapter of Genesis, has been tainted by the Fall. It has produced campaigns of terror when not restrained by a concept of Christian justice.

Second, strong Christian faith and spirituality are no guarantee of political competence, wise governance, or fairness in dealing with the public. To naively believe this can be dangerous and contrary to the evidence.

Third, the historical record shows that power tends to corrupt and even the most virtuous Christians can be (and are) corrupted by power.

Those who drafted the United States Constitution were well aware of the sinfulness of humanity and the inevitability of corruption, even among the truly religious. They denied the divine right of kings and understood the dangers posed by absolute monarchs who called themselves "defenders of the faith."

More important, those who framed the constitution knew that no sinful human being should be trusted with absolute power, and so they devised a system of checks and balances that would institutionalize restraint. James Madison and other Framers recognized that if men were angels, there would be no need for government. But men are not angels, so they designed a system for sinners.

In addition, the various Christian churches and organizations are at times not good examples of efficiency or consistent moral living. Christians, even of the same theological and political beliefs and who operate in the same organization, are often caught up in self-interest. How can those unable to successfully run their religious organizations realistically expect to rule a modern state, especially a state in which vast numbers of people disagree with those Christians who see themselves as "chosen" to rule?

Christians have every right to be involved in the political process, but they must rid themselves of the notion that they are destined to assume control of other people and governments and rule the world. The believer's claim must not be for absolute power but for equality of access to society's marketplace of ideas where true Christianity, and the worldview that springs from it, can more than hold its own. Claims of special holiness and a divine right to rule will not help Christians gain this equal access. Indeed, it may well, as discussed in chapter 8, create a reactionary backlash.

THE POLITICAL GOSPEL

Christians have the right to be involved in the political process and must do so if they are to fulfill their responsibilities of stewardship and care toward their fellow human beings. However, their loud assertion of this right in recent times has caused much distress to the secular establishment, which has tended to view religious people in general, and Christians in particular, as second-class citizens or even enemies, and which tries to exclude them from the public realm whenever possible.

There has been a tendency for Christians to put too much faith in the political process, which can be corrupt, to bring lasting moral and spiritual renewal. Although there are certainly many grievances that can and should be addressed through political channels, Christians above all people should realize that what can be accomplished through human institutions is limited in a fallen world and that matters of the eternal destiny of the spirit are of primary importance. Legislative influence, direct-mail campaigns, political action committees, press releases, lobbying, and other activities may be effective and appropriate in their place, but they are not the sum of the Christian faith.

Many Christians have lost sight of the truth that they struggle not against "flesh and blood" but against spiritual forces.[17] In like manner, "the weapons we fight with are not the weapons of the world. On the contrary, they have divine power to demolish strongholds."[18] Political action as a cure-all is an illusion. Although it is a valued and necessary part of the process in a democracy, the ballot box is not the answer to all mankind's ills. This is a purely humanistic hope based on the potential perfectibility of humankind.

HYPERACTIVITY

Those Christians who concentrate primarily on the political realm or throw themselves into frenzied activity in any other area, including local church activities, risk burning themselves out and jeopardizing their witness as well as their family stability.

As meaningful contact between parents and their children has decreased, parents and children have steadily become strangers, even in their own homes. This has caused a breakdown in human development because it is the family that builds healthy people—physically, mentally, and spiritually.

As we shall see later, parents must truly spend their time within the family environment. Fathers and mothers who are workaholics are not good parents, even if they are off "saving" America from so-called secular humanism. Children are more important than the causes, careers, cars, houses, and hobbies that occupy many modern parents.

SHOW BUSINESS CHRISTIANITY

Not so long ago, modern Christians discovered television as a form of evangelism, and many have since come to regard that medium as something of a savior. Through the miracle of technology, it is thought, one person in a studio can reach the masses.

However, there are several reasons why television may be an unsuitable medium for the presentation of the Gospel. Indeed, it is highly questionable whether any authentic religious experience can be communicated through television.

First, there is a sense in which the medium is the message, to use Marshall McLuhan's aphorism. Television is something you *watch*, and hence it favors moods of passivity and acceptance. Studies indicate that television is most successful when serious content of any kind is submerged. It is, above all, notorious for reducing communication to its lowest common denominator.

As Professor Neil Postman, author of *Amusing Ourselves to Death*, notes, television strips away everything that makes religion a historic, profound, and sacred activity. On television, "there is no ritual, no dogma, no tradition, no theology, and above all, no sense of spiritual transcendence." A television preacher may talk about God, but God is invisible, an off-stage character, and the viewers see only the preacher. "On these shows," Postman adds, "the preacher is tops. God comes out as second banana."[19]

It should be noted that television is not really communication, which requires reciprocity. The audience can see the preacher, but the preacher cannot see them. The transmission, such as it is, is only one way. Thus, television is a propagandist's dream. One may well imagine what Adolf Hitler and Joseph Stalin would have done with it.

Second, there is no way to consecrate the space in which a television show is watched. This is not to say that religious experience must take place only in special buildings or places. But for an encounter with God to take place anywhere, there is usually some change of symbol— candles, a cross, pews—some alteration of decor indicating a transfer from profane to sacred use. Behavior changes to include a sense of humility and awe.

While watching television, such as game shows, documentaries, and sitcoms, people often eat, talk, or even do push-ups. The images on the screen do not mind; they have no way of knowing what is going on. There is frequently no change from this distracted state of mind when the show has a religious purpose.[20] Another negative implication of televised Christianity is that, since you can watch it at home, there may seem to be less of a need for the local church.

Third, television has a strong and inherent bias toward a psychology of secularism. Professor Postman's observations are on target:

> The screen is so saturated with our memories of profane events, so deeply associated with the commercial and entertainment worlds that it is difficult for it to be recreated as a frame for sacred events. Among other things, the viewer is at all times aware that a flick of the switch will produce a different and secular event on the screen—a hockey game, a commercial, a cartoon. . . . Both the history and the ever-present possibilities of the television screen work against the idea that introspection or spiritual transcendence is desirable in its presence. The television screen wants you to remember that its imagery is always available for your amusement and pleasure.[21]

Fourth, as Malcolm Muggeridge observes, the effect of television is to "draw people away from reality" and into fantasy.[22] The camera "always lies,"[23] says Muggeridge, who also relates a fascinating "Fourth Temptation" in which the Devil offers Christ free television time. Far from seizing the opportunity to relay His message far and wide, Christ refuses the offer.[24]

Television is indeed an awesome force, but the inherently fanciful and mendacious nature of the medium clearly makes the communication of truth a difficult, if not impossible, matter.

THE ENTERTAINMENT GOSPEL

It seems evident that tele-Christianity, far from changing the medium itself for the better, has in fact adapted itself to the medium and become entertainment. Many religious shows appear to place a premium on music. Instead of solid teaching, there is a talk-show format (very similar to that popularized by Johnny Carson on the "Tonight" show) hosted by the "star," the high-profile "television personality," and sometimes his wife, along with celebrity guests. These, not God, are the stars of the show, even though the hosts might not wish it to be so. Professor Postman warns of the constant danger of idolatry and even of "blasphemy"[25] in such circumstances.

Television Christianity loves the instant, the sensational, the flashy. There are the theatrics of faith healers restoring the gallbladder of a viewer a thousand miles away or the televangelist selling prayer cloths, crosses that glow in the dark, or "holy dirt." All one need do is watch a little of this tawdry and dismal fare to see how bad things really are. One can only wonder what Christ's reaction to all this would be. Unfortunately, the entertainment dimension is far from the only pitfall of television Christianity.

THE GOSPEL OF WEALTH

Producing a television show of any size is an expensive proposition. This necessarily means that raising funds is an integral part of the survival of televangelism. Indeed, a study conducted by Professor Stephen Winzenburg found that television preachers spend approximately 22 percent of their time on the air fund-raising. One televangelist spent 84 percent of his time raising money.[26]

Those who would survive in this highly competitive world must therefore attract the largest audience possible, and this applies to religious broadcasters as well. A former executive director of the National Religious Broadcasters sums up the unwritten law of all television preachers: "[Y]ou can get your share of the audience only by offering people something they want."[27]

This is a grave issue for religious leaders who, instead of offering people what they want, must tell their listeners what they need or what they must sacrifice. Jesus Christ told people to count the cost before following Him and clearly indicated that, in this world, Christians would experience many troubles.

Religious programs, like their secular counterparts, are filled with good cheer (what media gurus call "happy talk"), and they "celebrate affluence." God will give you whatever you want if you just ask. It is precisely *because* the message is trivial that the shows have high ratings.[28] It is either openly proclaimed or subtly implied that by supporting a particular television ministry you too can be wealthy, just like the hosts.

The grim truth is that, on television, the big-name star and his prosperity gospel come across better than God and truth. True Christianity is difficult, serious, and on many points offensive to modern thinking. What might be called the "Lite" television version is too often easy and amusing, and one can argue that televised religion is really not religion at all.

What the early church [and] the Reformers . . . understood was that Christianity speaks to all of life: science, philosophy, art, politics. . . . Their view of life was comprehensive in regard to the truth.

Defenders of televangelism argue that some people are converted or gain spiritual help from the programs. But even assuming this is so, television is still not validated as a gospel tool any more than a few conversions justify the religious hucksters who distort the truth with fantasy.

The entertainment and prosperity gospels not only fail to do the job, but they hurt the witness of the church as well. One legacy of "television Christianity" is that far too many local churches are built around a celebrity pastor or music director and seem to be more oriented to entertainment than to teaching and worship. This is tragic.

Sexual and financial scandals may awaken Christians to the abuses of televangelism and hopefully lead to a wider debate about the validity of televangelism altogether. But whether it lingers on, as seems likely, or begins to fade away, televised religion fails to meet the challenge of secular culture. When it is not self-satirizing, it provides endless fodder for politicians, secularists, cartoonists, and comedians.

INTELLECTUAL ILLITERACY

In terms of their intellectual content, the purveyors of television Christianity certainly do not measure up to the substance provided by many pastors, elders, seminary professors, or even laymen. It is also true that many of the leaders of the evangelical world, as Neil Postman notes, "do not compare favorably with well-known evangelicals of an earlier period, such as Jonathan Edwards, George Whitefield and Charles Finney, who were men of great learning, theological subtlety and powerful expositional skills."[29]

These men, and others like them, widely influenced life and religion in Europe and in North America. For example, John Nelson Darby and William Kelly developed the theology of dispensationalism and are considered by some to be the originators of what is now called "fundamentalism." J. Gresham Machen argued the Reformed faith from an intellectual standpoint and won the respect of the secularists of his day. Yet these men were persons of enormous erudition, among the most learned of their time. Professor Postman also states: "In the eighteenth and nineteenth centuries, religious thought and institutions in America were dominated by an austere, learned, and intellectual form of discourse that is largely absent from religious life today."[30]

What the early church, the Reformers, and those mentioned above understood was that Christianity speaks to *all* of life: science, philosophy, art, politics, medicine, and so on. Their view of life was comprehensive in regard to the truth. For them, *all* truth was God's truth.

For the most part, religious intellectual rigor has declined to the point that much of contemporary Christianity can safely be characterized as anti-intellectual. The comprehensive view of life and truth has all but disappeared and has been replaced by a highly compartmentalized and fragmented view that keeps certain disciplines and areas of inquiry off-limits, often because they are considered worldly.

The fault does not lie entirely with the local church. Modern culture is also highly anti-intellectual, sentimental, and of course secularized, especially since the 1960s. The local church, however, has not provided a bulwark against these trends, as British writer Harry Blamires recognizes:

[U]nfortunately the Christian mind has succumbed to the secular drift with a degree of weakness and nervelessness unmatched in Christian history. It is difficult to do justice in words to the complete loss of intellectual morale in the twentieth-century Church. One cannot characterize it without having recourse to language which will sound hysterical and melodramatic.[31]

One sometimes hears it said of a preacher or scholar that he or she has "head knowledge" rather than "heart knowledge." The implication is that such a preacher or scholar is stuffed with theological theories but is essentially cold and unfeeling. That may be true in some cases, and God knows their hearts. But what it more likely indicates is that the listener's shallow brand of Christianity has simply rendered him or her incapable of understanding what was being said by the preacher or scholar. And instead of taking stock of his or her own deficiencies, the listener simply imputes the problem to the speaker. It is a form of blaming the messenger if one does not like or cannot comprehend the message.

Another clue to contemporary anti-intellectualism is that preachers are encouraged to "dumb down" their sermons, rather than present something intellectually challenging. Such sermons often aim at everyone in general and hence speak to no one in particular.

Above all, it is heard that one must "preach a simple Gospel," but this common formulation is misleading. One may preach the Gospel simply, but no Christian, if he or she is faithful to the truths of the Bible, preaches a "simple" Gospel, if this means being simplistic.

The Gospel is the eternal God's revelation of Himself in human form and in human history. It is an absolutely stupendous historical event that touches virtually all areas of life and raises countless questions, most of them quite complicated. To the extent possible, the Christian should be capable of providing honest and informed answers. Slogans and clichés will not do the job.

This is not an apology for a dry intellectualism, a highbrow or snobbish posture, or for a view that sees the Bible and what it has to say only in terms of ideas. Neither is it a denial of the role of the Holy Spirit in conversion and the Christian life. Rather, it is simply a recognition that a gospel that fails to grapple with all of life is a false gospel, certain to fail in view of the present strong secular opposition, and far removed from what was once characteristic of the Christian church. In the simplest possible terms, the contemporary church has lost its intellect and, therefore, its mind.

CULTURAL ILLITERACY

The traditional, historical view of Christendom has been that the arts, human creativity, and the beauty of the creation are gifts of God and thus need no justification on spiritual or utilitarian grounds. They are valuable in themselves and were put here for people's enjoyment. However, modern Christianity has largely lost this truth. One would be hard-pressed to find many leading artists who are true believers. The same could be said in the field of aesthetics at large.

Almost everywhere one looks in modern Christianity there is a lack of craftsmanship—in publishing, in music, and particularly in the hucksterism of television. Some prime samples of Christian endeavors in the arts may be found in the local Christian bookstore, which is not primarily a bookstore at all but rather a kind of accessory and paraphernalia shop. Much of its quality as "art" leaves much to be desired. Some of it rightly deserves the title "Jesus Junk."

At times artistic standards of the world are low, but this does not mean that Christians should accept mediocrity and then spiritualize it.

The lack of craftsmanship is also evident in the arts. Art provides the antennae of a culture, and it seems clear that too many Christians have ceased to pay attention. In the artistic realm, as in the spiritual, many have lost themselves in a religious ghetto where ideas are exchanged by and large only with other Christians. Thus they miss an important point of contact with precisely those non-Christians with whom they have at least some common interest.

Artistically, the result is usually pablum, and the "circle think" mentality hinders quality work and presents a form of unreality as to how believers should conduct themselves in the world around them. A root problem is the mistaken idea that anything outside so-called spiritual endeavors is evil. This is neither the view of the Bible nor of the historical Christian church through the centuries. The Reformers, for instance, held up the noble and redemptive purposes of artistic endeavors of all kinds.

Some Christians have no view of the arts because they do not view the arts. They have no view of cinema because they do not go to movies. They have no view of ballet or the theater because they do not attend a ballet or the theater. They have no view of music because they either refuse or are afraid to listen to anything other than so-called Christian music. They do not trust themselves to watch secular videos, even those that would be appropriate morally except for their non-Christian themes. Once again, I am not saying that one should not be prudent related to moral values, but we may throw the baby out with the bath water.

It should be stressed that being "tuned in" to the arts is an exercise in understanding the culture around us. It is not the same as accommodation—that is, adopting the beliefs and views of the dominant culture.

To cut oneself off from this vital area of life is to be culturally illiterate. Little wonder that Christians are often perceived as kooks, obscurantists, or cultural neanderthals. In certain areas related to the arts this perception is accurate.

A CHURCH UNDER JUDGMENT

The world is obviously under God's judgment. Few, if any, knowledgeable Christians would disagree with that assessment. However, this judgment is no cause for self-congratulation. The Bible is clear that judgment begins not with the world and those who oppose God but rather with "us," the family of God, the local church.[32]

Given the terrible condition of the world, the woefully inadequate work of churches and evangelicals, and the sure hand of God's judgment, it seems that the only viable response is a return to the true Christianity that nonbelievers can, to some degree, relate to and appreciate.

However, there is a sense of betrayal in the nonbelieving world. This may be best illustrated by world events. For example, some former Soviet Marxists have said that they were betrayed by the Marxist philosophy. They have compared this betrayal to that of a former lover who whispers "I love you" but all the time is raping his victim. Western Christianity, if it is self-centered and isolationist, is comparable to the feigning lover spoken of by the former Soviet Marxists.

The United States was, at one time in its history, a nation greatly influenced by Christianity. This stemmed from those who immigrated from Europe and established the original colonial governments. Up through the nineteenth century, the Judeo-Christian ethic pervaded the American culture. We were also more integrated into the culture, including the arts.

At one time, the Christian church, with leadership from pastors, helped provide a form of stability for the culture. Times have changed. It now appears that Christianity, as illustrated by the scandals that permeate modern Christendom and the general loss of ethics within Christian circles, whispered "I love you" and, like the feigning lover, betrayed the American culture. As a consequence, society views Christianity with great cynicism today.

To recover respect for the Christian faith, the practice of true Christianity is essential. We will now explore how this can be done.

10

THE
TRUE GOD

The essence of true Christianity is seeking communion (and eventually union) with God. Thus, although Christianity involves the life of the spirit and the internalization of truth, it also requires the externalization, or living out, of that same truth. As this takes place, the believer should be able to reflect the character of the Creator more closely.

The Creator, it should be understood, is the eternal and omnipotent God of the Bible, not a limited abstraction or wistful projection of human attributes. God is the all-loving, all-knowing God who created all things *ex nihilo,* or out of nothing, from the vast galaxies in space to the tiniest grain of sand.

This omnipotent God is an objective being who exists in real space-time history. Nothing is beyond His power. Hence, the true believer sees supernatural events as a natural and logical activity of the Deity and sees God's presence and imprint in all areas of life. God is the fundamental ground of all existence.

Christians believe that God has revealed Himself, specifically His character, through various laws and principles expressed in the Bible: the Ten Commandments, the Sermon on the Mount, and the teachings of the apostles found in the New Testament. The God revealed in the Bible is both a holy God and a righteous God; that is, God established a specific standard and conforms to that standard Himself.

A SUBSTANTIAL HEALING

True Christianity explains the nature and behavior of people and the world around us in terms of the flaws caused by the historic, space-time Fall.

The Fall brought depravity to all facets of the human being and blighted nature as well. Moreover, the effects of the Fall are pervasive and are inherent in every member of the human race.

Many modern philosophers assert that people are inherently good. However, they have no real answer to the fact that the supposedly noble attributes of people are marred by selfishness, cruelty, and vice. These philosophers view God as pure benevolence or a kind of "Life Force." However, this is not the God revealed in the Old and New Testaments. Richard Lovelace explains:

> The tension between God's holy righteousness and his compassionate mercy cannot be legitimately resolved by remolding his character into an image of pure benevolence as the church did in the nineteenth century. There is only one way that this contradiction can be removed; through the cross of Christ which reveals the severity of God's anger against sin and the depth of his compassion in paying its penalty through the vicarious sacrifice of his Son. In systems which resolve this tension by softening the character of God, Christ and his work become an addendum, and spiritual darkness becomes complete because the true God has been abandoned for the worship of a magnified image of human tolerance.[1]

As noted earlier, Christianity provides the restoration to the Fall in the atoning work of Jesus Christ on the cross. And through Jesus Christ's resurrection, a central doctrine of Christianity, Jesus Christ proved to be the firstborn Son of God. Jesus Christ was "declared with power to be the Son of God by his resurrection from the dead."[2] In addition: "[God has fulfilled his promise] by raising up Jesus, as it is also written in the second Psalm, "You are my Son; today I have become your father.""[3]

As the apostle Paul wrote, "If Christ has not been raised, our preaching is useless and so is your faith."[4] But Jesus Christ has been raised from the dead, and the empty tomb means that no mere man died at Calvary. Jesus Christ now reigns as Lord over a new spiritual community of believers. He is the second Adam, a "life-giving spirit."[5] Whereas the first Adam was an "earthly" being, "the second man [is] from heaven."[6] Jesus Christ is the new King of creation, "the faithful witness, the firstborn from the dead, and the ruler of the kings of the earth."[7]

God grants full forgiveness of sin to those who by faith accept Jesus Christ's redemptive work. This does not mean that those who believe are thereby perfect. To put it in medical terms, the fatal infection of sin is cured through Jesus Christ's work on the cross, but the symptoms remain. The believer is, therefore, substantially healed by Jesus Christ's work, but he or she is never perfect in this life. Through Jesus Christ's voluntary death for our sins, however, God's justice and love are reconciled, and the way of salvation is opened for those who accept the gift of God through faith in Jesus Christ.

This being true, humanity owes a debt of gratitude to Jesus Christ. However, more than gratitude is owed. In the words of the Westminster Catechism, the primary purpose of people should be to glorify God and enjoy Him forever. Such a statement often seems absurd to nonbelievers, but Malcolm Muggeridge, who was converted later in life, noted that one of the greatest attractions of Christianity is "its sheer absurdity." He writes:

> I love all those crazy sayings in the New Testament—which, incidentally, turn out to be literally true—about how fools and illiterates and children understand what Jesus was talking about better than the wise, the learned and the venerable; about how the poor, not the rich, the blessed, the meek, not the arrogant, inherit the earth, and the pure in heart, not the strong in mind, see God.[8]

SPIRITUAL POWER

Biblical absolutes are needed to transform, order, and direct the fallen nature of humankind. This remains true even when one is a believer, because the believer is always in a spiritual state of *becoming*— never attaining complete spiritual fulfillment because in this life there is only substantial healing of the fallen nature. As the apostle Paul notes, "Now we see but a poor reflection as in a mirror; then we shall see face to face. Now I know in part; then I shall know fully, even as I am fully known."[9]

Fortunately, however, God has not left believers without provision for growing spiritually, to become what they are capable of becoming in

Jesus Christ. They share in Christ's resurrected power and are part of a new spiritual community. This power is necessary, since all true Christians will be resisted by opposing forces in the spiritual realm. The apostle Paul recognized that "our struggle is not against flesh and blood, but against the rulers, . . . against the spiritual forces of evil in heavenly realms."[10]

Believers who practice consistent biblical living will inevitably be engaged in struggles against the spiritual forces of which the apostle Paul spoke. In the final analysis, that is the nature of true Christianity. Christians who are not being opposed must always examine the way in which they are living their lives, because something is wrong. Indeed, the very freedom promised to believers by Jesus Christ is lessened when they corrupt their spiritual walk and do not face some conflict. If darkness does not oppose us, we are probably impotent.

AWESOME FREEDOM

Jesus Christ is *the* truth incarnate, and He told His followers that "the truth shall set you free."[11] Believers are freed from the guilt of sin through the atonement of Jesus Christ. They are relieved, then, of the rigors and consequences of Old Testament laws and ceremonies and are also free from the petty legalisms modern evangelicals often inflict on themselves and those around them. Christians are, in short, free to become and be what God intended when He first created us.

Such awesome freedom is only possible through Jesus Christ. The believer is, in effect, "crucified with Christ" so that even though he or she continues in the natural world, in the words of Paul, "I no longer live, but Christ lives in me."[12] The life that believers live "in the body," they live "by faith in the Son of God, who loved me and gave himself for me."[13] Allowing Jesus Christ to live through the believers brings forth the fruit of the Holy Spirit: "love, joy, peace, patience, kindness, goodness, faithfulness, gentleness, self-control."[14]

Russian writer Fyodor Dostoyevsky describes this freedom in the novel *The Brothers Karamazov* in the context of the temptation of Jesus Christ. Satan first tempted Jesus Christ by saying, "If you are the Son of God, tell these stones to become bread."[15] Of course, being the very God that He is, Jesus Christ could easily have turned the stones into bread, and the people would have followed and worshiped Him for it.

Dostoyevsky notes that one reason Jesus Christ declined to perform this miracle was that He did not want to deprive people of their freedom, for obedience bought in this way is not the spiritual freedom that Jesus Christ desired for people.[16] Jesus Christ also refused because the request came from *Satan* and because, as He stated in His reply, the Bible proclaims, "Man does not live on bread alone, but on every word that comes from the mouth of God."[17]

The Word of God provides the substance and power of which true freedom is composed. It is, among other things, the freedom to forget one's past, the freedom of not having to look over one's shoulder, the freedom from addiction to earthly "powers," a freedom from guilt. Most of all, it is freedom to enjoy the Creator, a freedom to do those things pleasing to God.

The apostle Paul noted that believers were called to freedom but cautioned them not to "use your freedom to indulge the sinful nature."[18] Instead, true Christians are to serve one another in love, which is in keeping with the commandments to love one's neighbor as oneself.

One of the blessings of the Holy Spirit is joy. It is emphasized that the believer has the freedom to enjoy life. The rigid rules enforced by some churches constitute a form of bondage, and bondage is not true Christianity. God did not place His creatures in a concentration camp, but initially in a paradise. Moreover, Jesus Christ was a person who obviously enjoyed Himself. Indeed, this was one of the complaints against Him on the part of the self-righteous Pharisees. They called Christ a "glutton and a drunkard, a friend of tax collectors and 'sinners.'"[19]

In summary, freedom in its essence means the enjoyment of God and His creation and the enjoyment of life. It means to do good in service to both God and human beings. It is found only in Jesus Christ.

THE CHURCH

God has not left believers on their own. Indeed, wherever two or three Christians gather in His name, Jesus Christ promises that "there am I with them."[20]

All Christians are part of the *ecclesia,* a Greek term meaning "called-out company," from which our word "church" is derived. When Jesus Christ ascended into Heaven, the believers remaining on earth effectively became His body, energized by the Holy Spirit whom He sent to complete His work. Jesus Christ is the Head of that body.[21] When one is converted, the Holy Spirit baptizes that person into the body of Jesus Christ, the universal church. This universal church includes all believers of all times and places. The *visible* church is the worldwide body of believers, in all its diversity, in its institutional form.

The *local* church, it should be stressed, is not a building. In fact, the early concept of the local church had *no* connection with a building. For example, the apostle Paul sends his greetings to a group of believers by stating, "greet the church that meets at their house."[22] Paul's reference to the church is not to a building but to the "church" (believers) *in* the house.

The local church, then, is a congregation or gathering of Christians in a specific place. It is a living, *organic* entity that happens to meet in a building. In New Testament times, believers most often met in houses. In totalitarian countries, believers meet wherever and whenever they can. But wherever they meet, the Bible sets forth certain norms.

The first norm is that churches should be composed of believers in Jesus Christ. Second, these congregations should meet together in a special way on the first day of the week.[23] Third, there are to be elders who have responsibility for oversight of the church. Fourth, there are to be pastors and teachers who feed and care for the flock. Fifth, there are to be deacons, responsible for the material side of church affairs.[24] Scripture lists clearly defined standards for those who would hold all these offices.[25] The local church, it should be stressed, has no authority to change or diminish these standards, nor to elevate any other standards above them. Sixth, the local church is to take seriously the discipline of the believers within that congregation. Seventh, there is a place for organization on a wider basis than the local church, such as councils and conferences.[26] Eighth, baptism and the Lord's Supper are to be practiced.[27]

Some would question whether some of these are actually norms or whether other matters are in fact commanded. In any case, the primary point is that there is a place for the local church and the Bible contains guidelines for it. At the same time, however, there are vast areas of freedom for diversity. No one has the right to bind people morally where the Bible lacks a clear command.

One thing is clear about the local church: It is intended to be a place of holy worship. This is where many modern church ceremonies may come into conflict with New Testament modes of church conduct. This means that contemporary churches must divest themselves of the "entertainment" mentality and again become centers of worship, instruction, and true fellowship. Churches should restore the power-packed hymns of the past and eschew trivial songs that tell how the individual singer "feels" about Jesus, but little about the Savior Himself.

This does not mean that the local church is to be bound in a straitjacket. There is freedom in Christ. Yet our purpose should be to bring glory to Him in this way. Anything the New Testament does not *command* concerning church form is a freedom to be exercised under the leadership of the Holy Spirit for that particular time and place. In other words, the New Testament sets boundaries, but within those boundaries there is a good deal of freedom to meet the changes that may arise in different places and times.

CONFRONTATION

The church provides Christians with a place of fellowship, spiritual sustenance, and worship. But the local church is also the "pillar and foundation of the truth,"[28] and the present age often has no desire to hear truth (which it often finds offensive). True Christianity is likewise offensive to the secular juggernaut. Its light exposes their darkness. Confrontation is therefore inevitable if churches are faithful to their mandate.

It is often in moments of great confrontation and controversy that the truth is most effectively spoken. For example, the apostle Paul took advantage of every confrontational situation to speak about Jesus Christ. Paul had been arrested and beaten in Jerusalem for his stand for the truth. Paul so inflamed the people that he had to be guarded by Roman soldiers. As Paul was led away, he begged to be allowed to speak to the people,[29] and from there he proclaimed the gospel of Jesus Christ.

THE
CHRISTIAN
MENTALITY

Modern Christendom often depicts Jesus Christ as a meek, harmless friend of the world. However, that is not the picture found in the Gospels or the book of Revelation. Far from being passive and meek, Jesus Christ was both controversial and dogmatic.

Indeed, as theologian John R. W. Stott explains, true Christianity is inevitably and "essentially dogmatic." Why?

> It purports to be a revealed faith. If the Christian religion were just a collection of the philosophical and ethical ideas of men (like Hinduism), dogmatism would be entirely out of place. But if God has spoken (as Christians claim), both in olden days through the prophets and in these last days through His Son, why should it be thought "dogmatic" to believe His Word ourselves and to urge other people to believe it too?[1]

Stott adds that Jesus Christ was not "broad-minded" in the popular sense of the word; He was not prepared to accept as valid all views on every subject. Jesus Christ was not afraid to dissent from official doctrines He knew to be wrong (or not "politically correct") and to expose error. He called false teachers "blind guides," "wolves in sheep's clothing," "whitewashed tombs," and even "a brood of vipers."

Jesus Christ was literally on the offensive, with a message that offended those around Him to the point that He was killed. One illustration is Jesus Christ's action in the temple:

> Jesus . . . drove out all those who were buying and selling [in the temple]. He overturned the tables of the money changers and the benches of those selling doves. "It is written," he said to them, "'My house will be called a house of prayer,' but you are making it a 'den of robbers.'"[2]

In addition, Jesus Christ would not permit anyone to carry goods through the temple and He even blocked the doorways.[3]

In short, Jesus Christ took the truth to the world and commanded His disciples to do likewise:

> Then Jesus came to them and said, "All authority in heaven and earth has been given to me. Therefore go and make disciples of all the nations, baptizing them in the name of the Father and of the Son and of the Holy Spirit, and teaching them to obey everything I commanded you. And surely I am with you always, to the very end of the age."[4]

The early Christians took this mandate with the utmost seriousness. John Stott writes:

> The apostles also were controversialists, as is plain from the New Testament Epistles, and they appealed to their readers "to contend for the faith which was once for all delivered to the saints." Like their Lord and master they found it necessary to warn the churches of false teachers and urge them to stand firm in the truth.[5]

There are many examples of confrontation and controversy in the New Testament. For example, the apostle Paul preached in a Jewish synagogue in Thessalonica, with the result that some came to believe what he was saying. However, those who opposed Paul formed a mob and incited a riot.[6] In this case, the mere preaching of the truth caused the confrontation. The apostles would hardly have been described as men who "turned the world upside down," as the King James Version puts it,[7] if they had casually explained the truth or allowed other points of view to be taken on an equal basis. Truth and confrontation often go hand in hand.

But here the problem arises. Many modern Christians have a dislike for dogmatism and controversy. This relates to the posture of accommodation on the part of many Christians to the thinking of this age. As noted, the present secular age does not allow Christianity to have a voice in the pluralistic society. And if Christians are to confront the secular Goliath, they must not only have the willingness to engage in controversy, but also the proper intellect.

THE COMPREHENSIVE GOSPEL

Controversy, it should be stressed, flows from the collision of truth with falsehood. Controversy, however, should not result from the *manner* in which the truth is presented. In other words, in a confrontational situation, controversy should be a result of the message, not the messenger.

For example, when the Gospels note that the scribes and Pharisees were plotting to kill Jesus Christ, they give the reason: "For they feared him, because the whole crowd was amazed at his *teaching.*"[8]

Likewise, when the apostle Paul was in Athens, he was distressed by the idolatry he saw. However, he did not rant and rave or harangue the Athenians about their pagan religions. Rather, he "reasoned" in the synagogue, "disputed" with the philosophers, and calmly addressed a meeting of the Aereopagus.[9] In other words, Paul was able to *argue* effectively because he spoke the truth and also because he knew the minds of the listeners. He even quoted their own poets to them.[10] Some of the Athenians ridiculed Paul, but others found his message challenging and asked that he speak again. Had Paul attempted forcibly to indoctrinate his listeners, it is doubtful whether they would have given him a hearing at all.

True Christianity, it should again be emphasized, speaks to *all* of life, not just to narrowly "religious" concerns. The comprehensive nature of the truth expressed by the apostles, especially Paul, must be restored if Christians are to be effective in their work. Such a lack of comprehensiveness is a problem of lack of faith, to be sure, but it is also inherent in some of our institutions.

For example, far from constituting a real alternative to the diminishing academic and intellectual standards of most public education, many seminaries and "Christian" colleges have become soft in their teaching. In some cases, these neo-evangelical institutions are places where ideas already discarded by secular philosophers and intellectuals—ideas often hostile to Christianity, such as Marxism and Freudianism—are taken seriously and enjoy a long afterlife. In some cases, attempts are even made to integrate such ideas into Christian theology. It may be that those who would minister effectively to their generation may have to seek their education in the best so-called secular schools where there may be more rigorous academic and professional standards. Granted, the moral absolutes may not be present—but one at least may not be confused by mixing Christianity with secular thought.

Christian seminaries and Bible colleges must become institutions that equip Christians for the intellectual combat necessary to confront the world with truth. However, because of the inadequate intellectual developments of many Christian institutions, this will be difficult. C. S. Lewis wrote that Christianity had not been tried and found wanting, but rather found difficult and not tried. This is the challenge for Christian institutions of learning, especially in the area of the mind. Christianity provides answers to all the latest trends in secular thought, but Christians must develop "systems" to meet the challenge.

INTERNALITY-EXTERNALITY

Here I would like to bring in my own experience. I was converted from agnosticism to Christianity in 1974. In the first six months of my Christian experience, I trekked from church to church—Baptist, Methodist, Presbyterian, Pentecostal—seeking a coherent whole in terms of my new-found religious faith. While I found myself struck by the "other-worldliness" of some of the activities, I also found a one-dimensional view of spiritual reality, the idea that the church building was the center of the religious experience and Christian duty. There is, of course, a sense in which this is true, but it seemed to me that the local church should not hoard the truth within four walls. I was now a believer, but was I just to attend church services? Or was there something more?

It is true that Christianity is essentially internal. As a woman thinks in her heart, so she is; if a man commits adultery in his heart, he is an adulterer. Christianity is also internal because the Holy Spirit is invisibly inhabiting the believer. However, this spiritual power is for an external purpose, to create a morally fruitful life that people can *see* and *experience* externally, just as they experience Jesus Christ Himself internally. In like manner, the true believer reflects in his or her own small way the holiness of God.

Jesus Christ said that believers are to love God with their entire being.[11] But how does the believer love God? Such love is not the unctuous emotional product that many modern evangelicals associate with love. True love affects the emotion, but it is obedience and a direct act of the will at its heart. "If you love me," Jesus Christ says, "you will obey what I command."[12] Hence, love is both internal and external; it is living according to the principles of the Bible.

Believers are to love their neighbors as they love themselves.[13] It cannot be denied that self-love permeates all of society, Christian and non-Christian alike. It ranges from the athlete who exalts in the skill that has brought him victory to the institutions and monuments that Christians build and name after themselves.

In a properly externalized experience, true Christian belief shines out like a beacon.

Jesus Christ drew on this self-love and commanded the believer to treat others with equal amounts of love, service, and compassion. This is perhaps the clearest example of outward living. Suffice it to say that a Christian experience that is only internal stands against human experience and reason. It also stands against the authority of the Bible.

SALT, LIGHT, AND RADICALISM

At one point Jesus Christ said: "You are the salt of the earth. But if the salt loses its saltiness, how can it be made salty again? It is no longer good for anything, except to be thrown out and trampled by men."[14]

In Jesus Christ's time, salt was a preservative, used primarily to cure meats. In like manner, believers are to preserve and to cure. However, salt also makes one thirsty. If Christians are fulfilling their proper role, the culture should be thirsty for the knowledge of biblical truth.

Moreover, salt, if placed on metal and dampened with water, will slowly eat through steel. True Christians, who are the depositories of truth, should be able to penetrate and defeat the arguments and actions of the opposition. Christians who believe they cannot effectively answer the secularist's arguments either do not know the Bible or have not taken the time to study how to apply what they believe.

Christians are to accurately preach and teach the good news of Jesus Christ's atoning death and resurrection. In turn, that will have a curing and preserving effect on those who hear it and on society as a whole. Thus, the concept of "salt" is very much an "external" idea.

So is the concept of light. As Jesus Christ also noted:

> You are the light of the world. A city on a hill cannot be hidden. Neither do people light a lamp and put it under a bowl. Instead they put it on its stand, and it gives light to everyone in the house. In the same way,

191

let your light shine before men, that they may see your good deeds and praise your Father in heaven.[15]

A purely internal experience would be tantamount to putting one's light under a basket. In a properly externalized experience, true Christian belief shines out like a beacon.

By serving as salt and light, true Christianity can be a corrective influence on society and the dominant culture. The result will mean that more people will be receptive to the message believers are teaching and living out. It is also the only way to preserve society's foundations from crumbling.

Once, after I spoke on salt and light principles, a woman approached me and stridently informed me that I was a "radical." This was some time ago, and I did not quite know how to take it. I was new in the faith and simply believed what I was saying to be based on sound principles. Just what was a "radical"? As it happens, the root of the word radical is the Latin *radix,* meaning "root" or, by extension, "fundamental."[16]

In reality, then, a radical is someone who espouses fundamental principles that are the root and foundation of truth. This is not rebellious or revolutionary. Radicalism means that Christians should stand by the truth. It also means increased visibility for Christians. The great need is for a Christian radicalism that will seek out and challenge secularism on every point.

THE ETHICAL PROBLEM

As discussed in chapter 1, Christendom faces a grave ethical crisis. From the grass roots Christian to the well-known "star" televangelist, some modern Christians seem to have an immense difficulty telling the truth or living by a strong moral code, let alone the standards set for believers by Jesus Christ and the Bible.

William Barclay writes: "[T]he crisis of the present is not theological; it is ethical. Christian theology is not really under attack, for there are few outside the Church sufficiently interested in it to assail it, and the internecine wars of the technical theologians are not of any great interest to the general public."[17] Indeed, many modern Christians are, sadly so, ethically illiterate. Unfortunately, the Bible is no longer the norm it used to be. If anything, our modern culture is predisposed against the Christian ethic (including those who call themselves Christian). This means that "there has never been a time when the discussion of the Christian Ethic has been more necessary and more relevant."[18]

Christians have a massive educational task facing them. Education in contemporary society, however, may come in many forms: writing, speaking, protesting, picketing, defending, and even suing in court in addition to other forms of making issues public. However, believers will not be listened to if they are perceived as being unethical and fraudulent.

How can those who say they hold the truth speak effectively if they are liars and thieves? Indeed, this may explain why Christians are so ineffective in influencing contemporary culture.

However, Christians, if they practice their faith consistently, should not be afraid to challenge the modern secular culture. The present "air raid shelter" mentality of Christians will not alter the course of society. Timidity, likewise, will not bring about change.

NO COMPROMISES

Concession and dismay mark modern Christendom. Like the reports of ten of the twelve spies sent out by Moses to report on the military capacities of the Canaanites, our reports are filled with fear. Yet Rahab told the spies of the next generation that "when we heard of it, our hearts melted and everyone's courage failed because of you, for the Lord your God is God in heaven above and on the earth below."[19] We appear to be more like that first generation.

Therefore, the battle cry of faithful Christians should be that Jesus Christ is Lord of all things in heaven and on earth. He is not simply Lord of heaven above and impotent on the earth. He is Lord of the entire cosmos.

The misinterpretation of Jesus Christ's words in John 18:36—that His kingdom is not of this world—should be finally given the burial it deserves. In this verse, Jesus Christ was asserting to Pilate that His source of authority or Lordship was not earthly, but heavenly. This misinterpretation has nothing to do with the reality of Jesus Christ's authority over all things. He still retains authority over the earth.

The newspapers, entertainment media, and universities likewise speak of little else but defeat and alienation. Many secularists see their world crumbling about them. What an opportunity this is to inject a consistent Christian message into the sermons, evangelistic crusades, and bookstores filled with false pietism. Indeed, the fruit of secular presuppositions is here—and we are experiencing its bankruptcy.

Christians naively believe that they can retreat (note that Christian seminars are often called retreats) into a zone of social and political impotence and, therefore, social and political irresponsibility (just as

193

they have done for over a century). However, with the acids of relativism eroding the foundations of modern humanism, the social buffers are disappearing.

Drugs, pornography, lawlessness, economic disruption, witchcraft, random and serial murders, abortion, terrorism, and all the rest of secularism's children no longer respect the sanctuary of the churches. Like Joab, contemporary Christians are discovering that the horns of the altar no longer protect them from destruction.[20] They can no longer be "nice" Christians, the beneficiaries of the endless fruits of a former "Christian" culture, hiding in the "nice" colleges, "nice" churches, and "nice" ministries.

As a whole, modern evangelism, at least in the Western world, because of its pietistic base has little effect on contemporary cultures. As a consequence, the enemy is at the gates. Coupled with the fact that humanism is the end of the road spiritually, nothing is left to hold society together except brute force—in other words, tyranny.

There are no safety zones in the combat of faith. The only way to be effective is to apply true Christianity consistently to culture in all its aspects. As underground evangelist Brother Andrew has written:

> The first principle for any Christian work is this: the Lord Jesus Christ, who crushed Satan and conquered death, commands us to invade this enemy-occupied world and reclaim it for God. We march under his exclusive authority and are forbidden to make any deals with the foe. No compromises. No concessions. And no excuses![21]

If believers are not prepared to do this, then they have not learned the lessons of the past. And as history demonstrates, they will be bound to repeat them.

PART FOUR
ACTIVISM

Good citizenship requires both
discernment and courage—discernment
to assess soberly the issues and to know
when duty calls one to obey or disobey,
and courage, in the case of the latter, to
take a stand.

Charles Colson
Kingdoms in Conflict

12

THE
POLITICAL
QUESTION

hristians in the United States are increasingly becoming involved in politics and government. Thus, it is important to ana-
lyze both the positive and negative effects of such political
activism in terms of how true Christianity operates in our often chaotic
and torn world.

ACTIVISM

"Activism" or "social activism" is normally defined as "a doctrine or
practice that emphasizes direct vigorous action (such as a mass demonstration) in support of or in opposition to one side of a controversial
issue."[1] To what extent is this a legitimate activity for the believer?

The primary task to which the believer is called is the preaching of
biblical truths and the living of a moral life. In the Bible, there are no
commands to specific "social action" other than speaking and acting
on biblical truth. Undoubtedly, the believer can have an influence on
the world by speaking and acting on such truths. Indeed, the believer

must be a "social activist" to a certain extent if he or she is faithful to the general teachings of the Bible.

It should be added that activism is not necessarily "humanistic." There is a sense in which all people, including Christians, are humanists insofar as they believe in or practice humanitarianism, the concern for the dignity of humanity. But a "humanist," strictly speaking, is one whose belief system and activism deliberately exclude God and have no transcendent reference point.

The activism of the true believer, on the other hand, flows from a sense of loving care for what God has created. The Christian has a responsibility to assist in preserving both freedom and order—indeed, to work for justice—while keeping in mind one's spiritual priorities and the limitations of the political process.

PIETISM AND POLITICS

Even in light of the devastating developments concerning the threat to life and liberty discussed earlier, there are still many Christians who argue that believers should avoid all involvement in government, law, and politics. They voice concern over attempts by Christians to interact in political affairs. I often hear such statements as: "That preacher needs to get back in the pulpit and get his nose out of politics."

Although Christianity cannot survive if it neglects personal commitment and the spiritual life of the individual, it also inevitably declines if it devotes itself solely to the inward life.

This is not the way Christians should view their role in the world. It is time to drop the naive idea that Christians can avoid political and cultural involvement and remain somehow untouched by the results of corruption in modern society and government. Such ideas, if they continue to predominate, will actually contribute to the present drift toward the complete cultural and moral collapse of society.

Christianity can impact cultures. Early American Christianity is an example. A dominant aspect of the Christian influence on early nine-

200

teenth century America was the interest in and energy expended on the betterment of the external society. However, the increased importance of the pietist movement of the seventeenth century resulted in the decline of such interest and energy and turned Protestant Christianity *inward;* Christians began forsaking involvement in what was termed the "world" to pursue the development of their own internal spiritual life.

Although it was originally intended as a renewal movement, Pietism ultimately tended to degenerate into mere personal religiosity without much direct influence on society and culture. Religion became "privatized" and ceased to affect public life. Although the foundation laid by some of the American colonial Christians was so strong that Judeo-Christian theism (with its attendant ethical system) continued to affect society for decades thereafter, such influence eventually began to fade as the new generations of Christians turned inward and ceased any attempts to confront and, therefore, impact their society. Many took it for granted that society had a basic Judeo-Christian outlook.

Although Christianity cannot survive if it neglects personal commitment and the spiritual life of the individual, it also inevitably declines if it devotes itself solely to the inward life. To be effective, Christianity must be both. Inward redemption must flow outward and affect the temporal world.

American colonial Christianity saw God as working in the whole culture, not merely in the hearts of the people. In this respect, Christians themselves were seen as whole people, not merely as witnessing machines.

This is the same colonial Christianity that led to the drafting of the Declaration of Independence, the American Revolution, and the writing of the Constitution. This same attitude led to the abolition of the slave trade in Great Britain and effectively began the abolition of slavery in the United States. William Wilberforce and others in England spent a lifetime fighting evils such as slavery because of their determination to apply Christian principles to the external world. In America, Christian groups such as the Quakers fought slavery, applying their Christianity externally.

A few of the early pietists were active reformers, but the later wave of the pietistic movement looked inward. The movement's focus was, and still is, on the areas of life that were "believed" to be "spiritual" as opposed to secular or worldly, including politics and involvement in government. This view eventually led to a reduction of the Christian influence on the external world, leaving the field increasingly open to domination by those with non-Christian views and others with active *anti*-Christian viewpoints as well.

Pietism (or better yet, "false pietism"), especially in its present form, stresses only the personal "salvation" experience. Bible study becomes simplistic, based on emotions, and any form of intellectualism is considered unspiritual. False pietism inevitably resulted in the adoption by many Christians of a religious form of Platonism, a belief that the spiritual world is somehow superior to and above the physical-temporal world. This pietism, therefore, created a nonbiblical dichotomy between the spiritual and temporal worlds.

False pietism eventually produced a generation of Christians with a schizophrenic view of reality. While giving lip service to the idea that the Bible was the basis of all life, these pietists only applied it to their inward selves. The result of this tension is, of course, inaction. Its consequence is a Christianity that often appears impotent in a world that is being dominated by external as well as internal crises.

PHILOSOPHY AFFECTS BEHAVIOR

A personal philosophy of life is important because a person's philosophy dictates how he or she will act. If Christians continue to take the position that they are impotent in the face of the crises this generation is facing, they will continue to have little effect on a culture that appears to be collapsing. Indeed, people most often act in ways that reflect how they *think* of themselves and their work, as well as how these self-perceptions correspond to their role in society and the crucial issues they face.

> *If the democratic governments are to survive, Christian influence and involvement in government at all levels will be necessary, or Christian apartheid will result.*

Christians need to reevaluate the consequences of false pietism and reconsider the "eat, meet, and retreat" theology so prevalent in certain contemporary evangelical circles. The issues are too important for silence or apathy."

Christians may, so to speak, be holding "the truth in unrighteousness" when they remain silent on the issues and fail to act.[2] Many Christians, as is obvious, are stagnating in churches that have no external political, social, or moral impact upon the world. Truth cannot remain bottled up and be effective.

If Christians want to see a moral revival, then they must externalize the principles of their faith as practiced by believers during the European Reformation and in early America. The truths of the Bible must flow from the mind into the world. A false pietism, a false "spirituality," and all the exclusively internal activities that so often make up contemporary churches do not alone bring revival or reformation.

RESPONSIBILITY AND STEWARDSHIP

Christians, if they do not speak and act effectively on their faith, will continue to have very little impact on the culture that surrounds them. As noted earlier, Jesus Christ taught that true Christians will exert some moral influence on their culture. This is what Jesus Christ terms being "salt" to the culture.

There is a strong emphasis in some segments of Christianity at the present time on personal evangelism. That is admirable, but it is only one part of being "salt" to the world. It cannot be the only emphasis. Churches and Christians have to touch and influence the entire community.

Christians are not simply witnessing machines. Indeed, believers are *whole persons,* and they live in a *whole world.* To give a large section of the world over to secularism without a fight is to cheat God. Wholistic evangelism and service is required.

As theologian J. Gresham Machen pointed out in the early part of this century: "We may preach with all the fervor of a reformer and yet succeed only in winning a straggler here and there, if we permit the whole collective thought of the nation . . . to be controlled by ideas which, by the resistless force of logic, prevent Christianity from being regarded as anything more than a harmless delusion."[3]

This will mean a Christian perspective in *all* areas of life—including politics—in proclaiming the freedom found in the Gospel and the Lordship of Jesus Christ.

POLITICAL INVOLVEMENT
WITHOUT COMPROMISE

As one considers involvement in the political establishment, he or she must be mindful of an essential point: Although it is important to

203

become politically involved, the true believer must do it without compromising any Christian principle.

Jesus Christ, as we all know, did *not* seek political power, and, likewise, Jesus Christ did *not* command Christians to seek it either. Indeed, He said: "My kingdom is not of this world. If it were, my servants would fight to prevent my arrest by the Jews. But now my kingdom is from another place."[4]

However, Jesus Christ did not say that Christians should not be involved in political affairs. If the democratic governments are to survive, Christian influence and involvement in government at all levels will be necessary, or Christian apartheid will result. At the same time, Christians in politics must avoid being compromised by their involvement in the political establishment.

This will mean that the Christian in politics will have to tell the *truth*. This is especially so in light of the current ethical crisis in Christianity. However, the very words *political* and *politics* imply avoidance of the truth. In other words, Christians may run for government office and get elected, but they must avoid being politicians. Instead, Christians should be statesmen. The difference is that the statesman, unlike the politician, will go against the popular flow. Telling the truth may also cost elections, but that is the price Christians must pay.

This will mean, for example, that Christians may sometimes have to challenge their own political parties when they are wrong. This, in turn, means that the Christian in politics may not be very popular—and may not get reelected.

Yet if Christians do not tell the truth and, if need be, stand against the governmental and political establishment, they will lose their witness. To some extent, believers must always, as John the Baptist did, stand outside the political establishment and criticize (when necessary) the political Herods of this world.

Finally, Christians must also be mindful of the proper use of power. The legitimate use of power does not include using it to impose one's will upon others. From the Christian standpoint, the proper use of power is to implement God's plan for order and justice for all.

THE POLITICAL SAVIOR ILLUSION

Citizens of any country must be mindful that, even in a democracy, there are no heroes on white horses. This is also true of those who represent themselves as "Christian" candidates.

Jesus Christ rejected heroics, and Christians must reject spiritual leaders who seek to be political saviors. Religious leaders who identify themselves with a particular political view or party have, by definition, limited their leadership to those who hold such views or belong to that party.

Jesus did not categorize humans according to their political beliefs. In fact, Jesus commanded us, without qualification, to "[l]ove your neighbor as yourself."[5] Today's Christians and their leaders, no less so than the original followers of Jesus Christ, must include *all* people.

Religious leaders who politicize their influence have thus traded their moral imperative for a political imperative.[6] Jesus, as noted earlier, did not seek political power nor did He command Christians to seek it.

Christians, therefore, must be wary of spiritual leaders who, while posing themselves as political saviors, preach a sermon of political power. The goal of the true believer is for justice, not power. Believers must avoid forsaking their witness to humankind for a bowl of political porridge or short-term gains. Though we need to be active in politics, the real purpose is to allow the grace, mercy, and overall rule of Christ to be extended to all areas.

THE PROBLEM IS SPIRITUAL
AND NOT POLITICAL

As we speak of political involvement, we must be mindful that *our real problems are not political, but spiritual.* Abortion, for example, is a mere *symptom* of a deeper problem. The problem is moral and spiritual decay.

American Christians, for example, have, since the legalization of abortion, fought hard in the political arena to elect pro-life presidents. Yet, while American presidents Ronald Reagan and George Bush paid lip service to a pro-life stance, the number of abortions (1.5 to 1.6 million annually) did not decline during the twelve years these men were in office. Indeed, 19 million unborn babies were "legally" aborted during the terms of presidents who professed to be pro-life.

Western nations will not be positively changed through the political system. Therefore, unless there is a *spiritual revival,* there will be little alteration in the present course of such societies. If the hearts of people are not changed, then further decay is to be expected.

It will take leadership from pastors and churches for a spiritual revival to occur. Indeed, most of the books of the New Testament, as well as Jesus Christ's references in the book of Revelation, are letters written to local churches. This is because God first desires action to be taken there. Failing this, God obviously works through organizations and individuals outside the church.

Pastors who have voiced their dismay at the numerous "evangelical" groups who have organized outside the local church have only themselves to blame. Such evangelical groups exist largely because local churches and the institutional church, as a whole, have not fulfilled the needs such organizations meet. Tragically, most local churches have been apathetic to much of what has been going on outside their four walls.

Sermons, seminars, lectures, and books produced by the so-called Christian establishment most often are concerned with the "spiritual" enlightenment of the individual churchgoers. Very few pastors, as a result, ever consistently address such issues as the violation of human rights worldwide, the loss of religious freedom, or the holocaust of abortion. Fewer still relate these issues to how Christians in general can effect a remedy and bring about change through applying the Gospel to that issue.

The grave moral problems and decay of the contemporary world are the consequences of at least a century of church teaching that involvement in local church activities is more important than involvement in the affairs and institutions of society. The generation that preceded the past one thus lost its moral imperative and, therefore, lost the moral high ground to the secularists. In the process, Western societies became and presently remain biblically illiterate.

Moreover, the secularists who claimed this moral high ground taught a generation of young people the principles that have led to contemporary secular societies and the abortion holocaust. Thus, the so-called generation gap is really a spiritual gap created by a generation of nonthinking and nonacting people who referred to themselves as Christians.

Christian pastors of this present age, therefore, must once again teach the biblical requirement that involvement in *all* areas of the culture is a necessary part of true Christianity. A common response to this challenge from pastors is that they must only preach the Gospel. However, the Gospel (or Good News of Jesus Christ's coming, resurrection, and triumph over evil) speaks clearly to assisting the poor and helpless and preserving life.

Jesus Christ said His mission was "to release the oppressed."[7] This includes anyone, especially unborn babies. If pastors, whom God desires to take leadership, would consistently practice the Gospel and teach their congregations to stand against abortion, for example, such offenses as the deprivation of religious liberty and abortion could be eliminated.

We must never forget that there would be no United States as we have known the nation if the pastors of the 1700s had not stood against the British and preached resistance to governmental actions from the pulpit.[8]

The challenge to individual believers is this: They must confront pastors who are silent on the crucial issues of the day. Such issues are too important for spiritual leaders to sit idly by and allow the country to reach total cultural and moral collapse.

THE TRUE EMPHASIS

The future is in the hands of those willing to take moral stands and become actively involved in all aspects of life and culture. We have seen our freedoms threatened on numerous occasions by societies and governments virtually devoid of any Judeo-Christian worldview. The time to act is now. Tomorrow may be too late.

However, as mentioned earlier, in the willingness to become politically involved, one must be careful that the goal of gaining political power never becomes an end in itself. Otherwise, one may end up serving the god of politics.

Also, the believer must understand that involvement in politics does not mean compromising personal values. Indeed, the true Christian must always remain in a position to evaluate and remain critical of this world and its institutions (including government). This will not be an easy task because of strong opposition to the true Christian position on many political issues.

The true emphasis must be on preserving the freedom to present, to speak, and to act without undue government restraint. This should mean that the offer of Jesus Christ's Truth will gain a fair hearing, and a fair hearing is the main requirement for such truth to have the opportunity to prevail.

13

CAUTIOUS RADICALISM AND CIVIL DISOBEDIENCE

As secularism imposes its worldview on society, we can only expect continuing and increasing interference with the rights, liberties, and even the lives of humankind. The result will be an ongoing conflict between traditional theism and pervasive secular ideologies.

In order to counter expanding secularism, those holding to Judeo-Christian theism will have to practice "a cautious radicalism" and, in some instances, some may opt for civil disobedience. If not, the freedoms we take for granted will continue to wane.

Civil disobedience, however, is a very serious and frightening matter. This is even more true today because technology has globalized the impact of civil disobedience and, as a result, has attracted diverse groups to its possibilities. This includes some who may be mentally or ideologically imbalanced. Any concept or proposed action can, and most likely will, be extended or taken to its illogical extreme by someone. Even movements that have advocated pacifist acts of civil disobedience have found themselves embroiled in violence. In a fallen world, this is to be expected. However, the fact that there are those who will distort or exploit moral acts of civil disobedience compels us to examine this subject closely.

It must be remembered that civil disobedience is an important part of the American heritage. Its use dates prior to the establishment of the United States. Indeed, it has provided a means for significant changes in the law and policies of the United States, preventing the need to resort to armed rebellion or anarchy.

Numerous groups and causes throughout American history have resorted to civil disobedience as a way of expressing their dissatisfaction with governmental law and policies. These include movements as far-ranging as the abolitionists, the modern African-American civil rights movement, the Vietnam War protests, and antiabortion clinic sit-ins or "rescues."

Civil disobedience and resistance to the state, however, are subjects about which there is wide disagreement, even within the religious community. Nonetheless, civil disobedience has a long tradition in Judeo-Christian history and is sanctioned as a form of protest against certain governmental acts.[1]

A CRISIS

Twentieth-century religion, in particular Judaism and Christianity, has faced a potent opponent in civil governments worldwide. A prime example is the Nazi state erected by Adolf Hitler.

Hitler believed in neither God nor conscience, the latter of which he called "a Jewish invention, a blemish like circumcision." Hitler's tool was scientific reason. In the midst of World War II, Hitler said:

> The dogma of Christianity gets worn away before the advances of science. . . . Gradually the myths crumble. All that is left is to prove that in nature there is no frontier between the organic and the inorganic. When understanding of the universe has become widespread, when the majority of men know that the stars are not sources of light, but worlds, perhaps inhabited worlds like ours, then the Christian doctrine will be convicted of absurdity . . . . The man who lives in communion with nature necessarily finds himself in opposition to the Churches, and that's why they're heading for ruin—for science is bound to win. . . . Thousands of excursionists will make a pilgrimage there every Sunday. . . . It will be our way of giving men a religious spirit.[2]

Hitler did not see the state as secular. To him, the state was a *religious* institution intent on saving humanity through the use of its technology. This was later mirrored in Stalin's Russia and Mao's China, and it continues in modern authoritarian regimes. One can only hope that the democratic wind that has blown across various parts of the world will ameliorate the problem. However, with the fallen state of human-kind, the totalitarian possibility is always with us.

With the loss of Judeo-Christian theism as an integral part of Ameri-can public life, religious persons in the United States are finding them-selves increasingly in opposition to various government policies and laws. Indeed, as we have seen, traditional proponents of religion face "religious apartheid" in modern American society.[3]

Such religious opposition has led to a myriad of court cases. In some instances, such as the controversy surrounding the abortion is-sue, there have been numerous protests, sit-ins, and other opposition. These have led to arrests, jail, and/or prison sentences for religious people.[4] In these cases, Christians of conscience felt it was the logical outworking of their beliefs in opposing evil.

RADICAL AND HESITANT

When discussing the involvement of Christians in cultural concerns and a possible radical position on certain issues, Professor Glenn Tin-der states, "The Christian record in the annals of reform, it must be granted, is not impressive. Christians have accepted, and sometimes actively supported, slavery, poverty, and almost every other common social evil. They have often condemned such evils and principles but failed to oppose them in practice."[5]

Nonetheless, the crux of the matter is clear: "Christian ideas place one in a radical—that is, critical and adverse—relationship to estab-lished institutions."[6]

> The Kingdom of God is a judgment on existing society, and a symbol of its impermanence. Jesus was crucified because his presence and preaching were profoundly unsettling to reigning religious and politi-cal groups. Jesus did not seek the violent overthrow of these groups, but neither did he show much concern for their stability.[7]

Christianity thus compels the believer to act on its truths and count the cost. This is true, although in the fallen world our attempts to influ-ence society will fail in many instances. However, it is presumptuous to assume that failure is inevitable, because Christianity teaches that it is not only sinful human beings who are at work in history, but God as well. In the end, it is God who defines success and failure.

The believer, it is emphasized, must be cautious in how he or she acts on Christian ideas and must be mindful that true Christianity is defined by a series of checks and balances.

The Bible stresses that the believer is to love other human beings and exhibit an extreme humility but, at the same time, take strong stands on the truth. Thus, *Christianity will leave the believer cautious in the way he speaks the truth in love.* He or she should be aware of complexities and difficulties. This, in essence, expresses the spirit of reform inherent in Christianity, as Tinder points out:

> Christianity is radical, but it is also hesitant. This is partly, of course, because Christianity restrains our self-assurance. Efforts at social trans-formation must always encounter unforeseen complexities, difficulties, limits, and tragedies. Caution is in order. But Christian hesitancy has deeper grounds than prudence and more compelling motives than wariness of practical blunders. Hesitation expresses a consciousness of the mystery of being and the dignity of every person.[8]

This cautious radicalism demonstrates respect for God and for our fellow human beings. Those who disagree with us or work at cross purposes to God are still made in His image, endowed with common grace. Any acts that violate this respect are not acts of true Christian radicalism.

SKEPTICISM, RESISTANCE, AND DISOBEDIENCE

This cautious radicalism must be skeptical to some degree of all activities of individuals and the institutions they create, including soci-ety. This reluctance stems from the implications of the Fall and the corrupt nature the Fall cast upon all humanity.

Although the individual is exalted (because he or she is created in the image of God), every individual's flawed character multiplies to pro-duce institutions that thus present serious defects. This is often called "bureaucracy" or "mismanagement," but it really relates to the fallen-ness of individuals. In essence, then, a true Christian perspective is always skeptical about the intentions and activities of the state. As Pro-fessor Tinder writes:

> In the Christian view, while every individual is exalted, society is not. On the contrary, every society is placed in question, for a society is a mere worldly order and a mere human creation and can never do jus-tice to the glory of the human beings within it. The exaltation of the individual reveals the baseness of society. It follows that our political obligations are indeterminate and equivocal. If we recognize what God has done—so Christian principles imply—we shall be limitlessly re-spectful of human beings but wary of society.[9]

As a consequence of this position, believers can only give society and political institutions their "qualified" commitment.

Qualified commitment means that at certain points, times, and places the believer may be forced to resist governmental and societal laws and actions. Noncompliance with government directives is not foreign to Christianity. In fact, it has been a common strain throughout the history of Christianity to resist the state where its edicts violated God's laws. Virtually every era has some incident of resistance to a corrupt state, or for that matter, a corrupt church. As the late Francis Schaeffer wrote:

> The early Christians died because they would not obey the state in a civil matter. People often say to us that the early church did not show any civil disobedience. They do not know church history. Why were the Christians in the Roman Empire thrown to the lions? From a Christian's viewpoint it was for a religious reason, but from the viewpoint of the Roman State they were in civil disobedience, they were civil rebels. The Roman State did not care what anybody believed religiously; you could believe anything, or you could be an atheist. But you had to worship Caesar as a sign of your loyalty to the state. The Christians said they would not worship Caesar, anybody, or anything, but the living God. Thus to the Roman Empire they were rebels, and it was civil disobedience. That is why they were thrown to the lions.[10]

We must not forget that at one time the Christian church was "illegal" in the Roman Empire. To survive, the church had to go underground—literally—into the catacombs. In doing this, the church was violating the law. It was considered rebellion against the emperor, and Christians were viewed as subversives, criminals, and agitators.

BIBLICAL GUIDELINES

The Bible provides clear guidelines for resistance to illegitimate acts of the state.[11] A basic text for such resistance is found in the Bible in the thirteenth chapter of Romans. It is interesting that this chapter is often cited by those who claim the state has the authority to mandate anything and that Christians must blindly comply. This argument can be advanced only if Romans 13 is misunderstood.

In Romans 13:4, the Bible instructs that the state (or state official) is "God's servant to do you good. But if you do wrong, be afraid, for he does not bear the sword for nothing. He is God's servant, an agent of wrath to bring punishment on the wrongdoer." [12]

The Greek noun for the word *minister* (NASB; "servant," NIV) in Romans 13:4 is *diakonos,* which means a servant, attendant, or deacon. *Diakonos* is used by Christ when he states, "Whoever wants to become great among you must be your servant."[13] It is used in 1 Timothy by Paul to refer to "a good minister of Christ Jesus."[14]

Elsewhere, Paul refers to Timothy as a "minister of God"[15] and, in another book of the Bible, to Tychicus as "a dear brother and faithful servant in the Lord."[16]

In Romans 13:6, Paul again uses the term *servant* to describe a state official.[17] The Greek word used in this verse, however, is *leitourgous,* which describes earthly rulers who, though they may not consciously act as servants of God, discharge functions that are the ordinance of the Creator.

These particular Greek words are used in the Bible for a specific reason: to indicate that legitimate state officials or civil rulers are to be servants under God, not lords or sovereigns, "for there is no authority except that which God has established."[18] When the civil authorities divorce themselves from any responsibility to the Creator, they often become self-styled lords, lawless and predatory as to the citizens under their control. In St. Augustine of Hippo's opinion, such civil rulers are no more than bands of robbers.

In chapter 13 of Romans, the apostle Paul describes the authority and limits of civil government. The Creator has appointed civil magistrates to perform a twofold function that reflects the general purpose of the state. First, the state must protect and promote, not destroy or subvert, the good of society. Second, the civil government must deter crime and bring to punishment those who foster evil in society.

Paul states very clearly in Romans 13:1 that all government is ordained and established by the Creator. The Bible states that parents, pastors, civil authorities, employers, and others have received their authority to govern from God. This authority, however, is delegated authority. It should not be exercised in opposition to principles of higher law or natural law (as based upon Judeo-Christian principles). If so, subjection of people's rights is most often the result.

When the state is discussed in the New Testament, the scope and limits of its authority are generally defined. For example, Paul writes: "I urge, then, first of all, that requests, prayers, intercession and thanksgiving, be made for everyone—for kings, and all those in authority, that we may live peaceful and quiet lives in all godliness and holiness. This is good, and pleases God our Savior, who wants all men to be saved and to come to a knowledge of the truth."[19] Paul makes clear that the state is to create an atmosphere where knowledge and truth prevail as part of its task of protecting good. Paul links this idea to the prayers and attitude of humankind toward the state.

If the state is established by God to be "God's servant to do you good," then the question arises: What about a government that acts diametrically opposed to the higher law principles? Does the Creator also ordain such a government? If the answer is in the affirmative, then it can logically be argued that God was in support of Hitler's and Stalin's regimes. This is not to say that God did not sovereignly ordain these men as agents of judgment (like Pharaoh); nonetheless we must resist their immoral governments.

GOD OVER MAN

Despite the biblical support for resistance to the state, Christians through the centuries have fallen into two fundamental errors with regard to their relationship with the government. The first error involves the claim that the civil government represents the "god of this world." This view is totally illegitimate and has nothing to do with true Christianity.

The second erroneous view is that the state is divinely ordained in all respects and that Christians owe it absolute obedience. Romans 13 refutes both errors.[20] The state is a legitimate institution, ordained in principle by God, and intended to act as God's servant to promote justice in the civil and social realm.

> *Paul was not imprisoned because he was considered a model citizen; rather, he was in jail because he was considered a perpetrator of civil disobedience.*

However, the government's legitimacy is conditioned on its promotion of justice. If the state becomes incompatible with the ends for which it is ordained, then the state becomes lawless.

The question remains: What should be done when the state violates its authority? If the state commands or permits that which is contrary to the basic Judeo-Christian principles of justice and the sanctity of human life, then, as Francis Schaeffer noted: "There is not only the right, but the duty, to disobey the state."[21]

Theologian Alan Johnson writes in his study of Romans that "the proper role of government is in promoting good and punishing evil. . . . It can be assumed that if either of these conditions is not met there is ground for resistance or even disobedience. That state is not absolute in its demands over us, nor is it infallible or always on the side of justice."[22]

Some seek to justify their refusal to stand against illegitimate state acts by asserting that Christ and the apostles were pacifists. This is not true. The question of pacifism did not arise, but Christ was certainly not silent on matters of government. He felt free to criticize not only the Jewish civil leaders[23] but also the Roman-appointed ruler Herod Antipas, referring to him as a "fox."[24] Christ overturned tables and whipped the money changers from the temple.[25] The book of Revelation portrays Christ as ultimately exercising vengeance on the secular state.

Paul likewise accused one of the members of a grand jury who commanded him to be hit on the mouth of being a "whitewashed wall," although he apologized when he learned that the man who issued the order was the high priest.[26] Moreover, it must not be forgotten that the majority of Paul's epistles in the New Testament were written from jail cells. Paul was not imprisoned because he was considered a model citizen; rather, he was in jail because he was considered a perpetrator of civil disobedience. He obeyed the command to preach the gospel whether the civil authorities were pleased or not.

*B*iblical resistance does not include riots or armed revolution, nor does it sanction vigilante acts.

Peter's resistance in Acts 5 is a classic example of standing for religious principles against the illegitimate acts of the state. Peter and others were thrown in prison for preaching.

The Bible records in Acts 5 that even God defied the local authorities when an angel opened the doors of the prison, freeing the apostles. That was highly illegal. According to the biblical account, God identified with those who defied the state. God took Peter out of the prison and then instructed the apostles to stand in the temple and preach. Again, that violated the mandates of the authorities, and the apostles were brought before the Sadducees (or religious leaders) to answer for their "crime."

In response to the charges of preaching in Jesus' name, Peter replied: "We must obey God rather than men."[27] The apostles were then beaten and commanded not to teach about Christ. However, daily "in the temple courts and from house to house, they never stopped teaching and proclaiming the good news that Jesus is the Christ."[28] Nothing could stop them. They were too intent on "turning the world upside down" for Christ.[29]

REQUIREMENTS

Any type of resistance must meet certain basic requirements.

For example, when illegitimate acts of the state are perpetrated on the citizenry, resistance must be first directed to appropriate authorities. In particular, Christian resistance must be under the rule of duly appointed local officials. If citizens, for instance, believe they are being treated unfairly by some part of the government, they should contact their representatives in government and protest. The appropriate government official could then represent them by going directly to the agency of the state that is involved and attempt to correct the matter. Thus, it is important to note that *all resistance should be aimed at helping the government to act righteously, not toward tearing down the structure.* The Bible simply does not authorize anyone taking the law into his or her own hands.

The American colonists, for example, followed this biblical mandate in the American Revolution. They elected representatives from every state who, by way of the Declaration of Independence, protested certain practices of Great Britain that violated their rights. That approach failing, they defended themselves with force when presented with the demand for compliance.

Biblical resistance is not revolution. Biblical resistance does not include riots or armed revolution, nor does it sanction vigilante acts. There is no example in the Bible of any person of God who intended to overthrow the government by violence. To the contrary, the biblical emphasis (as illustrated by Jesus Christ, Peter, and Paul) is that living consistent lives based upon Judeo-Christian principles, without regard to consequences, will bring about true cultural reformation.

Obviously, protest is the most viable alternative at this time in history in terms of resistance. The freedom yet exists for citizens to utilize their democratic right of protest to the maximum. However, we must realize that protest can be a *form* of force. When, for example, the apostle Peter was ordered not to preach about Jesus Christ in the temple, he ignored such illegitimate commands and reentered the temple to preach the gospel. This is civil disobedience and a form of force—compelling others to listen to something they do not want to hear.

"HAIL, CAESAR!"

"Hail, Caesar! We who are about to die salute you!" The gladiators of first century Rome raised their right hands straight out, signifying full allegiance. Thousands of others assembled in the crowded Roman Coliseum cheered, voicing their total commitment to the man-god Caesar while a large band played a rousing march. The same vibrant salute was repeated much later in history by thousands of goose-stepping soldiers with "Heil, Hitler!"

The leaders of Rome and the Third Reich claimed to be divine. When a state claims divinity, history illustrates that conflicts inevitably occur between those who hold Judeo-Christian beliefs and the state and society that envelop them.

The religious fervor of the gladiator salute "Hail, Caesar!" has its counterpart today. Candidates in modern election campaigns (even those claiming to be Christians) present themselves as heroes whose election will mark the advent of a new society. More and more, even in the United States, they claim that the state will provide all the answers to our woes. Perhaps that is why veneration of former American presidents and other leaders has drastically declined. People must understand that politicians are not the saviors of the modern world.

Yet, as American Christians, for example, have become more and more involved with the right or the left in the political arena, their candidates have all too often been characterized as "the" hope for a new America. The danger in this lies in the fact that, for the believer, Jesus Christ is the *only* true hope. Unfortunately, the fervor with which many Christians pursue politics and certain candidates seems to ignore this truth.

Modern secularists place their hopes largely in politics because the secularist ideology posits the state as the ultimate order and authority. For the believer, it is not and cannot be. Consequently, believers and local churches must avoid becoming merged with the state or politics, that is, becoming partners in ultimate goals. As Professor Johnson notes: "A Christianity tied too closely to the civil authorities soon finds itself being used as a tool to sanction the particular policies and acts of a government which uses the church to win citizen approval."[30]

A government leader may declare himself or herself to be "born again" and take an active role in congregational worship. However, this is no guarantee that the state that he or she heads will not continue as before and even intensify its struggle against Judeo-Christian beliefs, practices, and even Christians themselves. This is especially true with the current view that private beliefs should not influence public action.

Simply put, *believers must only approach government and society with skepticism and great caution.* This includes laws, goals, policies, promises, and the like. If not, modern believers are likely to repeat the grave mistakes of the past.

For example, in pre-Nazi Germany, there was ample German readiness to accept the existing political order without criticism and to grant unqualified obedience to the state. As the historian J. S. Conway recognized,

> The illusions entertained by churchmen about their Nazi rulers, even after the horrifying consequences . . . and the overrunning of neighboring countries, can be explained—if not explained away—by the traditional acceptance that "the powers that be are ordained of God." The German Church was not equipped with the theology adequate to sustain any critical attack upon the actions of its political rulers, and for that reason, even at the end of the Nazi era there was no more than . . . reluctant resistance.[31]

Some German churchmen cooperated with the Nazis in the German state's call for a renewal of the nation and a revival of the "spiritual" life. Unlike the Protestant churches, the Catholic church committed itself to a policy of official opposition to the Nazi party. Nonetheless, the Catholic Students Union endorsed the Nazi effort and issued the following proclamation on July 15, 1933:

> The Catholic Students Union hails the National Socialist revolution as the great *spiritual* breakthrough of our time. It is the destiny and the will of the Catholic Students Union to embody and disseminate the idea of the Third Reich . . . and therefore the Catholic Students Union will be led in the National Socialist spirit. . . . Only the powerful National Socialist state, rising out of the Revolution, can bring about for us the re-Christianization of our culture. Long live the Catholic Students Union! Long live the Greater German Reich! Heil to our Führer, Adolf Hitler.[32]

This type of rhetoric is a call for the state to do what believers would not do—that is, bring about a spiritual revival. By shifting their hopes for revival from the local churches to the state, Christians were forced to identify closely with the state and German nationalism. This made it much easier for Hitler to manipulate Christians and, therefore, German society in general.

Also, as one author notes, the German churches' "basically conservative outlook . . . led them to accept without question the claim of Nazism to be the only alternative to communism."[33] In other words, because Nazism *appeared* to be conservative, Christians leaned in its direction. This same danger is posed, for example, to American churches that espouse a conservative politicism cloaked in a claimed biblical theology. However, mere labeling of a philosophy as "conservative" does not necessarily mean it has any real relationship to true Christianity.

For these basic reasons, the German church, in general, failed to stem the Nazi tide. Through its lack of resistance, the church became as silent as a tomb. It would not interfere or protest acts of the state.

Those who oppose the truth want churches that will not interfere. In Germany, Nazi Joseph Goebbels said: "Churchmen dabbling in politics should take note that their only task is to prepare for the world hereafter."[34]

Too many Christians have, albeit unknowingly, taken Goebbels's advice. There is nothing that the world would like so much as silent churches. However, as believers practice a cautious radicalism, they will speak out, protest, and stand actively for the truth.

PRO-LIFE
STRATEGIES

Within the current legal and social context and in accordance with Judeo-Christian principles, what can—and what should—be done to stem the anti-life crisis in our world?

Within this book, there are other concepts such as the demonstration of love and compassion that apply to preventing future killing. However, in this chapter, I will propose some additional ideas I believe will stem the tide of secularism and end the American holocaust of unborn children.[1]

As we look at ways to affect our culture, we must be honest in recognizing that the pro-life movement as a whole does not seem to have a coherent strategy. No one seems to be in charge. If there is to be any hope in the killing fields for the unborn children, we must consider the overall strategies and philosophies of the pro-life movement in general.

I would like to preface all of my following strategies with the comment that I am, and always have been, deeply impressed with the commitment and religious beliefs of pro-life activists. That is one reason I have always been, and still am, committed to the defense through the legal system (and through many other means) of all pro-life people (including picketers and rescuers). Yet I believe we need to rethink strategies in light of the continued killing of babies and a spiritual, political, and legal climate that, unless drastically changed, only portends more killing in the future.

A PHILOSOPHY

It must be recognized that *Roe v. Wade* is no longer a case. It is a philosophy. As I noted earlier, most of the judicial, executive, and legislative authorities have accepted the Supreme Court's redefinition of human life. Although most Americans find abortion repugnant at some point during pregnancy, basic support for the "right to choose" is accepted by a large segment of Americans today.

The pro-life community looked to the Reagan conservatives on the Supreme Court and believed that at last *Roe* would be repudiated. *Casey* was the Court's response—*Roe* is, in the words of the justices, still "good law."[2] The pro-life community must stop placing a lasting hope in and directing its every effort toward the overturning of *Roe* by the Supreme Court.

The pro-life community faithfully supported twelve years of so-called conservative government under presidents who paid lip service to the right to life. Yet, the number of abortions remained relatively constant—since 1975 an incredible 1.5 to 1.6 million per year.[3] This means that approximately 20 million babies were killed while religious people, conservatives, and others kept hoping that the "conservative" president would end the holocaust. The pro-life community must recognize that it is unlikely that any president—Republican or Democratic—will ever make an unqualified commitment to ending abortion. Presidents of either party may, for whatever motivation, be willing to express their so-called personal philosophy against abortion, but we all have to understand that no president of the United States will stop abortion.

If the pro-life community will turn its attention from the straw man of a Supreme Court case to the real issue of the religious, spiritual, and moral health of this nation, we may see some real changes. Several times a week, pro-lifers tell me that they have invented the so-called perfect case to overrule *Roe*. There will probably never be such a case.

Pro-lifers must realize that *Roe* is, in many ways, like prohibition. The people of America manufactured, sold, and consumed alcohol despite—or to spite—the law. There was no widespread moral imperative supporting prohibition.

So it is with abortion. In today's moral climate, *even if Roe v. Wade* were overruled, there is no question that abortion would still continue in this country. That means that *cultural support* for the *Roe* philosophy of individual rights even over the lives of others must be discredited.

TO BE SAVVY

Those in the pro-life movement must become savvy. Pro-lifers must claim the phrase "a woman's issue." Under the proposed Freedom of Choice Act, for example, *states may not prevent abortions undertaken for reasons of sex selection.* Abortions based on sex selection almost always occur when the baby to be killed is a girl—a future woman. This is sexism to the ultimate degree, yet many feminists support it.

Thus, we must look beyond the rhetoric. The pro-life community must also look beyond illusions of hope and into the face of reality.

TACTICS AND RESCUES

Pro-life people must always be vigilant concerning the "goals" of their own organizations. Most rescuers and pro-life activists are sincere, courageous, and good people. I am well aware of the horrendous treatment of some rescuers by the police, as well as the abusive behavior of some pro-abortion activists.

However, many are concerned that, at some point in time, the goals of some of the leadership of the pro-life movement have become, or at least appear to be, somewhat confused and distracted from the goal of ending abortion. For example, one journalist, describing her impressions of the first rescue she had seen, said "[the off-limits rule regarding the street] was sporadically violated by Operation Rescue protesters trying to get themselves arrested."[4] The journalist described her impression at the day's end: "On the anti-abortion side, protesting is considered good Christian work, but getting arrested—well, that is the deed of the truly holy."[5]

In other words, the journalist left with the impression that the goal of the rescuers was to get arrested, not to save babies or stop abortion. The journalist believed that the rescuers placed their highest value on "getting arrested."

Unlike this journalist, many individual rescuers and other pro-life activists understand that *being willing to accept punishment for civil disobedience* is different from seeking arrest merely to clog municipal jails and disrupt the court system. To prevent misunderstanding, how-

223

ever, pro-lifers should discourage estimates of the success of anti-abortion activities that are gauged by such statements as "The total number of rescuers arrested in front of abortion clinics since the movement started will reach 70,000 this month,"[6] or, "More than 2,600 pro-lifers were arrested."[7] Such statements may confuse those who are not in the pro-life movement, including the media, and may in addition indicate a need for pro-life leaders to personally re-examine their goals.

In any case, the pro-life movement must come to grips with another fact: Although there have been organized rescue activities on a national scale since 1987, *there has been no significant decrease in the number of abortions.* Some babies have been saved by those who block access to abortuaries—and I do not diminish the importance of this fact—but the pro-life community must recognize that such activities have little impact on the *Roe* philosophy of America. Although disruptive activities at abortion clinics have somewhat heightened public awareness of the issue in general, such activities have served as well to polarize the issue and stereotype in a negative way all those who support life.

That also means that various tactics of civil disobedience must be reconsidered. Again, I admire the courage and moral witness of rescuers in general. In putting their bodies on the line for their beliefs, rescuers have often endured savage treatment from police with no retaliation and without notice from the press.

However, as John Leo of *U.S. News & World Report* writes,

> it is possible to doubt their wisdom. I hate the hectoring of pregnant women at clinics. I think it's wrong to carry the fight to the homes of abortionists, putting pressure on children and spouses. And I think there's a contradiction between commitment to nonviolent moral witness and the growing use of intimidation, stalking and harassment as tactics. Op-R's "No Place to Hide" campaign against doctors doesn't look much like King and Gandhi. It looks like ACT UP.[8]

It is legitimate to publicize and list the names of abortionists. Shame and embarrassment is one reason the number of doctors doing abortions has declined. However, there is a point at which the line is crossed in the wrong way. For example, holding up a "Wanted" poster containing a doctor's name on it seems like incitement to violence, perhaps murder. The logical extension of "Wanted" is "Dead or Alive." Indeed, "[the] current climate includes such things as butyric acid attacks on clinics, bombings, gunfire at a Michigan Planned Parenthood office, arson at clinics in Texas and Florida, plus death threats to doctors and stalking of clinic personnel."[9]

As such, "Operation Rescue really ought to reassess its tactics. If its goal is to shut down clinics at all costs, it will be pulled in the direction of terrorism. If it is more interested in moral witness, it will start treating women and doctors as potential converts rather than as enemies."[10]

Finally, John Leo comments:

Mostly, I don't think Operation Rescue is helping to create conditions under which abortion will begin to recede. The sheer practical fact is that abortion will become rarer only when more women come to see it as wrong. Instead of shrieking at women entering clinics, abortion protesters ought to take them seriously as moral decisionmakers.

There are other practical considerations. The press is totally bored by abortion demonstrations (the same boredom problem has affected ACT UP, too). So if vast publicity is the goal, it will come only if violence occurs—a no-win situation. More important, the increased pressure on clinics and pregnant women could invite the Supreme Court to cite it as an undue burden on women seeking abortions. If so, the modest abortion regulations now in effect could be struck down."[11]

Against this background, the very concept of rescues may need to be reconsidered and their effectiveness reevaluated.

THE MEDIA

The pro-life movement must work to get the support of the media. An eighteen-month investigation, as reported in *Citizen* magazine, documented abortion bias in the media.[12] According to the investigation, "the bias manifests itself, in print and on the air, almost daily in content, tone, choice of language or prominence of play."[13] Indeed: "Most major newspapers support abortion rights on their editorial pages, and reporters are decidedly pro-abortion. A 1985 *Los Angeles Times* poll found that 82 percent of journalists on newspapers of all sizes say they favor abortion rights. . . . The nation's largest newspaper chains, including the Gannett Foundation and the Knight Foundation, give money to pro-abortion groups,"[14]

Another reporter believes that "[o]pposing abortion, in the eyes of most journalists . . . is not a legitimate, civilized position in our society."[15] Thus, "[j]ournalists tend to regard opponents of abortion as 'religious fanatics' and 'bug-eyed zealots' . . . . Among reporters, the anti-abortion movement is perceived as one of those . . . 'fringe' things somewhere out there in Middle America or Dixie. . . . Journalists . . . not only are not part of the anti-abortion movement, but don't know anyone who is."[16]

Part of the problem here is the tight alliance between the newsroom and the abortion-rights lobby. The campaign to diversify newsrooms has not yet reached the critical turning point where most managing editors can truthfully say they have hired a journalist who actually

225

knows someone who opposes abortion. So reporters write about Operation Rescue people as if they were covering Martian invaders.[17]

The pro-life community must change this state of affairs. Pro-lifers should consider diplomatic tactics: Get to know media people personally; *develop relationships;* practice the art of diplomacy. For example, pro-lifers should regularly keep in contact with local journalists and do such things as take a journalist to lunch—everyone knows about "power lunches." Make them realize that pro-lifers are compassionate, intelligent, "everyday" people.

Pro-lifers should regularly write serious and reasoned articles of quality and then get them published—even if it means raising the funds for publishing within the community.

The pro-life community should run ads in the media—print and otherwise. Television ads by the De Moss Foundation are a good example. These ads are effective, no doubt in part because they do not resort to hysteria or religious elitism.

In other words, it is time to stop screaming at the media and instead attempt to work with journalists. There is no dispute regarding the power of the media. Instead of being the object of its disdain, pro-lifers must harness its power to save the lives of our unborn.

A WOMEN'S ISSUE

Pro-lifers should insist that the truth of abortion be told. Information that is never mentioned in the rhetoric about a "woman's right to control her body" is that abortion adversely affects a woman's health—physically and mentally. A great deal of respected medical literature exists documenting the negative consequences to women who "choose" abortion over life.[18]

Those effects include subsequent drug or alcohol abuse. For example, a 1990 random questionnaire survey of American women aged 24–44 found that 34 percent who reported a prior abortion also reported substance abuse, compared with only 12 percent for non-aborted women. A 1981 random survey of American women reported that 13 percent of the women reporting prior abortions were heavy drinkers, while abstainers had a reported abortion rate of only 4 percent. Among women in general, only 6 percent were heavy drinkers. Likewise, a 1984 Boston City Hospital study among inner city women enrolled for prenatal care found that those who reported cocaine use were more than twice as likely to report two abortions and were three times as likely to report three abortions compared to a non-cocaine-using control group.

A prior induced abortion is also a risk factor for pregnant women who intend to carry a subsequent pregnancy to term. Since abortion became legal in 1973, the incidence of repeat abortions has risen rapidly from 12 percent in 1973 to at least 43 percent in 1987.

One woman, whose story is drawn from numerous studies, said she obtained her abortion at the urging of her doctor who feared birth defects. Alcohol and drug abuse followed. Her second abortion was done in anger and "triggered a coolness about abortion," she recalled. Promiscuity followed, and the woman laughed about the third abortion. The fourth she called a "quickie," and she admitted that, by now, she was "deadened to pain, to right and wrong."

The abortion rate is much higher among the population of women who have already had at least one abortion. A 1984 study of 31,000 teenagers in New York City found that those who had experienced one induced abortion were approximately four times more likely to terminate a current pregnancy by abortion than teenagers with no previous abortions.[19]

As women repeat abortions, their communication with others tends to break down. They more often make the decision by themselves. They are less likely to be happily married, and they tend to have more difficulty than other women in getting along with people.

Replacement pregnancies are common following abortion as women attempt "atonement" or "restitution" for the initial loss. Masochism or self-punishment has been identified as a factor in repeat abortions as well.

Researchers have also found that the socioeconomic status of women tends to deteriorate as abortion is repeated.[20]

Thus, the real message to women regarding abortion is that abortion is not "therapeutic." Rather, it is very harmful when considered objectively. Repeat abortions lead not to economic prosperity or good health or social well-being, but to an increasing "feminization of poverty."

The media is not going to make this information widely available. Medical practitioners involved in abortion won't either. The pro-life community must build bridges of communication to pro-choice women so that all women understand the truth. The pro-life community must hold educational seminars in neutral settings regarding these issues and make serious efforts to educate without inflaming. The teach-ins of the 1960s—informal, lengthy discussions on topics such as the Vietnam War—are a good example of this tactic. They provided a forum for controversial, but open, discussion that was not available elsewhere.

USE THE JUDICIAL SYSTEM

The pro-life community must learn to use the judicial system and stop undermining it. Most of the judicial system is, without question, misguided with respect to the issue of abortion, and many courts have exhibited great hostility toward rescuers, for example, during their trials.[21]

Some rescuers have refused to provide arresting authorities with identification information and have succeeded not in disrupting jails and courts, as they had hoped, but only in receiving unusually long jail terms, both before and after sentencing.[22]

The personal addresses and telephone numbers of judges have even been distributed by rescue organizations in order to facilitate personal harassment of judges.

Many in the rescue movement who have been arrested have publicly attacked the judges involved in their cases and have organized letter campaigns against such judges. Some rescuers have destroyed court orders in the faces of their judges.

These tactics are wrong. As a practical matter, they will backfire.

Of course, there are judges who distort and misapply the law and, as a consequence (even if it is not intentional), end up advancing a pro-abortion agenda. This is to be condemned. Judges are instructed to apply the law as they find it and not to be "activist" courts. Unfortunately, much modern law fails to preserve life; it is, instead, on the side of personal freedom. As such, the target of activism should be those who make the laws rather than those who apply them.

The strategy of harassing judges and their families and neighbors also undermines the historic independence of the judicial branch and reduces it to a mere reflex of the prevailing opinion or passion of the day. Under this strategy, law becomes a matter of majority will or at least a matter of brute force. American freedoms, our constitutional rights, and our Christian witness are ill-served by furthering such a strategy.

Although we may condemn the acts of a particular judge, we should respect the office. Strong-arm tactics will not reverse the opinions of judges who have ruled adversely to the pro-life position. Judges swayed by political pressure, as opposed to the sound reasoning of the law, are unlikely to be moved by this approach.

Moreover, many judges favorably disposed to the rights of the unborn will be undercut by a blatant strategy to manipulate the judicial process. Harassment strategies will further undercut the efforts of pro-life attorneys—who are, after all, officers of the court—sacrificially standing in the gap on behalf of the unborn.

There is another reason to abandon judicial intimidation and harassment. There is little doubt that the Supreme Court will, much like Pontius Pilate, wash its hands of the abortion issue by preserving the overall right to abortion but leaving it to the states individually to permit or regulate. Thus, state responses to the issue will be the subject of widespread litigation. Commencing such litigation in courtrooms filled with judges who are already threatened by and angry with the pro-life community will not serve the interests of the unborn or freedom in general.

USE CITIZEN POWER

Pro-lifers should continue to use their powers as American citizens. Although the pro-life community has been active in forming political groups and in lobbying activities, these efforts become even more important as the abortion issue returns to the state governments. Pro-life attorneys should be recruited to immediately begin drafting well-crafted legislation favoring life. Although the Supreme Court will undoubtedly strike down legislation it views as "burdensome," the process of litigating all the way to the Supreme Court could be too expensive and burdensome for the proponents of "choice." Working at the state level can prove to be more efficient.

In addition to seeking to limit abortion through state regulations, pro-life people should also become involved in regulations that protect the health and safety of the mother. Though that may be difficult for some, we must care for the mothers undergoing abortion as well as the babies they kill. Efforts in this regard produce the side benefit that the expenses associated with providing abortions increase. Thus, requirements for licensure, medical malpractice insurance, and the like serve restrictive purposes, and pro-life activists should therefore diligently pursue them. Abortions are quite unsafe from a medical standpoint, though the pro-abortion groups attempt to suppress that fact.

As suggested earlier regarding the media, pro-lifers should use diplomacy and become personally acquainted with their governmental representatives, the local health agency officials, and everyone else concerned with the abortion issue.

ECONOMIC PRESSURE

The pro-life community must become skilled in exerting economic pressure. For example, consider the case of the delicatessen owner who refused to deliver sandwiches to an abortuary.[23] The owner of the delicatessen was fined by the city for violating its "nondiscrimination" provisions. Although the fine was overturned on appeal,[24] the deli was put out of business because all the pro-abortion people in the area boycotted him.

The pro-life community has done some boycotting of national and international businesses. However, this strategy should include local businesses as well. For example, it is more effective to boycott the local dry cleaners, the local pharmacy, and the local card store where local owners and managers support abortion. It is true that people in this country have a right to believe what they will—but your dollars need not contribute to their success.

TEACH YOUR CHILDREN WELL

After all is said and done, any true change in our country will come through a healthy family structure. Although the family is discussed in detail in chapter 15, I want to comment briefly on why the family is important to preserving life.

The family is at the heart of traditional Judeo-Christian theism. To destroy Christianity or Judaism, for example, all one has to do is destroy the family. That's how crucial the family is, and that is why the traditional family concept is constantly questioned and redefined in modern society.

Since contemporary secularism is undermining the institution of the family, those who advocate Judeo-Christian ideals must take a hard look at what they are doing in their own families. The family should be the center of spiritual life. No other institution (including the church) or activities should get in the way of strong family relationships. Parents must develop relationships with their children—and that means spending time with them.

Parents must make sure their children are being reared as fully informed citizens. That means instructing them in the realities of their culture as well as the spiritual principles. For example, are you teaching your children that Christianity is a system of thought that applies to all of life? Are your children being educated to be a generation that will vigorously resist secularistic values and infringements on their rights? Are you guiding your children to help them understand twentieth-century problems so they can handle the crises of the next generation?

Children must be guarded and protected but not divorced from reality. Reality, however, like strong medicine, must be provided in intermittent, small doses. That means that the family should be the center of "reality education" in the life of the child. That is true whether the child is educated in a public, private, or home school.

It is within the family system that children must learn about the world around them. We live in a world resounding with devastating crises. Children should know the truth about what is happening around them and that there are viable ways of providing Christian alternatives.

I am the father of five children. My wife and I were teaching our children, as early as five years of age, for example, about abortion and its impact on our culture. Children have a much greater capacity to deal with reality than we may think. Indeed, I find that many children are more capable of dealing with reality than so-called adults.

That does not mean, however, that parents should rob children of their childhood. Just as adults deal with different phases of life at a certain level, so should children.

A popular secular television show recently asserted that the pro-life community is "using" children as pawns in their anti-abortion struggles. To the contrary, children properly raised in a healthy family setting are not protesting abortion as "pawns"—they already know it is wrong, and why, and they are proceeding to engage the issue like the young Christians they are.

THE INDIVIDUAL

You, the one solitary individual, can make a difference. There is hope in the killing fields if we roll up our sleeves and join in the battle for cultural reform.

I would not be honest with you if I did not recognize that one of the most difficult tasks facing the present generation as we move into the twenty-first century is that of maintaining hope. The problems and crises seem overwhelming. Therefore, it is common to see people burn out and become enveloped in despair.

We live in a disheartening century. To many, it appears to be the worst in the history of humankind. This fact is borne out by what the twentieth century has produced in terms of world wars, racism, poverty, cruelty, and terrorism.

Any stand on the truth, therefore, will be difficult. Unfortunately, stands on the truth do not draw large groups of support. That will often mean that those "radicals" standing on the truth, based on hope, will be standing with little human support.

However, it is often that one solitary person or movement changes the course of history. For example, if the apostle Paul had turned east instead of west, the entire course of world history would have been altered. Thus, the individual, through involvement and articulating the truth, can likewise change the course of the future.

As an individual (or as a group) you can perform works of mercy and oppose injustice.

NO SILENCE

Finally, those who call themselves Christians *must not remain silent.* Silence is the mortar that keeps the prison walls standing.

Alexander Solzhenitsyn speaks of how the Russian people would kneel inside the door of their apartments, pressing their ears to listen when the KGB came at midnight to arrest a neighbor. He says that if all the people would have come out and driven off the officers, sheer public opinion would have demoralized the effort to subdue an otherwise free people. But their own personal peace and longing for security were more important.

Babies are being killed before they are even allowed to be born. Infanticide and euthanasia are tragedies that are here and now.

It is shocking to realize that these things are occurring with very little moral comment from the majority of Christians and the churches they occasionally inhabit. Again, this has a parallel to the Nazi period. We are not there yet, but silence will certainly not deter its possibility.

The lack of resistance of the Christian churches to the Nazi state's Jewish policies has been the concern of extensive and still unconcluded research. The Nazis noticed early that the churches took their stand, not on the issue of the human rights of all Jews, but on an expedient and self-serving concern for "Christian Jews." The churches, by their submission to expediency and lack of political involvement, were eventually neutralized by the state.

Sadly, the same thing has happened in the United States. Through books, films, and the work of the pro-life movement, the American churches and the Christian community have been amply alerted to abortion as the primary issue facing the country today. Still, very little in the way of true resistance to the wanton slaughter of human life is coming from individual churches.

In all this, one principle must be understood: Although Christians may cry for religious freedom from here to eternity, a state that will not protect human life will ultimately protect no freedom of any kind. Instead, such a state will systematically attack God-given rights until the only freedom left is the "freedom" to die, whether it be by abortion, infanticide, or euthanasia. Religious freedom will have no ultimate value to a state that does not value life. The result—greater religious apartheid.

15

THE FAMILY AND THE HUMAN ELEMENT

If there is to be any recovery of the basic values that give form and freedom to society and provide worth and dignity to individuals, it will originate from healthy families. In this respect, Christians in particular must take a close look at how their families function.

A vibrant Christian life starts at home. A Christian can evangelize the world but neglect his own family in the process, thus denigrating the personal value of his work. Evangelization and love for one's fellow creatures begin in the family unit.

If Christians are to consistently speak and stand for the truth, it will be due not only to core beliefs but also to a strong, undergirding family structure. The need is therefore great to revitalize the biblical family structure.

This need does not deny the reality that many contemporary homes have no traditional family structure, with perhaps only one, or neither, parent present. However, as Christians, we must never abandon the biblical ideal. That means that all families, no matter how they are configured, should emulate the biblical ideal as much as possible.

FUNCTIONS

Historically and biblically, the family is the central institution in society, with obvious procreative functions. Ideally, believers marry because they share a bond of faith and love and resolve to maintain this bond for life under God. They thus create a family system that cannot be duplicated by either science or liberal social engineering as the ideal institution for raising children.

There are many reasons why the family is the foundational institution of a free society. First and foremost, the family should be society's basic health and welfare institution, caring for and educating its own without any outside compulsion.[1] When the family begins to break down, however, the state assumes the basic responsibility for health, welfare, and education and generally does an ineffective job in carrying out these duties. There is no possibility that the state can fully replace the parental function; hence, its performance will always be deficient and, as we saw in chapter 5, oftentimes becomes coercive.

The family is a person's first school, and parents are the educators, performing the most difficult of all educational tasks, teaching the child to speak. That is an important task, but it comes simply and naturally in the family as the result of a parent's love and the child's response to that love.

SELF-GOVERNMENT

The family is also the first government in the life of a child. Within the family setting, children should learn submission, self-government, motivation, and guidance. Again, this instruction flows naturally from the parents' natural love for their children. The children thus receive the highest order of motivation to become productive, ethical citizens.

In a biblically structured family, the father serves as the head of the household. He is the authority within the family relationship. The Bible is very clear, however, that the father should not be a dictator. Parents and children, therefore, learn from, and are governed by, the biblical family model.

The father is governed by the necessities of providing for the family, protecting family members, and giving them the example and leadership they need. Conversely, a father who will not provide for his family will not be respected and will have neither the authority nor the ability to govern with wisdom and honor. The Bible states clearly that if anyone does not provide for his own, especially those of his own household, "he has denied the faith and is worse than an unbeliever."[2] In the biblical model, the mother is voluntarily governed in her activities by the requirements of her husband and children.

SPOUSAL LOVE

Other biblical injunctions deal with a current problem in the church. Many Christian men imprison their wives in the house and treat them like slaves. Such behavior runs counter to the high estate placed upon women in the Bible and, in particular, to the reverent relationship men are to have with women.

The Proverbs 31 "virtuous wife" is a good example of how God views women. This chapter of the Bible clearly indicates that women (including wives) are to be afforded a great deal of respect. For example, in Proverbs 31:16, the wife owns property and acts as a business person. This biblical view runs counter to the way women are often viewed in Christian circles today.

Husbands, both Christian and non-Christian, need to reevaluate the relationship they have with their wives. A necessary element in the spousal relationship is the attention and love shown by the husband toward his wife. Indeed, the husband is to love his wife "just as Christ loved the church and gave himself up for her."[3] Men are also to love their wives "as their own bodies."[4] Failure to do so will interfere with God's blessing on that family.

Men need to shed arrogant, macho posturing and help their wives, even if that means staying home and performing tasks normally thought of as "wifely" functions. Jesus Christ set the example by washing the feet of His disciples. In view of Jesus Christ's great sacrifice, surely the Christian husband can love his wife sacrificially. To do less is simply wrong. The wife is a full partner, equal to her husband in every way.

THE EDUCATION FACTOR

It is clear that Western societies generally do not produce happy or well-balanced people. The high rate of suicide in all age categories is evidence of that. However, most of the distressing signs we see in our society are most likely related to malfunctioning families.

Thus, the answer to what seems to be a perplexing problem can be summed up in one sentence: *We must have better families.* And that can be done by returning the basic functions of parenting to the families once again. It also means returning children to the world of adults in restructuring adult-child relationships.

A basic function of parents that must be recovered from the state is *education*. The assembly-line education of both the state and private (including Christian) schools must be rethought.

The idea that only "professional" educators are qualified to teach children is a myth perpetrated by the educational establishment. Another absurd myth is the concept that teachers must be certified by the state in order to be qualified to teach. It is worth remembering that the men and women who built America, for example, were essentially home taught either by their "uncertified, nonprofessional" parents or by tutors who assisted the parents.

The family can recover the education function. In some ways, that is happening today, primarily through the growing home school movement and "parent-run" private schools.

Christian schools that are not parent-run are falling into the same trap as the state schools in usurping the function of the family. That can be easily remedied by putting parents in control of the school—which does not mean merely having parent meetings at the school. It means having parents on the school board and heavily involved in every aspect of the school. Otherwise, even private Christian schools can tend to be anti-parent, even unknowingly.

If at all possible, Christian and other private schools should cooperate with those parents teaching their children in the home. Christian schools should allow home education parents the use of their facilities and allow their children to take certain courses of instruction at the school, providing a type of learning center for them to customize their education.

Moreover, Christian schools and churches should work closely with home education parents in getting state laws amended to protect home education. Also, compulsory school attendance laws should be revised to allow children to spend fewer hours in formal schooling. Children should be encouraged to spend more time at home with their parents. There is much "dead-time" during the school day, and if that could be eliminated, less time at the school building would be required and more interaction with parents would be possible.

TO BE HUMAN

Children need both other children and adults in order to reach their full human potential. Isolation of children from adults simultaneously threatens the growth of the individual and the survival of society. *Child-rearing is not something children can do for themselves.* They cannot be "dragged up," as Professor Urie Bronfenbrenner recognizes:

It is primarily through observing, playing, and working with others older and younger than himself that a child discovers both what he can do and who he can become—that he develops both his ability and his identity. It is primarily through exposure and interaction with adults and children of different ages that a child acquires new interests and skills and learns the meaning of tolerance, cooperation, and compassion. Hence to relegate children to a world of their own is to deprive them of their humanity, and ourselves as well.[5]

What we are experiencing is a breakdown in the process of making human beings human. Bronfenbrenner adds: "By isolating our children from the rest of society, we abandon them to a world devoid of adults and ruled by the destructive impulses and controlling pressures both of the age-segregated peer group and the aggressive and exploitative television screen, we leave our children bereft of standards and support and our own lives impoverished and corrupted."[6]

Many have simply reversed their priorities. Other things have become more important than children. That is a betrayal of our children. It further underlines the ever-increasing disillusionment and alienation among young people in all segments of society.

Those who grew up in a setting where children and families were respected, loved, and taught are able to react to the frustrations of modern secular society in positive ways. Their families provide them with a strong sense of security, stability, and confidence. However, those who came from situations in which families and children were a low priority are striking out. The alienated child, for whatever reason, sets up his or her parents and society as objects of resistance.

It is the family that builds productive people. That means, again, that parents and children must be together. It also means that parents and children should be with each other in the family setting as much as possible. Parents should do what some may consider to be old-fashioned; that is, *keep their children at home,* away from some of the extracurricular activities that tend to disrupt families today. They should provide meaningful activities within the home.

That, in turn, means that parents themselves must remain within the family environment. Fathers and mothers who are workaholics or overly involved in other interests are not good parents.

All current trends point to the increasing participation of women and mothers in the work force. One may disagree that women are naturally more gifted and effective in the care of young children than are men. However, the fact remains that in today's society our children desperately need mothers.

Contrary to what some militant feminists may assert, one of the most important functions any human being serves is that of being a mother. When a mother works outside the home, however, the richness of the traditional family may suffer and in many instances be lost. Children deprived of a mother for any reason are children who have been robbed. We should do everything possible to avoid "latch-key" children. The child must have the security, nurture, and training that only a mother can give. If she is absent, the chances are that the child will develop personal problems.

There are instances where it is necessary for mothers to work. If they have small children they should attempt in-home employment opportunities as one solution. Or fathers and mothers who wish to be close to their children could both work out of the home at different times and split the work hours. Also, part-time work for mothers is another option.

> *Children are the living messages we send to a generation we will not witness. . . . They are the future leaders who will carry the message of the good news to a world of increasing darkness, and they are our legacy to the future.*

One caveat must be made, however. Mothers with small children should avoid working outside the home. Mothers have their greatest formative impact on children in their younger years. Small children need a mother's nurturing, modeling, and direction in their early years.

With the withdrawal of societal support of the family, older and younger women have become more isolated. Young mothers are removed from career women and society in general. An increasing responsibility for the care and upbringing of children has fallen on the young mother. Many rebel and put their children in day-care. Under dire circumstances, it is not surprising that many young women in America are in the process of revolting.

I, for one, understand and share their sense of rage. However, I fear that the consequences of the solutions advocated by some will have the effect of isolating children still further from the kind of care and attention described above. Parents should try at all costs to share responsibilities for the care and guidance of children.

If parents do not begin to increase the time they spend with their children, the "alienation gap" is going to increase. As a result, children will become even more estranged. Simply put, it is much easier to assert "children's rights"—as described in an earlier chapter—against parents who are strangers in their own homes.

A family is made or broken on the quality of human relationships. It takes effort, time, planning, and imagination on the part of parents to develop relationships with their children. It means reading aloud to them, playing with them, working with them, shopping with them, listening to their mundane joys and pains. Without this, we cannot build relationships.

Children are the living messages we send to a generation we will not witness. They are the combined images of their parents, and they are unique. They must be molded with love, positive discipline, and compassion. They are the future leaders who will carry the message of the good news to a world of increasing darkness, and they are our legacy to the future.

THE TELEVISION TRAP

That brings us to the subject of television. Nielsen company surveys of American viewers reveal that the average family watches television seven hours a day. As Pete Hamill says, "This has never happened before in history. No people has ever been entertained for seven hours a *day*."[7]

Television, besides consuming precious time, invades the privacy of the home. It almost always teaches an ethic that runs contrary to the foundation of the traditional family. It is at least a very subtle (although sometimes overt) attack on the family.

One Michigan State University study in the early 1980s offered a group of four- and five-year-olds the choice of giving up television or their fathers. One-third of the group said they would give up their fathers.[8]

Obviously, television has had a devastating impact on the American culture. It is a dominating force that alters behavior. Author Pete Hamill notes:

> Viewers can't work or play while watching television; they can't read; they can't be out on the streets, falling in love with the wrong people, learning how to quarrel and compromise with other human beings. In short, they are asocial. So are drug addicts.[9]

Hamill continues:

> In short, television works on the same imaginative and intellectual level as psychoactive drugs. If prolonged television viewing makes the young passive (dozens of studies indicate that it does), then moving to drugs has a certain coherence. Drugs provide an unearned high (in contrast to the earned rush that comes from a feat accomplished, a human breakthrough earned by sweat or thought or love).[10]

What should we do with television? Malcolm Muggeridge offered one solution: "I think the best thing to do is not to look at television, and to that end, I have, as has been said, disposed of my set."[11] It was Muggeridge's opinion—and that of others—that television is a medium doomed to mediocrity and incapable of much improvement.

Although I tend to agree with that assessment, I believe Christians must participate in the real world. They should not deprive their children altogether of a cultural reality such as television. Disposing of the television set will not make it disappear; monitoring it can in large part tame it.

"As a beginning," writes Pete Hamill, "parents must take immediate control of the sets, teaching children to watch specific *programs,* not 'television,' to get out of the house and play with other kids. Elementary and high schools must begin teaching television as a subject, the way literature is taught, showing children how shows are made, how to distinguish between the true and the false, how to recognize cheap emotional manipulation. All Americans should spend more time reading. And thinking."[12]

In other words, selective and limited television viewing is a large part of the answer. Of course that will not prevent erroneous or destructive material from seeping into your children's heads. It will, however, provide you with the opportunity to spend time with your children in educating them on what to watch. That means that parents, if at all possible, should watch programs with their children. If questions arise, they can then be answered in the context of the larger program. If parents cannot do that, they should watch at least one episode of each show and approve it *before* their children watch the show. They can have the children report on and evaluate future episodes.

These principles also apply to "Christian" programs as well. Because of its manipulative nature, much of so-called Christian programming is not healthy for adults or children (any more than secular programming is). Its main purpose may be to get you to buy some Christian product or it may be merely to perpetuate the show.

Television is also an intruder that prevents family unity. Many television programs and commercials are highly destructive to young minds.

They eschew moral judgments and program viewers only to buy products. In the realm of the commercial, nothing is sacred—which is evident in ads depicting computers dropping out of the sky to waiting monks, or ads depicting executives posing as angelic beings publicizing their products as they walk through clouds. Ads are often relativistic, materialistic, hedonistic, and often blasphemous.

I must add that I am not anti-television. In our family, however, we place restrictions on our viewing and screen what our children watch. We have found that videotapes provide a good alternative to regular television fare. There are many good movies and educational videotapes that are both enjoyable and instructive.

> *Christians need to emerge from their "evangelical" ghettos and acquire the capacity to understand and discuss the arts intelligently. . . . The believer should be able to interpret art and art forms in terms of their ideas and underlying ethical perspectives and respond in an enlightened way.*

In any event, we have found that the best way to watch television is as a family, which allows both parental critique and interplay with the children in discussing the content. What we do not allow is the television to serve as a baby-sitter. Intentionally or not, television is a teacher and an influence on behavior and, if not controlled, is a teacher of the worst sort.

CREATIVITY AND INTERACTION

Christian endeavors in the arts are in a dismal state. The biblical and traditional view of the arts and creativity as gifts of God has largely been discarded. However, any Christian revitalization in terms of the arts will begin in the family. It is there that parental direction and guidance could help produce an entirely new generation of artists.

241

Christians need to emerge from their "evangelical" ghettos and acquire the capacity to understand and discuss the arts intelligently. That does not mean that they must become absorbed with the respective works or subjects, nor does it mean that the Christian necessarily approves of the content. It simply means that the believer should be able to interpret art and art forms in terms of their ideas and underlying ethical perspectives and respond in an enlightened way. The arts, after all, often indicate the direction in which a society is heading. Picasso's paintings, for example, effectively foretold an era of mass inhumanity.

In terms of entertainment, Christians should relinquish the notion that all rock music is evil or that all movies are evil. Christians must not be flippant condemners of everything under the sun, but should be able to praise what is good from an artistic level, even if they do not agree with the lifestyle of the author or the content of the message. In other words, the form may be creative and valuable in itself, even if the context is not "Christian."

For example, one may not agree with the point of view of a particular film but may still recognize merit in technical aspects such as direction or cinematography. At the same time, however, one must be careful not to allow brilliant cinematography to seduce one into accepting an anti-Christian message. Although one may not be fond of jazz, one should be able to recognize a skilled jazz musician.

Whereas all Christians should be able to interpret the arts, some will want to be participants—and there is no good reason why they should not. Indeed, there is every reason why they should. Artistic creativity is a gift of God. As such, it is the imagination of the Christian that should soar beyond the stars.

Just as the arts need no justification, Christian participation in them should not have to be defended. Involvement in the arts cannot be opposed on the grounds that the world is divided into "spiritual" and "secular" spheres. Indeed, the word *secular* does not even appear in the Bible.

There is much that a family can do in the way of becoming involved in the arts. The key, once again, is parental participation.

By way of example, we have decorated our home with inexpensive prints of some of the great artists of our time, such as Rembrandt, Raphael, Matisse, and others. Our home is, in effect, an art gallery.

My wife and I also take time to listen to music with our children. We take in music all the way from the classical to the modern. For some forms of music, including rock, we have taken time for specific instruction of our children, listening to the music with them and pointing out problems in certain content and structure.

Thus, our children have been taught to take art seriously and be able to evaluate it through a Judeo-Christian worldview. If this type of instruction is not done with children, they are likely either to disregard the arts completely or, when they do imbibe, be ignorant of the meaning of what they are listening to and/or viewing.

An important caution needs to be given at this point. Believers who are inclined to the arts must understand that Christian faith and spirituality, however genuine and robust, do not necessarily guarantee artistic brilliance or even general competence. Triumphalism—the assumption of Christian superiority—is not only out of line, but can cause much embarrassment if the final product is less than brilliant. In addition, the fact that someone is a well-known "Christian personality" may help him get a hearing but does not necessarily ensure that his artistic efforts will be of high quality. We do not necessarily need to emulate secular standards, but our craftsmanship should be at least as good.

Whatever the Christian does, he or she is to do it while keeping in mind that God sets excellence as the standard. A Christian must be satisfied with nothing less than the best. We may never reach it, but we should always try. In practical terms, that means coming to grips with our own abilities, or the lack of them, and settling down to a long and sometimes grueling apprenticeship. Simply put, art is difficult. Making a living as any kind of artist is more difficult still.

At present, there is little reason why the world should necessarily take much Christian art seriously. Before Christians can be heard or taken seriously in the artistic world, they need to earn the *right* to be heard by developing their skills and artistic vision to the highest level. In view of the present state of things, that is going to take quite a while, whether the artistic medium be music, art, literature, or cinematography.

PRACTICALITIES

As I have said repeatedly, the properly functioning Christian family is the central source of power and social energy in any society. Because the Christian family is the great locale of power, it has often incurred the enmity of other claimants to power. One of those has been the church.

The older asceticism, because of misinterpretation of certain passages in the Bible dealing with "celibacy," saw marital life as a lower way of life and at times showed no little hostility toward the family. This attitude is still present in many evangelical churches in a disguised form. The family is, in effect, "saved" from itself by being drawn into the church night after night for church activities. Effort is directed toward encouraging attendance at weekday church prayer meetings and Bible study. Yet in days past, even when marital life was considered less "spiritual" than single ministry to the church, the family was considered important enough that church elders made annual visits to all homes in the parish to ensure that the parents were teaching the catechism to their children and were practicing regular family prayer and Bible study. The focus today has definitely shifted from such a standard.

Emphasis needs to be returned to the family. The local church should stress the importance of the family (and, therefore, the home) as *the* center of worship, education, and development of human beings— that is, the center of power. That, in turn, will have the effect of decentralizing society in general.

The church and pastor must loosen their authoritarian control over the congregation, especially families. That will mean cutting down on activities that tear parents and children away from the home. The family, instead, should be able to reach out to other hurting families.

These principles should be taught in the local church. Moreover, the church as a teaching institution should provide families with the necessary instruction and educational materials on developing strong families. One of the key efforts of a local church should be to build up families, giving them the tools to thrive spiritually within their own unit and grow relationally as well. Those strong families will, in turn, make strong churches and probably have as great an evangelistic impact as any other program.

Concern for the family goes beyond the churches. Other Christian organizations, regardless of their professed purposes, should have as a central function strengthening the family units of those who work for and with them. Many Christian organizations, because of their zeal to "win the world for Jesus," are inadvertently hurting families.

The entire "jet-setting" mentality of modern Christianity is harmful. The evangelists and Christian "celebrities" who have families and are on the road more than they are at home with their wives and children are not doing the "Lord's work" in the truest sense. The basic ministry of a father and a mother is to their children. Saving the world but losing one's children is a heavy price to pay for being a "success"—even in furthering God's kingdom. Everyone is hurt, including the local church.

What are our priorities now? Do we want to help our families grow as God intends, or do we want to attend the endless string of "Christian" seminars and conferences that too often characterizes the weekend (when parents should be with their children) in the Christian community? This is not to say that seminars and conferences are not beneficial in moderation. It is to say that there should be a rough balance, with the family holding the greater weight in the scale.

STRANGERS IN THE LAND

If parents and adults will commit themselves to restructuring the family and caring for children, then the children, who have become strangers in the land, will return. If not, society will continue to disintegrate, and the power of the state will continue to grow and threaten our rights to life and liberty. The state will become our "family," wielding the authority of father and mother over us.

As those who call themselves Christians look into the cold eyes of children who have become completely estranged and who battle their parents and others, let us remember that there was a time when action could have been taken that would have made it possible for this confrontation to have been avoided. Even now, the conflict can be lessened, but it will take commitment—commitment to each other in pursuit of a better future for all of God's children through stronger families. May the words of Malachi come true—that the hearts of fathers (and mothers) will return to their children.[13]

16

THE
BLOODY FACE
OF HISTORY

To live a truly Christian life in a secular age is a difficult and demanding task requiring all the measures I have suggested throughout this book. There is one element of Christianity without which even the most vibrant faith, the most fearless posture, the most brilliant apologetic, and the most selfless service is incomplete. That element is love.

When a lawyer asked Jesus Christ which was the greatest commandment in the law, He replied that it was to love God with all your heart, soul, and mind, and to love your neighbor as yourself.[1] Jesus Christ also said:

A new command I give you: Love one another. As I have loved you, so you must love one another. By this all men will know that you are my disciples, if you love one another.[2]

Given that this is a command, it follows that its violation is sin. Francis Schaeffer writes:

> In the midst of the world, in the midst of our present culture, Jesus is giving a right to the world. Upon His authority He gives the world the right to judge whether you and I are born-again Christians on the basis of our observable love toward all Christians.[3]

In other words, if people challenge whether or not believers are Christians because believers have not shown love toward other Christians, it must be understood that they are only exercising a prerogative which Jesus Christ gave them. Schaeffer also adds:

> We must not get angry. If people say, "You don't love other Christians," we must go home, get down on our knees, and ask God whether or not what they say is true. And if it is, then they have a right to have said what they said.[4]

In the midst of Jesus Christ's prayer in John 17:21, He prays that "they all may be one; even as thou, Father, art in me, and I in thee, that they also may be in us: that the world may believe that thou hast sent me" (KJV). Here Jesus Christ is praying for oneness among Christians; that is, that Christians love one another.

Note the reason for this unity: "That the world may believe that thou hast sent me." This means that love is the ultimate apologetic, or persuasion to the world. We simply cannot expect the world to believe that the Father sent the Son unless the world sees the reality of Jesus Christ in believers.

A DEFINITION OF LOVE

To reflect their love for God, believers must love others as they love themselves. This love is effectively described and defined in 1 Corinthians 13:4–8 (NASB):

> Love is patient, love is kind, and is not jealous; love does not brag and is not arrogant, does not act unbecomingly; it does not seek its own, is not provoked, does not take into account a wrong suffered, does not rejoice in unrighteousness, but rejoices with the truth; bears all things, believes all things, hopes all things, endures all things. Love never fails . . .

Love, then, requires an "otherness," a focus away from oneself, a total respect for others as a way of reflecting Jesus Christ. This is the kind of expression and action that draws people toward the truth. It concerns what we may call "humanness." Indeed, a primary task for this generation of believers is keeping humanness in the human race— that is, to upgrade and then maintain the individual person's high place in the universe. This is being a God-centered humanist.

As explained earlier, all people bear the image of God and have value, not simply because they may or may not happen to be believers but because they are God's creation and made in God's image. Modern men and women who have rejected this truth have no clue as to why they exist or their place in the universe. Because of this, they often feel lost and find life absurd. Modern culture further degrades and depersonalizes people; or, if it is perceived that an individual's "quality of life" is insufficient (according to society's standards), he is killed, as for example, in the case of unborn babies, or he is urged to die, as in the case of the aged.

The Christian believer, however, should know the value of people as God's creation and act on that knowledge. *All people are our neighbors.* We are to love them as ourselves, even if they are not believers, and even if the cost of such loving is great.

This means that the Christian must show love toward *all* fellow human beings. If, for example, we are going to preserve the right to life, Christians must truly love others as they love themselves. Crisis pregnancy centers and their work, as an illustration, are an important manifestation of this biblical principle.

Several years ago, I was told by an ardent pro-life activist that it would be biblical to bomb an abortion clinic, even if there was a pregnant woman inside who was seeking or having an abortion. This prolifer said that the pregnant woman could not be a Christian because of the abortion and, thus, it would be biblical to dispose of her along with the aborutary. This is yet another manifestation of the *Roe* redefinition of human life discussed earlier. It must be absolutely rejected by believers practicing true Christianity.

The same love must be exhibited to the homosexual. Homosexuality and lesbianism are growing by leaps and bounds. And, of course, the militancy of the homosexual groups, such as ACT-UP and Queer Nation, aggravate the often homophobic attitudes of many Christians. Homosexuals are, however, also made in God's image and must be treated with the same respect as God's other creatures. That means showing compassion. But it does not at the same time mean moving from the Bible's absolutes into modern permissive society. One can deal with the homosexual with compassion and not completely alienate him if he is met at a genuine human level, as a unique person, and shown the love of Christ. The same can be said, for instance, concerning liberal journalists in the media.

GIVING

In many ways, giving is the essence of love. C. S. Lewis noted:

I am afraid the only safe rule is to give more than we can spare. In other words, if our expenditure on comforts, luxuries, amusements, etc., is up to the standard common among those with the same income as our own, we are probably giving away too little. If our charities do not at all pinch or hamper us, I should say they are too small. There ought to be things we should like to do and cannot do because our charitable expenditure excludes them.[5]

In other words, giving that is not *sacrificial* is not true giving. But giving is not limited to money or material items. It includes giving time to others, opening one's home to others, and the general giving of one-self to serve others' needs.

I once had the privilege of working with a Christian theologian who was a tireless giver. In the last year of his life, this man was riddled with cancer. However, this did not cause him to forsake his work or keep him from one of his more tiring tasks—lecturing. Sometimes he would have to stop and sit down for a few minutes, but then he would rise and finish the lecture. Further, although it was very tiring and painful, he would often remain for hours after his speech to answer questions and discuss people's problems. This man, Francis Schaeffer, continued this until his death. A similar spirit must prevail in all believers if God is to be reflected in them.

COMPASSION

True compassion must start with assisting those who need help the most. For example, why aren't more believers on the front line assisting the homeless? Why aren't more believers working with AIDS victims? Why aren't more believers visiting nursing homes? Why aren't more Christians battling for the rights and lives of the unborn, infirm, and aged? Christians should know that helping with physical needs is a condition precedent to meeting spiritual needs. Indeed, the apostle Paul admonishes: "We who are strong ought to bear with the failings of the weak and not to please ourselves."[6] Jesus reminds us that what we do to the least of these we do to Him.

In one of my travels, I met a Christian man who worked as a barber in his spare time to meet living expenses. The major amount of his time was spent working without pay at a half-way house for AIDS victims, most of whom were homosexuals. The man told me that when he first sought out what he saw as a ministry opportunity, he was told that

Christians were not welcome because they were negative and lacked compassion. He asked if he could simply wash dishes. This he was allowed to do. Eventually this man worked his way into the living quarters and has since ministered and preached the Gospel to dying homosexuals (with astounding results). Many have accepted Christ on their deathbeds.

This is what true compassion is all about. It has nothing to do with weeping at tragedy, which might be more indicative of sentimentalism. Compassion is bringing justice and mercy to real-life situations.

> *Then there is the excuse that, if one stands for truth, it will offend people and the Christian will lose his or her "witness." This is a fundamental way to avoid the difficult task of taking a stand.*

However, true compassion often has an emotional accompaniment: *outrage.* Outrage is a legitimate reaction for believers who see inhumanity. Unfortunately, the lack of outrage is a striking characteristic of a modern Christianity that allows some of the most heinous crimes in history—terrorism, abortion, genocide, and oppression—to be committed before its very eyes without a response.

Perhaps that happens because of a lack of identification with the suffering of others. There is such a thing as concentrating too much on the blessings we've received at the expense of empathy with others' pain. Identification, however, as Os Guinness notes, is at the heart of the Incarnation:

> As God became man in Jesus, he was no . . . Pentagon chief, making quick flying inspections on the front line, but one who shared the foxholes, who knew the risks, who felt the enemy fire. No other God has wounds. It is because God identified so fully with us that we can know him and trust him.[7]

In view of Jesus Christ's example, Christians must not merely entertain themselves in million-dollar cathedrals while poverty and death reign a few blocks away.

PERSECUTION

If it happens that believers proceed in a manner consistent with true Christianity, they may not demand or expect to move from victory to victory. In a depraved culture that often rivals Sodom and Gomorrah, believers should expect opposition of the most hostile sort, even persecution.

John the Baptist spoke out against corruption in the court of Herod, and his actions cost him his life. Believers can expect the same, or even more, violent treatment, since modern technology provides persecutors with a variety of new and terrifying alternatives. And believers in foreign lands might find persecution even heightened by nationalistic prejudice or the hostility of non-Christian religions.

Western Christians currently have it easy. They do not compare well with the first Christians, nor with those solitary souls throughout the world who are persecuted simply because they are believers who will not be silenced. Unfortunately, I have had American Christians tell me that they would not fight for their freedom to speak the truth because they might lose their jobs.

Then there is the excuse that, if one stands for truth, it will offend people and the Christian will lose his or her "witness." This is a fundamental way to avoid the difficult task of taking a stand. One may be disliked or ridiculed for being a true witness, but one will not lose that witness for speaking the truth.

In the final analysis, persecution will follow any strong stand for God. One must be prepared. And, above all, one must count the cost.

SUFFERING

Suffering, then, is not an optional choice in the faith but rather an essential aspect of true Christianity. Jesus Christ foretold that the true believer would be hated.[8] And He specifically noted that suffering and persecution would follow: "In this world you will have trouble. But take heart! I have overcome the world."[9]

For Christians, suffering for what is right is never meaningless. Jesus Christ uses suffering as a way to mature and perfect the believer. The Bible states: "In bringing many sons to glory, it was fitting that God, for whom and through whom everything exists, should make the author of their salvation perfect through suffering."[10] How then shall followers of Jesus Christ escape the need for a similar process?

Suffering is also preparation for the Christian's eventual union with God. "We must go through many hardships," writes the apostle Paul, "to enter the kingdom of God."[11]

Moreover, the Scriptures state that those who suffer for the sake of righteousness are "blessed"[12] and may keep on rejoicing[13] because of the prospect of eventual exultation with God.

PROVISION FOR FAILURE

Practicing true Christianity and living consistently as a believer is a difficult task which at times seems impossible. The believer is told to run the race of life "in such a way as to get the prize,"[14] but failure is a definite possibility. In fact, *we all fail.* That is the human dilemma; that is a reality we cannot escape.

None of us is capable of doing everything. However, Jesus Christ does not expect the believer to do everything and has assured believers that His yoke is easy and His burden light. Jesus Christ promises to give the Christian rest.[15] In short, there is no cause for despair or pessimism. There is hope.

REASON FOR HOPE

Who would have thought that a ragtag band of Jewish radicals from an obscure Roman colony could have changed the course of history? And yet that is precisely what happened. The fact that they prevailed against all odds is an inspiration.

Because of the breakdown of Western society, the present situation is often compared to that faced by the early Christian church. However, one can make a good case that modern times, especially with the explosion of new technologies, have much in common with the sixteenth-century world of the Reformation: social ferment, religious corruption, an outburst of learning, a dissatisfied populace, and so on. Os Guinness says: "There was the period between the Renaissance and the Reformation when there was protest and re-evaluation everywhere. Renaissance humanism with all its brilliance had burst on the West, bringing with it not only the highest in art but also unrest, chaos, violence and disruption."[16]

The Reformation confronted all that, and its institutional source was one person in an obscure school. Today, Martin Luther would be considered an upstart, and the University of Wittenberg would be shrugged off as an insignificant junior facility, only fifteen years old, with a total complement of one hundred, and whose professors were mostly in their twenties.

However, equipped with great spiritual and intellectual power, along with fervent devotion to Jesus Christ, those professors greatly affected the world around them as well as the world to come. They are evidence of the biblical truth that with God all things are possible and that one need not despair.

THE BLOODY FACE OF HISTORY

Although one need not despair, the fact is that speaking for truth and taking moral stands is not and will never be easy. Persecution and suffering inevitably follow such stands.

Truth is precisely what true Christianity has to offer. Curiously, it is sometimes the non-Christian who sees the need for such stands. For example, French existentialist Albert Camus claimed to believe in nothing and to consider everything absurd. But he was an honest thinker, and perhaps because of this honesty, along with his absence of belief, Camus was able to see the needs of the age in a way matched by few of his peers. He wrote:

> The world expects of Christians that they will raise their voices so loudly and clearly and so formulate their protest that not even the simplest man can have the slightest doubt about what they are saying. Further, the world expects of Christians that they will eschew all fuzzy abstractions and plant themselves squarely in front of the bloody face of history. We stand in need of folk who have determined to speak directly and unmistakably and come what may, to stand by what they have said.[17]

Notice that there is no doubt in Camus' mind that Christianity is inherently *opposed* to the spirit of the age, what he calls the "bloody face of history." By his standard, the posture of noninvolvement is fatal. Camus expects Christians to spurn abstractions and hold clear, well-defined beliefs. They must not only raise their voices, but do so loudly, and in such a way that there is no doubt as to what is being said. That done, Camus says, they must stand by what they have said. One could hardly put it any better.

The believer who would practice true Christianity in our torn world will, even against great odds, speak the truth and work to assist his or her fellow human beings. Moreover, those believers will respond to God when He calls for the Christian to stand in the bloody face of history. Indeed, those believers will share the spirit of Isaiah the prophet and say, "Here am I. Send me!"[18]

If we shrink from this task, we may be faced with greater religious apartheid. We have seen many examples in this book already. In South Africa, in the heyday of apartheid, nonwhite races had no voice in the affairs of state whatsoever. People with religious convictions in the United States may follow suit—in terms of their religious beliefs. The difference is, in South Africa nonwhites became powerless. Yet here in America, the Judeo-Christian tradition was the foundation of our government. It will be a difficult battle in keeping alive religious liberty as an influence in all realms of culture, but surely it is worth fighting for—for both ourselves and our children.

... in South which flourished because ... power pass ... before in ... the Jews ... nation but ... was the foundation of our ... In ... 3 ... in bond ... ... the Bible religion ... ...

STUDY GUIDE

*T*he following questions will assist you, the reader, in mastering the key issues of *Religious Apartheid.* The questions will help you to better understand the book's important facts and the meaning, implications, and applications of the material.

These questions may be used for personal study as well as group discussion, such as a small group setting or Sunday school class. They are presented thematically, rather than chronologically. Thus the table of contents may be helpful for locating specific references.

The first section addresses the concerns and principles of both Judeo-Christian and secular worldviews. Section two examines specific social crisis points of modern America. The third section examines the role of the church in today's society and the need for a true Christianity. Section four evaluates the need for true activism as Christians operate within the culture.

PART 1: CONCERNS AND PRINCIPLES

1. Censorship was once a tool used against obscenity and treason. What are the new targets of censorship, and how is censorship being applied?

2. How is the increasing power of secularism corrupting the values of pluralism and tolerance?

3. How is the decline of Judeo-Christian values manifested in modern society?

4. How has modern medicine changed our view of the sanctity of human life?

5. Abortion kills unborn babies based on a "right to choose." Who are the potential victims of this "right to choose" philosophy?

6. What new methods may the modern authoritarian state use to manipulate people?

7. How does Christianity provide a solution to protect people from tyranny?

8. What is the basis for the concept of the exalted individual?

9. What central ideas of Nietzsche, Marx, Freud, and Darwin have contributed to a devalued view of human worth?

10. How does a system of absolutes differ from the current system of relativism regarding its view of the role of God in society?

11. What are the political results when the "immeasurable dignity" of a person disappears?

12. What happens to personal freedom when the state is idolized?

PART 2: CRISIS POINTS

1. Identify the worthwhile goals of political correctness as well as its present dangers. How is the implementation of political correctness through policy and law problematic?

2. How does censorship affect the classroom, our cherished free marketplace of ideas?

3. What group of people is most endangered when free speech is restricted?

4. Who is responsible for a child's well-being, according to the child savers?

5. How would the "rights of the child" change the structure of the family?

6. What other groups of people are placed at risk with the emergence of a *Roe* culture?

7. How does the media censor discussions of abortion?

8. In what areas of life are homosexuals demanding "rights"?

9. Why is eligibility for military service critical to the homosexual agenda?

10. How are the major corporations fostering acceptance of homosexual behavior through re-education and preferential treatment?

11. New laws grant unique protection from discrimination for homosexuals. What are some of the possible effects of these laws on religious employers?

12. Why can conservative Christians be called the newly oppressed minority?

PART 3: A TRUE CHRISTIANITY

1. According to George Gallup, the relationship between belief and behavior is changing among evangelicals. How is it changing?

2. How do legalism and holiness differ from each other?

3. What negative patterns have contemporary evangelicals borrowed
from the Pharisees?

4. Both evangelism without social concern and utopianism are defended by some as biblical norms. How do they differ in their effects
on the mission of the church in the world?

5. What are some weaknesses of television in presenting the Gospel?

6. What are the dilemmas Christians face when they serve in politics?

7. What are the signs that Christians lack intellectual and cultural literacy? How does this weaken their ability to present the Gospel effectively?

8. What commands of God help to keep us from being too "other-worldly" or too internalized?

9. If being salt and light makes one "radical," is that good or bad? Why?

10. What is the true nature of freedom? How should we use our freedom?

11. What is the mandatory, biblical pattern for the church?

12. How did Jesus show tolerance and broad-mindedness?

PART 4: ACTIVISM

1. How has false pietism caused a split between inward (personal) renewal and external (cultural) renewal?

2. What key virtue is critical for Christian politicians? Why?

3. Is abortion primarily a political problem or a symptom of a deeper spiritual problem of our society? Why?

4. What are some of the dangers of civil disobedience campaigns?

5. Why should radical Christians act hesitantly?

6. What does the apostle Paul say about government authorities? How should his statement impact our behavior as Christians?

7. What limitations does civil government face?

8. How does America's hope in politics and politicians parallel pre-Nazi Germany?

9. What steps can we take to become more "savvy" in promoting the pro-life agenda?

10. What are some responsibilities parents should reclaim in their children's education?

11. Why should parents share experiences in the arts with their children?

12. Why are persecution and suffering almost inevitable if Christians take a loving, uncompromising stand against unrighteousness?

NOTES

PREFACE

1. See James Davison Hunter, *Culture Wars: The Struggle to Define America* (New York: Basic, 1992).
2. Brian Lapping, *Apartheid: A History* (London: Paladin, 1987), 13.
3. 330 U.S. 1 (1947).
4. Id. at 15–16.
5. Id. at 18.
6. See *DeSpain v. DeKalb County Community School District,* 384 F.2d 836, 837 (7th Cir. 1967).
7. *ACLU N.J., et al. v. Black Horse Pike Board of Education, et al.,* No. 93-5368 (Third Circuit, June 25, 1993).
8. Lapping, 14.
9. Although I disagree with some of the author's conclusions, Stephen L. Carter has discussed the results of such domination in *The Culture of Disbelief* (New York: Basic, 1993).

CHAPTER 1: De-Christianizing the American Psyche

1. Richard Brookhiser, "The Cultural Right Is Here to Stay," *Time,* 31 May 1993, 74.
2. William Barclay, *The Ten Commandments for Today* (Grand Rapids: Eerdmans, 1973), 9.
3. Chuck Colson, "Can We Be Good Without God?" *Imprimis,* April 1993, 2.
4. Ibid.
5. Ed Briggs, "Only 1 in 10 Held Deeply Committed," *Richmond Times- Dispatch,* 27 November 1982, B-3.
6. Kenneth L. Woodward and David Gates, "How the Bible Made America," *Newsweek,* 12 December 1982, 45.
7. Colson, 2.
8. In Colson, 3.
9. Ibid., 3 (italics added).

10. Harvey Cox, *The Secular City: Secularization and Urbanization in Theological Perspective* (New York: Macmillan, 1965), 21.

11. Ibid., 18.

12. See, for example, Whitehead, "Avoiding Religious Apartheid: Affording Equal Treatment for Student-Initiated Religious Expression in Public Schools," 16 *Pepperdine Law Review* 229 (1989).

13. *The Williamsburg Charter Survey on Religion and Public Life* (Washington, D.C.: Williamsburg Charter Foundation, 1988), 21.

14. Ibid., 7.

15. Ibid., 8.

16. Ibid., 29.

17. Colson, 2.

18. Michael Harrington, *The Politics at God's Funeral: The Spiritual Crisis of Western Civilization* (New York: Holt, Rinehart & Winston, 1983), 11, 10.

CHAPTER 2: The Fire Storm

1. Chuck Colson, "Can We Be Good Without God?" *Imprimis,* April 1993.

2. Alvin Toffler, *The Third Wave* (New York: Morrow, 1980).

3. See Philip Elmer-Dewitt, "Cloning: Where Do We Draw the Line?" *Time,* 8 November 1993, 65.

4. Ibid.

5. It is interesting to note that the response of scientists at the American Fertility Society in Montreal reassured Jerry Hale, the director of the in-vitro lab at George Washington University who successfully cloned seventeen microscopic human embryos, that his experiment was merely "a modest scientific advance." See Elmer-Dewitt.

6. See B. F. Skinner, *Beyond Freedom and Dignity* (New York: Knopf, 1971).

7. Betty Friedan, *It Changed My Life* (New York: Random, 1976), 122.

8. 410 U.S. 113 (1973).

9. Friedan, 124.

10. 410 U.S. at 162.

11. Id. at 153.

12. 112 S. Ct. 2791 (1992).

13. Russell Hittinger, "What Really Happened in the *Casey* Decision?" *Crises,* September 1992, 20–21.

14. Ibid., 22.

15. See Barbara J. Logue, *Last Rights* (New York: Maxwell Macmillan International, 1993) (after assessing the alternatives, "compassionate death control" should be as available as birth control).

16. *Zorach v. Clauson,* 343 U.S. 306, 313 (1952).

17. 112 S.Ct. 2649 (1992).

18. Id. at 2656.

19. Id. at 2685 (Scalia, J., dissenting).

20. 494 U.S. 872 (1990).

21. This problem is somewhat altered by the enactment of the Religious Freedom Restoration Act. But this act may pose new and more difficult questions. See John W. Whitehead and James J. Knicely, "Religious Freedom Restoration Act: Wolf in Sheep's Clothing," *Plymouth Rock Foundation Leadership Memo* (1991). For copies of this paper, contact The Rutherford Institute, P. O. Box 7482, Charlottesville, VA 22906-7482 (804) 978-3888.

22. *Roberts v. Madigan,* 921 F.2d 1047 (10th Cir. 1990), *cert. denied,* 60 U.S.L.W. 3878 (U.S. June 29, 1992).

23. For a detailed discussion of rights in the public schools see John W. Whitehead, *The Rights of Religious Persons in Public Education,* 2d ed. (Wheaton, Ill.: Crossway, 1991, 1993).

24. Bertram Gross, *Friendly Fascism: The New Face of Power in America* (New York: M. Evans, 1980), 3.

25. Roland Huntford, *The New Totalitarians* (New York: Stein & Day, 1972), 11.

26. William Irwin Thompson, "'What's Past Is Prologue,' The Past—What's That?" *New York Times,* 10 June 1976, 37.

27. Ibid.

28. Aldous Huxley, *Brave New World* (1939; New York: Bantam, 1968), xii.

29. Albert Einstein, "Why Do They Hate the Jews?" reprinted in *Ideas and Opinions* (New York: Crown, 1954), 191.

30. C. S. Lewis, "The Humanitarian Theory of Punishment," *God in the Dock* (Grand Rapids: Eerdmans, 1971), 292–93.

31. Robert Bolt, *A Man for All Seasons* (New York: Vintage, 1960), 38.

32. Paul Johnson, *A History of Christianity* (London: Weidenfeld, 1976), 516.

33. Ibid., 515–16.

34. Ibid., 517 (italics in original).

35. James Dobson, "Are You There?" *Citizen* 6, no. 9 (21 September 1992), V-1.

CHAPTER 3: Judeo-Christian Principles

1. Chuck Colson, "Can We Be Good Without God?" *Imprimis,* April 1993, 2.

2. See, for example, John W. Whitehead, *An American Dream* (Westchester, Ill.: Crossway, 1987).

3. See John 3:16.

4. Glenn Tinder, "Can We Be Good Without God?" *Atlantic Monthly,* December 1989, 70.

5. Colossians 1:15 (NASB).

6. 2 Corinthians 5:17 (NIV).

7. However, it is interesting to note how quickly this concept can yet evoke emotion. For example, when the human-embryo cloning was announced, a Time/CNN poll revealed that "58% said they thought cloning was morally wrong, while 63% said they believed it was against God's will. . . . For many, the basic sanctity of human life seems to be under attack, and it made them angry" (Elmer-Dewitt, 69).

8. Tinder, 72.

9. Ibid.

10. Galatians 3:28 (NIV).

11. Lucien Goldman, *Le Dieu Cache* (Paris: Gallimard, 1955), 45.

12. As the scientist who first cloned human cells put it, "It's up to the ethicists and the medical community, with input from the general public, to decide what kind of guidelines will lead us in the future" (Elmer-Dewitt, 70).

13. Tinder, 79.

14. James Hitchcock, *What Is Secular Humanism?* (Ann Arbor, Mich.: Servant, 1982), 8–9.

15. Adolf Hitler, *Mein Kampf* (1925; New York: Houghton Mifflin, 1971), 214–15.

16. Albert Camus, *The Rebel,* trans. Anthony Bower (New York: Knopf, 1969), 10.

17. Tinder, 76–77.

18. Ibid., 77.

19. Ibid.

20. Ibid., 77–78.

21. Ibid., 79–80.

22. Ibid., 80.

23. As quoted by Francis A. Schaeffer, *Back to Freedom and Dignity* (Downers Grove, Ill.: InterVarsity, 1972), 20.

24. Tinder, 80.

25. Ibid.

26. Francis A. Schaeffer, *Genesis in Time and Space* (Downers Grove, Ill.: InterVarsity, 1972), 21 (italics added).

CHAPTER 4: The New Concentration Camps

1. Jerry Adler, "Taking Offense," *Newsweek,* 24 December 1990, 48.

2. See *Doe v. University of Michigan,* 721 F. Supp. 852, 865 (E.D. Mich. 1989). The graduate student was not a party to the case.

3. Hyde and Fishman, "The Collegiate Speech Protection Act of 1991: A Response to the New Intolerance in the Academy," 37 *Wayne Law Review* 1469, 1483 (1991).

4. Anderson, "Political Correctness on College Campus: Freedom of Speech v. Doing the Politically Correct Thing," 46 *S.M.U. Law Review* 171, 172 (1992).

5. Ibid., 173.

6. Adler, 48.

7. Ray Bradbury, *Fahrenheit 451* (New York: Ballantine, 1979), 182.

8. See *UVM Post v. Board of Regents of the University of Wisconsin System,* 774 F. Supp. 1163 (E.D. Wisc. 1991); *Doe v. University of Michigan,* 721 F. Supp. 852; Adler, 48.

9. Christine Haynes, "Taking America Back," *Chronicles,* January 1993, 43–44.

10. Strossen, "Thoughts on the Controversy over Politically Correct Speech" (hereinafter, "Politically Correct Speech"), 46 *S.M.U. Law Review* 119, 129–31 (1992).

11. Ibid., 128, quoting Wills, "Peeling Off Political Labels," *Sacramento Bee,* 28 December 1990, B11.

12. An example of how language could play a definitive role in group equality was found by "PCers" in the women's suffrage movement. After the 1868 ratification of the Fourteenth Amendment (The Fourteenth Amendment to the United States Constitution states: "all persons born or naturalized in the United States . . . are citizens of the United States" and "no state shall . . . abridge the privileges and immunities of citizens of the United States." U.S. Const. amend. XIV, sec. 1.), some leaders in the women's suffrage movement argued women were persons within the Amendment and should therefore be guaranteed the right to vote.

    During the 1872 presidential election, Susan B. Anthony and a group of other women sought to cast their ballots at the polls in Rochester, New York. However, upon arrival Anthony was arrested, indicted, prosecuted, convicted, and fined. In rejecting Anthony's claim of being protected by the Fourteenth Amendment, government officials stated "the use of the masculine pronouns, he, his and him in all the constitutions and laws, is proof that only men were meant to be included in their provisions." See Strossen, "Politically Correct Speech," 128–29, quoting Susan B. Anthony, "Women's Right to Vote," reprinted in *The American Reader: Words That Moved a Nation*, ed. Diane Ravitch (San Francisco: HarperCollins, 1991), 160–62.

13. Not all agree with this view. For example, an essay in *Time* notes:

    > Talk of mosaics and quilts is both an attempt to describe the way America is headed and an effort to hurry it along. The description is inaccurate, and in a world of ungorgeous mosaics and fraying quilts, the goal is undesirable. The U.S. has had historic success with heavy bursts of immigration, interspersed with decades of digestion, but only because people are asked to check their identity at the door. If the mild-mannered Czechs and Slovaks couldn't hold a multiethnic country together, and if the even milder-mannered Canadians are having trouble, we Americans should have second thoughts about becoming a true mosaic. Fortunately, we're not one yet, except at the level of boiler plate. Let's hope we never take our speeches seriously.

    Richard Brookhiser, "The Melting Pot Is Still Simmering," *Time,* 1 March 1993, 72.

14. For a listing of institutions, both public and private, that adopted hate speech codes or positions advocating the tenets of the PC movement, see Hyde and Fishman, 1470–71, nn. 5, 6.

15. For some examples of racial incidents on college campuses, see Lawrence, "If He Hollers Let Him Go: Regulating Racist Speech on Campus," 1990 *Duke Law Journal* 431, 431–34 (1990); Matsuda, "Public Response to Racist Speech: Considering the Victim's Story," 87 *Michigan Law Review* 2320, 2333 n. 71 (1989).

16. The quoted language was taken from the University of Michigan's "Policy on Discrimination and Discriminatory Harassment," which is cited in *Doe v. University of Michigan,* 721 F.Supp. at 856.

17. Sedler, "The Unconstitutionality of Campus Bans on 'Racist Speech': The View from Without and Within," 53 *Univ. of Pittsburgh Law Review* 631 (1992); see, for example, Lawrence, 446–48, 462–66.

18. See Matsuda, 2322.

19. See Anderson, 180–81; Sedler, 650–51; Strossen, "Regulating Racist Speech on Campus: A Modest Proposal" (hereinafter, "A Modest Proposal"), *Duke Law Journal* 484, 502–3 (1990). The Supreme Court has alluded that freedom of expression should have heightened protection within the academic environment: *Sweezy v. New Hampshire,* 354 U.S. 234 (1957); *Keyishian v. Board of Regents,* 385 U.S. 589 (1967).

    To impose any straight jacket upon the intellectual leaders in our colleges and universities would imperil the future of our Nation. . . . Teachers and students must always remain free to inquire, to study and to evaluate, to gain new maturity and understanding; otherwise our civilization will stagnate and die.

    Sweezy, 354 U.S. at 250.

20. *Keyishian v. Board of Regents,* 385 U.S. 589, 603 (1967).

21. Id. (quoting *United States v. Associated Press,* 52 F.Supp. 362, 372 [1993]).

22. For example, in *Tinker v. Des Moines Indep. Community School District,* 393 U.S. 503 (1969), the Court upheld the students' right to wear black armbands in class to show their objection to the Vietnam War. In *Healy v. James,* 408 U.S. 169 (1972), the Court ruled unconstitutional the refusal by the university to grant official recognition to a student group (Students for a Democratic Society) on the grounds that the college disagreed with the group's philosophy.
    However, the Supreme Court has permitted some restrictions on free speech if it pertains to designating the time, place, or manner of the speech. Further, restraints may be permissible if there is a material disruption to the educational process. See Anderson, 183.

23. Anderson, 184–86; Sedler, 650.

24. *Texas v. Johnson,* 491 U.S. 397 (1989).

25. Id. at 414.

26. *Cohen v. California,* 403 U.S. 15, 25 (1971).

27. *Collin v. Smith,* 578 F. 2d 1197 (7th Cir. 1978), *cert. denied,* 439 U.S. 916 (1978).

28. See Anderson, 187; Sedler, 648–49. This concept of viewpoint neutrality was the basis for the Supreme Court's invalidation of federal and state laws banning flag desecration (*United States v. Eichman,* 110 S.Ct. 2404 [1990]; *Texas v. Johnson,* 491 U.S. 397 [1989]).

29. *American Booksellers Assn. v. Hudnut,* 771 F.2d. 323, 324 (7th Cir. 1985), *aff'd mem.,* 475 U.S. 1001 (1986).

30. See Anderson, 177.

31. Cf. Strossen, "A Modest Proposal," 535; Hyde and Fishman, 1486; Sedler, 651 n. 81.

32. Hyde and Fishman, 1484. See also Scott Gottlieb, "A Mockery of Justice on Campus" (hereinafter, "Mockery") *The Wall Street Journal,* 27 September 1993, A22.

33. Gottlieb, "Mockery."

34. Ibid., 1484.

35. Ibid.

36. Ruchlak, "Civil Rights, Confederate Flags, and Political Correctness: Free Speech and Race Relations on Campus," 66 *Tulane Law Review* 1411, 1428 (1992). See also William A. Henry, III, "Upside Down in the Groves of Academe," *Time*, 1 April 1991, 66.

37. See "Speech and Reason at GMU," *Washington Post*, 13 September 1993, A–20.

38. Ruchlak, 1425, n. 60, quoting Presser, "The Politically Correct Law School: Where It's Right to Be Left," *American Bar Association Journal*, September 1991, 52–53.

39. See Hyde and Fishman, 1484.

40. Ibid., 1484–85.

41. Nat Hentoff, "Gregorian's Chant," *Washington Post*, 13 April 1991, A19.

42. Strossen, "Politically Correct Speech."

43. Hyde and Fishman, 1472–73.

44. Ibid., 1472–73.

45. See Strossen, "A Modest Proposal," 559.

46. Ibid., 554 n. 358.

47. Ibid., 559.

48. See Kurt Andersen, "Big Mouths," *Time*, 1 November 1993, 60.

49. Ibid., 561.

50. Hyde and Fishman, 1489.

51. See "From Equal Opportunity to Affirmative Action—A Leap of Policy," 70 *Texas Law Review* 1525, 1533 (1992).

52. Hyde and Fishman, 1489.

53. For a discussion on the British experience with such problems, see Strossen, "A Modest Proposal," 555–60.

54. Hyde and Fishman, 1489.

55. Strossen, "A Modest Proposal," 560.

56. Strossen, "Politically Correct Speech," 132.

57. Hyde and Fishman, 1490.

58. Suzanna Sherry, "Speaking of Virtue: A Republican Approach to University Regulation of Hate Speech," 75 *Minnesota Law Review* 933, 940 (1991) (italics added).

59. Ibid., 941–42.

60. Ibid., 937. This type of "virtue prodding" is not limited to the university setting. While it is a prime example, subliminal "mind controlling" is occurring elsewhere. Newspaper articles refer to minority groups in certain terms. Articles to the editor often contain scathing words for those who do not comply with "PC"-chosen terminology. Television shows are careful to be politically correct when addressing controversial issues. Even on network comedy shows, characters are quick to say "not that there's anything wrong with that" when referring to homosexuality and other items of discussion.

61. Ibid. (citing Matsuda, 2361–70).

62. Strossen, "Politically Correct Speech," 129.

63. Paul Richard, "Scrawling in the Margins," *Washington Post*, 5 March 1993, C1, C8.

64. Strossen, "Politically Correct Speech," 130–31.

65. See Alessandra Stanley, "Militants Back 'Queer,' Shoving 'Gay' the Way of 'Negro,'" *New York Times*, 6 April 1991, sec. 1, p. 23.

66. Mary Jordan, "College Repeals Speech Code," *Washington Post*, 12 September 1993, A1, A7.

67. "Polynesian P.C.," *Chronicles*, October 1993, 50.

68. Ruchlak, 1425 (citing Arthur R. Miller, *Miller's Court* (Boston: Houghton Mifflin, 1982), 87.

69. As quoted by John Leo, "Not the Way to Stop Abortions," *U.S. News & World Report*, 29 March 1993, 17.

70. Ibid.

71. See "While We're at It," *First Things,* August/September 1993, 73.

72. Richard A. Baer, Jr., "The High Court's 'S' Word," *Christianity Today,* 8 September 1989, 20 (italics in original).

73. Ibid.

74. Ibid. (italics in original).

75. Judith Bat-Ada (Reisman), "Freedom of Speech as Mythology, or 'Quill Pen and Parchment Thinking' in an Electronic Environment," 8 *New York University Review of Law and Social Change* 271, 272 (1978–79).

76. Strossen, "A Modest Proposal," 567.

77. Aryeh Neier, *Defending My Enemy* (New York: Dutton, 1979), 4–5.

CHAPTER 5: Uncle Sam's Children

1. Allan Carlson, "Uncle Sam's Child," *Chronicles* (January 1993), 12–13.

2. *DeBurgh v. DeBurgh,* 39 Cal. 2d 858, 863–64, 250 P.2d 598, 601 (1952). The United States Supreme Court has relied on several principles to identify family rights as "fundamental" and therefore according them constitutional protection. In *Palko v. Connecticut,* 302 U.S. 319 (1937), it was said that the fundamental liberties to be protected, though not found in the text of the Constitution, included those "implicit in the concept of ordered liberty," so that "neither liberty nor justice would exist if [they] were sacrificed." See also Robert H. Bork, *The Tempting of America: The Political Seduction of the Law* (New York: Free, 1990), 113, 118–19, citing Palko, 302 U.S. at 325, 326.

   Forty years later, in *Moore v. East Cleveland,* 431 U.S. 494 (1977), the formulation of protected freedoms was those that are "deeply rooted in this Nation's history and tradition" (id., citing Moore, 431 U.S. at 503). As was earlier noted, the common law structure also relied on history and tradition to protect parental rights. A basic reason for classifying parental rights as fundamental is based on the presumption that parents have innate affection for their children and are the adults most able to determine the child's best interests and the means of protecting those interests (*Parham v. J.R.,* 442 U.S. 584, 601–4 [1979], and cases cited therein). Although the holding in *Parham* recognizes strong parental rights, the case does not explicitly characterize parents' rights as fundamental.

3. Barbara DaFoe Whitehead, "Dan Quayle Was Right," *Atlantic Monthly,* 271, no. 4 (April 1993), 84 (italics added).

4. See generally R. Collin Mangrum, "Religious Constraints During Visitation: Under What Circumstances Are They Constitutional?" 24 *Creighton Law Review* 445 (1991).

5. Ibid., 474. See also J. Rawls, *A Theory of Justice* (Cambridge: Harvard Univ. Press, 1971).

6. Thomas Fleming, "Puppets and Their Masters," *Chronicles* (October 1993), 11.

7. Carlson, 13.

8. Ibid.

9. Ibid.

10. Ibid.

11. Ibid.

12. Ibid.

13. Ibid., 13–14.

14. Barbara DaFoe Whitehead, 47.

15. Carlson, 14.

16. Ibid.

17. George Orwell, *Nineteen Eighty-Four* (New York: Harcourt, Brace, World, 1949), 136–37.

18. *Newkirk v. East Lansing Schools,* No. 1:91: CV: 563 (U.S. Dist. Ct., W.D. Mich.).

19. Id. at 13.

20. Urie Bronfenbrenner, *Two Worlds of Childhood: U.S. and U.S.S.R.* (New York: Russell Sage Foundation, 1970), 95.

21. Urie Bronfenbrenner, "Socialization and Social Class Through Time and Space," in Eleanor E. Maccoby, Theodore M. Newcomb, and Eugene L. Hartley, eds., *Reading in Social Psychology* (New York: Holt, Rinehart & Winston, 1958), 400–425.

22. Ibid., 424.

23. Bronfenbrenner, *Two Worlds of Childhood,* 98 (italics added).

24. Ibid., 98.

25. Alvin Toffler, *The Third Wave* (New York: William Morrow, 1980), 45.

26. Ibid.

27. Ibid., 81.

28. Havy C. Bredemeier and Richard M. Stephenson, *The Analysis of Social Systems* (New York: Holt, Rinehart & Winston, 1962), 119.

29. James Coleman, *The Adolescent Society* (New York: Free Press of Glencoe, 1961), 3 (italics in original).

30. "Outcome-Based Education: A Brief Overview," Charlottesville, Va.: The Rutherford Institute, July 1993.

31. Elizabeth Hurlock, *Child Development* (New York: McGraw-Hill, 1942), 359.

32. Bronfenbrenner, *Two Worlds of Childhood,* 101.

33. Id.

34. Id.

35. Ibid., 102 (italics added, in part).

36. Ibid., 96.

37. See, for example, Leslie Milk and Harry Jaffe, "Saturday Night," *The Washingtonian* (September 1993), 78.

38. Ibid., 97.

39. Ibid., 99.

40. A nineteenth-century English court explained the justifications for judicial interference in parental authority:

    A father has a legal right to control and direct the education and bringing up of his children until they attain the age of twenty-one years . . . and the Court will not interfere with him in the exercise of his paternal authority, except (1) where by his gross moral turpitude he forfeits his rights, or (2) where he has by his conduct abdicated his parental authority.

    In re Agar-Ellis, 24 Ch. D. 317 (Ca.) (1883). Even the modern United States Supreme Court has required clear and convincing evidence in cases involving the termination of parental rights. In the 1982 decision of *Santosky v. Kramer,* 455 U.S. 743, 745, 768–69 (1982), the critical issue of burden of proof in parental rights termination hearings was argued. The statute in New York required a "fair preponderance of the evidence," and a 5-4 majority held this standard to be unconstitutionally low. The Court imposed a "clear and convincing evidence" standard as a Fourteenth Amendment norm. Id.

41. Karen Dorros, Ph.D., and Patricia Dorsey, "Whose Rights Are We Protecting Anyway?" *Children Today,* May-June 1989, 8.

42. Robert Horowitz, J.D., Associate Director, National Legal Resource Center for Child Advocacy and Protection, American Bar Association, "Tighten Standards for Termination of Parental Rights," *Children Today,* May-June 1989, 9.

43. Richard A. Gardner, "Modern Witch Hunt—Child Abuse Charges," *Wall Street Journal,* 22 February 1993, A, 10:3.

44. Ibid.

45. Ibid. Dr. Gardner cites several examples of cases of false accusations that he personally evaluated. One such case was as follows: On March 5, Raymond and Shirley Souza (both 61) of Lowell, Massachusetts, will be sent to prison, possibly for the rest of their lives.

They are accused of having performed a series of perverted sexual acts on three of their grandchildren. The accusations began when one of the Souzas' daughters had a dream in which she envisioned her parents and her brother sexually abusing her when she was a child. In the dream her mother had a penis. She concluded that the dream indicated that she had actually been abused as a child by her parents and that the Souza grandchildren had probably been abused as well. She suggested that her siblings question the grandchildren. Thus began the wave of hysteria that ultimately resulted in the Souzas being found guilty of these alleged crimes. The full story of the Souza case was reported by Dorothy Rabinowitz, who wrote about this in the Leisure & Arts page of the *Wall Street Journal,* 22 February 1993.

Dr. Gardner went on to say that on the basis of his investigations, there wasn't one scintilla of evidence that they had committed these crimes. Rather, he concluded that the conviction was the result of coercive interviews, overzealous prosecutors, and the system in general.

This is not to say that there is no evidence of genuine child abuse. According to the *Statistical Handbook on the American Family* (edited by Bruce A. Chadwick and Tim B. Heaton [Phoenix: Onyx, 1992], in 1989 2.4 million reports of suspected child maltreatment were filed in the United States, and more than 900,000 cases were officially substantiated. In 1989, at least 1,200 and perhaps as many as 5,000 children died, and more than 160,000 were seriously injured at the hands of their parents (ibid.). Coupled with the statistics are real-life horror stories, such as the Stephen Hill case. Beginning at age nine, he was repeatedly chained to a kitchen cabinet and starved until the age of thirteen, when he finally died of starvation ("Doctor Recalls Starved Boy," *Dallas Morning News,* 8 August 1992). His parents contended that they only wanted to punish Stephen for his bad behavior, not kill him (ibid.). The matter of genuine child abuse undeniably exists. Consequently, significant measures of protection should be available to children who are victims of this type of abuse.

The problem is that there is a frightening increase of cases where the parents are erroneously accused of abusing their children. As a consequence, children are taken away from their parents and the entire family is emotionally ravaged by state legal mechanisms. Child abuse prevention legislation has contributed to this problem.

46. John E. B. Myers, "A Survey of Child Abuse and Neglect Reporting Statutes," 10 *The Journal of Juvenile Law* 1, at 4 (1986). As of August 1993, the states of Minnesota (MINN STAT. ANN § 626.556 10.(b) [West Supp. 1986]), Rhode Island (R.I. GEN LAWS §40-11-7 [Supp. 1984]), and Virginia (VA. CODE ANN. § 63.1-248.10 [1980]) authorize investigators to interview children without parental knowledge, and Arkansas (ARK. STAT. ANN § 42.816 [Supp. 1985]), Colorado (COLO. REV. STAT. § 19-10-104(4)(b)[1978]), Montana (MONT. CODE ANN §41-3-207 [1985]), and New York (N.Y. SOC. SERV. LAW § 420 2. [McKinney 1983]) expressly provide for civil liability for failure to report. Texas (TEX FAM. CODE ANN. §34.07(b) [Supp. 1985]), Utah (UTAH CODE ANN. § 78-3b-10 [Supp. 1985]), and Wisconsin (WIS. STAT. ANN § 48.981(6) [West Supp. 1985]) currently impose criminal liability for failure to report child abuse.

47. *Roman v. Appleby,* 558 F. Supp. 449, 459 (E.D. Pa. 1983).

48. See Myers, 4.

49. Ibid., 6.

50. Ophelia D. Johnson, "Parents Feel Besieged by Suspicions," *Richmond Times-Dispatch,* 3 May 1992, A-11.

51. Ibid.

52. Ibid.

53. Elizabeth F. Loftus and Laura A. Rosenwald, "Buried Memories, Shattered Lives," *American Bar Association Journal,* November 1993, 70.

54. Ibid., 71.

55. Carlson, 18 (italics added).

56. See, for example, Ellen Hopkins, "Abusing the Rights of Parents," *Newsweek,* 18 October 1993, 26.

57. Andrea Sachs, "Home Smoke-free Home," *Time,* 25 October 1993, 56.

58. The Council of State Governments, *The Book of States, 1990–91*, 417, Table *.3 (1990); see also *Thompson v. Oklahoma*, 487 U.S. 815 (1988) (Appendix D lists parental consent statutes).

59. *Moe v. Dinkins*, 533 F. Supp. 623 (S.D. N.Y. 1981), *aff'd*, 669 F.2d 67 (2d Cir.), *cert. denied*, 459 U.S. 827 (1982). The courts have reasoned that although some parents make decisions that are not in their child's best interest, "the law presumes that parents 'possess what the child lacks in maturity' and that 'the natural bonds of affection lead parents to act in the best interest of their children' (533 F. Supp. at 629, citing *Parham v. J.R.*, 442 U.S. 584, 610 [1979])." One federal court held that the minor's right to marry was not a "fundamental right," and it could be denied if the restriction on the minor's right to marry had a "rational relation" to the state's interest in protecting "minors from immature decision making and preventing unstable marriages" (533 F. Supp at 629). Thus, parents can veto their child's marriage for virtually any reasons—if they dislike the prospective spouse or to enable them to continue collecting the child's welfare benefits (533 F. Supp. 623.)

60. See generally James Shortall, *"Hodgson v. Minnesota:* Balancing the Competing Interests of the State, Parents and Minor—A Missed Opportunity?" 69 *Denver Univ. Law Review* 539 (1992).

61. 110 S.Ct. 2926 (1990).

62. MINN. STAT. ANN. § 144.343 (West 1989).

63. *Hodgson*, 110 S.Ct. at 2931 n.3, applying MINN. STAT. ANN. §§ 144.341–42 (West 1989). The Supreme Court agreed with Minnesota case law that the definition of an emancipated woman was one who is living apart from her parents or who is either married or has borne a child. See *Streitz v. Streitz*, 363 N.W.2d 135, 137 (Minn. Ct. App. 1985).

64. MINN. STAT. ANN. § 144.343(3) (West 1989) provides in part: "'[P]arent' means both parents of the pregnant woman if they are both living, one parent of the pregnant woman if only one is living or if the second one cannot be located through reasonably diligent effort, or the guardian or conservator if the pregnant woman has one."

65. MINN. STAT. ANN. § 144.343(2) (West 1989) provides in part: "[N]o abortion operation shall be performed upon an unemancipated minor or upon a woman from whom a guardian or conservator has been appointed . . . until at least 48 hours after written notice of the pending operation has been delivered [to the parent]."

66. For more information on the constitutionality of the delay requirement see Debra Harvey, Note, *"Zbaraz v. Hartigan:* Mandatory Twenty-Four Hour Waiting Period After Parental Notification Unconstitutionally Burdens a Minor's Abortion Decision," 19 *John Marshall Law Review* 1071 (1986).

67. MINN. STAT. ANN. § 144.343 (c)(i) (West 1989).

68. *Hodgson*, 110 S.Ct. at 2947.

69. Id. at 2961. More recently, the Supreme Court let stand a Mississippi law requiring minors under 18 to obtain both parents' permission before having an abortion, except in certain circumstances and where a judicial by-pass procedure is available (*Barnes v. Mississippi*, ——— U.S. ——— (October 1993).

70. Douglas Kirby, "The Effect of School-Based Health Clinics in St. Paul on School-Wide Birthrates," *Family Planning Perspectives* 25, no. 1 (January/February 1993), 12.

71. The Committee on Child Psychiatry, Group for the Advancement of Psychiatry, *How Old Is Old Enough?: The Ages of Rights and Responsibilities* (New York: Brunner/Mazel, 1989), 51.

72. Ibid., 51.

73. *Wisconsin v. Yoder*, 406 U.S. 205 (1972). See also *LeDoux v. LeDoux*, 452 N.W. 2d 1 (Neb. 1990) (where there is a conflict between the religious practices of divorced parents, the religious practices of the custodial parent prevail).

74. *Martin v. Martin*, 123 N.E.2d 812 (N.Y. 1954) (age 12); *In re Vardinakis*, 289 N.Y.S. 355 (Dom. Rel. Ct., N.Y. Co. 1936) (ages 13 and 15). See also Justice Douglas's dissent in *Wisconsin v. Yoder*, 406 U.S. 205, 241–49 (1972).

75. Pat Wingert and Eloise Salholz, "Irreconcilable Differences," *Newsweek* (21 September 1992), 88.

76. Bill Hewitt and Meg Grant, "The Home of His Choice," *People,* 12 October 1992, 57–58.

77. Mark Hanson, "Boy Wants 'Divorce' From Parents," *American Bar Association Journal* 78 24(1), July 1992.

78. Ibid.

79. Bob Cohn, "From Chattel to Full Citizens," *Newsweek,* 21 September 1993, 89.

80. Ibid. Lewis Pitts, the attorney who argued the case on behalf of the National Child Rights Alliance claims that the ruling will not encourage children to sue to terminate the rights of their parents. Rather, it will let the child accomplish what state officials charged with protecting children fail or refuse to do—terminate the parental rights in a timely manner.

81. Wingert and Salholz, 88–89.

82. Cohn, 88.

83. Ibid.

84. *Mays v. Twigg,* 543 So.2d. 241 (1993).

85. See, for example, Carlson.

86. Barbara DaFoe Whitehead, 47–48.

87. Convention on the Rights of the Child, G.A. Res. 44/25, U.N. GAOR Annex, U.N. Doc. A/44/736 (1989), reprinted in *International Legal Materials* 28 (1989), 1456.

88. Mason, D., "The Rights of Australia's Children in a Global Context," *Children Australia* 15 (1990), 6; Hammarberg, T., "The U.N. Convention on the Rights of the Child—And How To Make It Work," 12 *Human Rights Quarterly* 97 (1990); "Convention on the Rights of the Child," G.A. Res. 44/25, U.N GAOR Annex, U.N. Doc. A/44/736 (1989).

89. George A. Stewart, "Interpreting the Child's Right to Identity in the U.N. Convention on the Rights of the Child," 26 *Family Law Quarterly* 221 at 233 (1992).

90. Hammarberg, "The U.N. Convention on the Rights of the Child—And How to Make It Work," *Human Rights Quarterly* 12 (1990), 97.

91. Byrne, J., "Anti-Parent Charter Worry," *Australian Association for Adolescent Health Newsletter* 22 (1990); Phillips, D., "The Risk to Family Relationships from the U.N. Convention on the Rights of the Child," 60 *Light* 8 at 11 (1990).

92. Hammarberg, 98–99.

93. Ibid.

94. Margaret Otlowski and B. Martin Tsamenyi, "Parental Authority and the United Nations Convention on the Rights of the Child: Are the Fears Justified?" 6 *Australian Journal of Family Law* 137 (1992).

95. "Divorce, Clinton-Style," *National Review,* 19 October 1992, 18.

96. Ibid.

97. Ibid.

98. Ibid.

99. Hillary Rodham [Clinton], "Children Under the Law," 43 *Harvard Educational Review* 487, 497 (November 1973).

100. Ibid., 505–6.

101. Ibid., 506–7 (italics in original).

102. "Children in Crisis," *American Bar Association Journal,* October 1993, 38.

103. Christine Gorman, "When AIDS Strikes Parents," *Time,* 1 November 1993, 76.

104. Barbara Bush, address to Wellesley, May 1992.

CHAPTER 6: The Killing Fields

1. James S. Dennis, *Christian Missions and Social Progress* (Old Tappan, N. J.: Revell, 1909), 2:130 (italics added).

2. 410 U.S. 113 (1973).

3. Lawrence Tribe, *Abortion: The Clash of Absolutes* (New York: Norton, 1990), 3.

4. Ibid., 30.

5. Ibid., 30–31, citing James Mohr, *Abortion in America: The Origins and Evolution of National Policy, 1800–1900* (New York: Oxford, 1978), 165.

6. Ibid., 34, citing Kristin Luker, *Abortion and the Politics of Motherhood* (Berkeley: Univ. of California Press, 1984), 49.

7. Ibid., 35, citing Faye Ginsburg, *Contested Lives: The Abortion Debate in an American Community* (Berkeley: Univ. of California Press, 1989), 32.

8. Ibid., 35.

9. Ibid., 37, citing Lawrence Lader, *Abortion II: Making the Revolution* (Boston: Beacon, 1973); Kristin Luker; and Eva Rubin, *Abortion, Politics and the Courts,* 2d ed. (New York: Greenwood, 1987).

10. Ibid., 38, citing Kristin Luker, 77.

11. Ibid., 38.

12. Ibid., 40 (citations omitted).

13. For example, Susan B. Anthony said:

> I deplore the horrible crime of child murder. We must reach the root of the evil. It is practiced by those whose inmost souls revolt from dreadful need. No matter what the motive, love of ease, or a desire to save from suffering the unborn innocent, the woman is awfully guilty who commits the deed; but oh, thrice guilty is he who drove her to the desperation which impelled her to the crime.

As quoted in George Grant, *Third Time Around* (Brentwood, Tenn.: Wolgemuth & Hyatt, 1991), 100, citing *The Revolution,* 8 July 1869. Elizabeth Cady Stanton summed it up eloquently:

> When we consider that women are often treated as property, it is degrading to women all the more that we should treat our children as property to be disposed of as we see fit.

Grant, 100, citing Letter to Julia Ward Howe, 16 October 1878.

14. Betty Friedan, *It Changed My Life* (New York: Random, 1976), 122.

15. Ibid., 124.

16. Tribe, 41 (citations omitted).

17. Ibid., 45.

18. Ibid., 45, citing Ginsburg, 39–40.

19. Ibid., 46 (citations omitted).

20. Ibid., 79.

21. See Tribe, 49–50, citing Professor Mary Ann Glendon of Harvard Law School, who argues that "the Roe decision interrupted an evolutionary process within state legislatures" that "represented a trend" followed by Western Europe in the subsequent period (Mary Ann Glendon, *Abortion and Divorce in Western Law* [Cambridge, Mass.: Harvard, 1987]).

22. Ibid., 51.

23. Ibid., 135, quoting Guido Calabresi, *Ideals, Beliefs, Attitudes and the Law: Private Law Perspectives on a Public Law Problem* (Syracuse, N.Y.: Syracuse Univ. Press, 1985), 95–96 (italics in original).

24. 112 S. Ct. 2791 (1992).

25. Id. at 2804.

26. Id. at 2831.

27. Id. at 2819–20.

28. "Challenges, 'Executive Disorders,'" *Life Insight* (a publication of the NCCB Secretariat for Pro-life Activities) 4, no. 2 (February 1993), 1. Hereinafter, "Executive Disorders."

29. Tribe, 193–94.

30. "Post-Abortion Fetal Study Stirs Storm," *Medical World News,* 8 June 1973, 21.

31. "Executive Disorders," 1.

32. See Theodore M. Hess-Mahan, "Human Fetal Tissue Transplantation Research: Entering a Brave New World," 23 *Suffolk University Law Review* 789 (1989), 812.

33. "Are There No Limits?" *National Right to Life News,* 23 February 1993, 2.

34. Hess-Mahan, 793.

35. "Are There No Limits?" 2.

36. Richard D. Glasow, Ph.D., "D & X Kills Late-Term Unborn Babies By Sucking Out Brains," *National Right to Life News,* 23 February 1993, 4.

37. Ibid.

38. Dennis D. Spencer, M.D., "Unilateral Transplantation of Human Fetal Mesencephalic Tissue into the Caudate Nucleus of Patients with Parkinson's Disease," *The New England Journal of Medicine* 327, no. 22 (26 November 1992), 1541–48. See also Curt R. Freed, M.D., "Survival of Implanted Fetal Dopamine Cells and Neurologic Improvement 12 to 46 Months After Transplantation for Parkinson's Disease," *The New England Journal of Medicine* 327, no. 22 (26 November 1992), 1549–55.

39. Robert J. White, M.D., "Fetal Brain Transplantation: Questionable Human Experiment," *America,* 28 November 1992, 422 (italics added).

40. Hess-Mahan, 813.

41. Ibid., 794 n. 29, citing Note, "Fetal Experimentation: Moral, Legal, and Medical Implications," 26 *Stanford Law Review* 1191, 1195–97 and nn. 42–67 (1974).

42. Philip Elmer-Dewitt, "Cloning: Where Do We Draw the Line?" *Time,* 8 November 1993, 65.

43. Ibid., 67.

44. Ibid., quoting from Arthur Caplan, director of the Center for Bioethics at the University of Minnesota.

45. Rick Weiss, "The Ethics of Cloning: Who Decides?" *Washington Post Health,* 16 November 1993, 13.

46. Ibid.

47. Russell Hittinger, "When the Court Should Not Be Obeyed," *First Things,* October 1993, 13.

48. Sponsors' Statement at 2.

49. See *Belotti v. Baird,* 443 U.S. 662 (1979); *H. L. v. Matheson,* 450 U.S. 398 (1981); *Planned Parenthood Association v. Ashcroft,* 462 U.S. 476 (1983); *Hodgson v. Minnesota,* 497 U.S. 417 (1990); *Ohio v. Akron Center for Reproductive Health,* 497 U.S. 502 (1990); and *Barnes v. Mississippi,* ―――― U.S. ―――― (October 1993).

50. Sponsors' Statement at 3.

51. See *Akron v. Akron Center for Reproductive Health,* 462 U.S. 416, 450 (1982).

52. 1993 S. 25 and 1993 H.R. 25, § 2(b).

53. In *Connecticut v. Menillo,* 423 U.S. 9 (1975), the Supreme Court upheld a statute prohibiting the performance of abortions by non-physicians. The Court stated:

> The insufficiency of the State's interest in maternal health is predicated upon the first trimester abortion being as safe for the woman as normal childbirth at term, and that predicate holds true only if the abortion is performed by medically competent personnel under conditions insuring maximum safety for the woman.

> Id. at 11. It would seem, then, that nonmedically competent personnel could be prohibited by statute from performing abortions. It is not clear, however, if physicians' assistants or other nonphysician hospital personnel would be considered medically competent.

> States could only require abortion clinics to be licensed if they could show that this was medically necessary to protect the health of the woman. This is likely to be an extremely fact-specific issue and would probably turn on the degree of the medical profession's support for the provision.

54. See *Margaret S. v. Treen,* 597 F.Supp. 636, *affirmed* 794 F.2d 994.

55. See, for example, *Barnes v. Moore,* 970 F.2d 12 (5th Cir. 1992) *cert. den.* 113 S.Ct. 656

(1992) (holding 24-hour waiting period for abortion is facially constitutional). For a general discussion of this issue from the abortion rights perspective, see Tribe, 203–4.

56. Jill Smolowe, "New, Improved and Ready for Battle," *Time*, 14 June 1993, 48.

57. Ibid., 49.

58. Carolyn Hax, "No Birth, No Pangs," *Washington Post*, 21 March 1993, C1.

59. Ibid., C1, C4.

60. Ibid., 49.

61. Ibid., 51.

62. Ibid., 54.

63. "The Second Woman Justice," *American Bar Association Journal* (October 1993), 42.

64. Ibid.

65. *LegisLetter* 2, no. 1 (Winter 1993), 2 (American Life League).

66. Ibid., 3, citing *Louisville Courier-Journal*, 15 April 1992.

67. Ibid., 3.

68. "Abortion TV Ads Catch on in Campaigns, Candidate Gets Graphic Images Past Censors," *Washington Post*, 20 July 1992, A1.

69. Ibid., A7. See sections 312(a)(7) and 315.

70. FCC Mass Media Bureau Letter Ruling of August 21, 1992.

71. *LegisLetter*, 4, citing *The Abortion Report*, 2 November 1992, 5.

72. Ibid., 6.

73. "Pro-Choice, Anti-Speech," *Wall Street Journal*, 30 November 1992, A12.

74. See Knight-Ridder, "Free Speech Ruling on Abortion Protest Seen Bound for Supreme Court," *Washington Post*, 24 October 1993, A21.

75. See *Cheffer v. McGregor*, 6 F.3d 705, 708 (11th Cir. 1993). The Supreme Court case is *Madsen v. Women's Health Center, Inc., et al.*, No. 93-880 (October Term, 1993.)

76. James Podgers, "Debate Grows Over Euthanasia," 78 *American Bar Association Journal* (May 1992), 62, quoting John Pickering, a leading opponent of the euthanasia resolution rejected in February 1992 by the ABA House of Delegates.

77. Ibid., 62, quoting Dubler.

78. Ibid., 62.

79. Michael Kramer, "Pulling the Plug," *Time*, 4 October 1993, 36.

80. Tribe, 229–30 (citation omitted).

81. Hax, C4.

CHAPTER 7: The Gay Agenda

1. Chandler Burr, "Homosexuality and Biology," *Atlantic Monthly*, March 1993, 48, describing a scene in James Harrison's 1992 documentary film *Changing Our Minds* taken from a 1950s educational film produced by the U.S. Navy and from a 1940s film clip.

2. Daniel P. Dromm, "America Needs This Curriculum," *The American Teacher*, published by American Federation of Teachers (February 1993). Dromm, according to the article, is a gay fourth-grade teacher at P.S. 199 in Sunnyside, N.Y. and has taught for the last fifteen years. He is currently a member of the Lesbian and Gay Teachers Association in New York City.

3. Burr, 47.

4. Ibid.

5. For example, in a study of homosexual obituaries compared to heterosexual obituaries, the median age of death of married men was 75, the median age for unmarried men was 57, for married women 79 and unmarried women 71. Yet, where AIDS was the listed cause, the median age of death was 39; the median age of death from unlisted causes was 38 if the individual had a long-time sexual partner, 45 if he did not. For homosexuals

who died of non-AIDS, the median age of death was 43. Homosexuals apparently more frequently died violently with 10 times the rate of nonmotorized vehicular accidental deaths, 17 times the motorized vehicular accidental death rate, 20 times the suicide rate, and 83 times the murder rate of white males from 25 to 44 years of age. See Paul Cameron, Ph.D., William L. Playfair, M.D., and Stephen Wellum, "The Homosexual Life-Span," Family Research Institute, Washington, D.C.

A 1978 study found that 43 percent of male homosexuals estimated they had sex with 500 or more different sexual partners, and 28 percent had more than 1,000 partners. See Eugene T. Gomulka, "Homosexuality in Uniform: Is It Time?" *First Things,* February 1993, 41, 43.

6. Eric E. Rofes, "Mobilizing for a Freedom March in 1993," *March on Washington for Lesbian, Gay & Bi Equal Rights and Liberation,* publication of Newspaper Project of the Committee for the March on Washington, Inc., February 1993, 2 (hereinafter, *March on Washington*).

7. Yet "[t]he equation of homosexuality with the noble history of civil rights in this country serves only to dilute, distort, and denigrate true civil rights" according to Anthony Evans, executive director of The Urban Alternative, quoted in Marco, "Oppressed Minority, or Counterfeits?" *Citizen* 6, no. 4 (20 April 1992).

8. Rofes, 2 (italics in original).

9. Ibid.

10. Gomulka, 43.

11. Thomas Fleming, "Cultural Revolutions," *Chronicles,* January 1993, 5–6.

12. Derek Charles Livingston, "A Look Beyond the Inaugural," *March on Washington,* 6.

13. See *March on Washington,* 20.

14. See Armistead Maupin, "Boycott Colorado," *New York Times,* 21 November 1992, A19.

15. *Evans v. Romer,* 854 P.2d. 1270 (1993).

16. See Howard Kurtz, "Gay Journalists 'Asserting Themselves in the Media,'" *Washington Post,* 12 September 1993, A4.

17. James D. Wilson, "Gays Under Fire," *Newsweek,* 14 September 1992, 36. See also "Straight Talk About Gays," *U.S. News & World Report,* 5 July 1993, 42ff.

18. Bob Cohn, "Discrimination: The Limits of the Law," *Newsweek,* 14 September 1992, 38 says: "Only six states and about 110 municipalities have statutes barring discrimination against gays."

19. For a discussion of these issues, see Major Melissa Wells-Petry, *Exclusion: Homosexuals and the Right to Serve* (Washington, D.C.: Regnery Gateway, 1993).

20. In *Bowers v. Hardwick,* 478 U.S. 186 (1986), the United States Supreme Court merely held that the Due Process Clause of the federal Constitution does not prohibit states from prosecuting consensual homosexual sodomy committed in a private home.

21. The concern of individuals *qua individuals* with respect to the orientation issue is beyond the scope of this book.

22. One of the books recommended by the Rainbow curriculum, *Heather Has Two Mommies,* by Leslea Newman (1989), describes the artificial insemination of a woman so that "Heather" had two mommies (lesbians). *Daddy's Roommate,* by Michael Willhoite (1990), pictures daddy and his male roommate in bed together. (These books are published by Alyson Publications, Dept. H80, 40 Plympton St., Boston, MA. This organization is also a publisher for NAMBLA.)

23. An approximation of this notion is embodied in President Bill Clinton's July 1993 "Don't Ask, Don't Tell" Policy for homosexuals in the U.S. military forces. Thus, one commentator posits:

    What if homosexuals do not freely choose their sexual identity? "Are they to be despised and rejected because of what they are—because of a status nature gave them?" pleads Anthony Lewis in the *New York Times.* The empirical evidence that homosexual orientation is biologically determined is mixed. But even if a biological link were established, that would not justify sanctioning the behavior, any more than it would justify condoning other aspects of anti-social human behavior for which biological links have been established, such as crime. As James Q. Wilson and Richard Hernn-stein point out in their book *Crime and Human Nature* (1985), although there is sub-stantial evidence that those who bear certain biological traits will commit certain crimes, those traits do not cause the criminal behavior: "The existence of biological predispositions means that circumstances that activate criminal behavior in one per-son will not do so in another." Similarly, persons whose sexual orientation is homo-sexual still make decisions about their behavior.

Linda Chavez, "Homosexuality and the Moral Order," *First Things*, April 1993, 160. For an exhaustive discussion of this issue written by a homosexual, see Burr, 47–65.

24. The dilemma of causal identification on an individual level is presented in "The Twilight of the Golds," by Jonathan Tolins, the "story of a family thrown into turmoil when a pregnant woman is told through genetic testing that her fetus will most likely be homo-sexual." See Jonathan Tolins, "A Playwright's Insight—And Warning," *Time*, 26 July 1993), 38.

25. Chavez, 15.

26. "The March Demands," *March on Washington*, 3; quotation reformatted for clarity and emphasis.

27. Donna Minkowitz, "Forward March," *March on Washington*, 3.

28. Ibid. (italics added).

29. Eloise Salholz, "The Power and the Pride," *Newsweek*, 21 June 1993, 54.

30. Robert Dunn, "Why Levi Strauss & Co. Stopped Funding the Boy Scouts," *Washington Times*, 28 August 1992, F2 (Dunn, vice president of corporate affairs for Levi Strauss, explains Levi's boycott in a letter to the editor); Roy Rivenburg, "Of Boy Scouts and Boycotts," *Los Angeles Times*, 31 August 1992, E1.

31. Maria Goodavage, "Boy Scouts: No Gays Despite Bans at Schools," *USA Today*, 17 Sep-tember 1991, A, 1:4.

32. San Diego Unified School District's non-discrimination policy allows Boy Scout activities after school but not during school hours.

33. Samuel Francis, "Gay Activists Are Silencing Their Critics," *Human Events* 52, no. 50 (12 December 1992), 16 (radio station WMZQ in Washington, D.C.).

34. Jacqueline Trescott, "After Warning, WMZQ Airs Gay Alliance Ad," *Washington Post*, 22 October 1992, C2.

35. Studds declared his homosexuality in 1983 after being charged with sexual misconduct when his improprieties with underaged male congressional pages came to light. "Com-mittee Recommends House Reprimand Two for Sexual Misconduct," *Washington Post*, 15 July 1983, A1. Subsequently, Studds was formally censured by the House of Represen-tatives (*Congressional Record*, 20 July 1983, 20037).

36. Studds chairs the House Merchant Marine and Fisheries Committee, which oversees the U.S. Coast Guard. John A. Farrell, "Conservative Accuses Studds of Censorship," *Boston Globe*, 7 February 1993, 25.

37. Letter to Representative Gerry Studds from Gary Bauer.

38. Bill Nichols, "Clinton: Gay Policy 'Right,'" *USA Today*, 20 July 1993, 1.

39. See John Lancaster, "Clinton and the Military: Is Gay Policy Just the Opening Skirmish?" *Washington Post*, 1 February 1993, A10.

40. General Colin Powell, letter to Rep. Patricia Schroeder, 8 May 1992, reprinted in *Crisis*, July/August 1992, 46.

41. Chavez, 15.

42. See *Washington Times*, 10 February 1993.

43. See *National & International Religion Report* 7, no. 4 (8 February 1993), 5.

44. See Gustav Niebuhr, "Lesbian Ousted from the Military Is Hoping to Return as a Chap-lain," *Washington Post*, 10 February 1993, 4. However, the Supreme Court has left intact a federal court ruling in a lesbian chaplain's favor that social disapproval of homosexu-ality is insufficient justification for the military's exclusion of homosexuals (*Pruitt v. Che-ney*, 963 F. 2d 1160 [9th Cir. 1992], *cert. denied*, 61 U.S.L.W. 3418 [1992]).

45. William P. Hoar, "Emasculating the Military: The Legalized Homosexuality Edict," *The New American*, 8 March 1993, 4.

46. Ibid.

47. See generally Wells-Petry.

48. See id.

49. In any case, the Clinton compromise is still in doubt until the courts rule in *Meinhold v. Department of Defense*, 808 F.Supp. 1453 (C.D.Cal 92), where the military's policy is being challenged as unconstitutional for violation of the First Amendment and Equal Protection (See Joseph E. Broadus and William B. Rubenstein, "Don't Ask, Don't Tell," *American Bar Association Journal*, October 1993, 54).

50. Howard L. Hurwitz, "It Undermines Traditional Family Values," *American Teacher*, American Federation of Teachers, February 1993, 4. According to the article, Mr. Hurwitz served as a teacher and principal in the New York City public schools. He is the author of twelve books on the social sciences and chairman of the Family Defense Council.

51. Chavez, 15.

52. Chavez, 15–16. See also "Sexual Disorientation," (1992) Family Research Council, 700 Thirteenth Street, N.W., Suite 500, Washington, D.C.

53. Rorie Sherman, "Gay Law No Longer Closeted," *National Law Journal*, 26 October 1992, 1; *Baehr v. Lewin*, 852 P.2d. 44 (May 1993).

54. See Annotation, "Marriage Between Persons of the Same Sex," 63 A.L.R.3d 1199 (1975 & Supp. 1992) (hereinafter "Same Sex"); *Matter of Estate of Cooper*, 564 N.Y.S.2d 684, 687 (Sur. 1990), *aff'd*, 592 N.Y.S.2d 797 (A.D. 2 Dept. 1993) ("This court could find no authority in any jurisdiction of the United States, either authorizing marriages between people of the same sex, or elevating homosexual unions to the same level achieved by the marriage of two people of the opposite sex").

55. *Singer v. Hara*, 522 P.2d 1187, 1196 (Wash.App. 1974) ("Appellants were not denied a marriage license because of their sex; rather, they were denied a marriage license because of the nature of marriage itself"); *Adams v. Howerton*, 486 F.Supp. 1119 (C.D.Cal. 1980) (applying U.S. and Colorado law), *aff'd* 673 F.2d 1036 (9th Cir. 1982), and *cert. denied*, 458 U.S. 1111 (1982).

56. *Meyer v. Nebraska*, 262 U.S. 390 (1923) (the liberty guaranteed under due process includes, inter alia, the rights to marry, to establish a home, and to raise children).

57. *Black's Law Dictionary* 972 (6th ed. 1990); 55 C.J.S. *Marriage* § 1(a) ("Marriage is a contract under which a man and a woman reciprocally engage to live with each other during their joint lives, and to discharge toward each other the duties imposed by law on the relation of husband and wife"); *Singer*, 522 P.2d at 1192–93, 1197 ("they are being denied entry into the marriage relationship because of the recognized definition of that relationship as one which may be entered into only by two persons who are members of the opposite sex;" marriage "has been deemed a private relationship of a man and a woman [husband and wife]"); see generally, "Same Sex," 63 A.L.R.3d 1199 (discussing cases declining to extend marital status to include those seeking same sex marriages).

58. Nan D. Hunter, *The Rights of Lesbians and Gay Men* (Carbondale, Ill.: Southern Illinois Univ. Press, 1992), 77.

59. Ibid., 78.

60. See, for example, *Phillips v. Wisconsin Personnel Com'n*, 482 N.W.2d 121, 123–24 n.1 (Wis. Ct. App. 1992) ("whether to allow or disallow same-sex marriages . . . is a legislative decision, not one for the courts"); *Singer*, 522 P.2d at 1197 ("The societal values which are involved [in defining marriage] must be left to the examination of the legislature"); *Estate of Cooper*, 564 N.Y.S.2d at 688 ("The Legislature has chosen to restrict the right to marry to people of the opposite sex").

61. Chavez, 16.

62. For a discussion of the evolution of legitimacy in the law, see, for example, Walter Wadlington, *Cases and Other Materials on Domestic Relations* (Westbury, N.Y.: Foundation, 1990), 299.

63. See Kimberly Scott, "Making Babies," *Washington Blade*, 23 October 1992.

64. Amy Rubin, quoted in "Homosexuals Make Babies," *Christian American,* February 1993, 8.

65. Sherman, 35.

66. See, for example, *Alison D. v. Virginia M.*, 77 N.Y. 2d 651 (1991) (partner of mother is not a parent and has no standing to seek visitation rights); *Sporleder v. Hermes,* 162 Wis. 2d 1002 (1991) (partner of mother is not a parent and has no standing to seek visitation rights).

67. Sherman, 35.

68. Ibid., quoting and paraphrasing Nancy D. Polikoff, family law professor at American University Washington College of Law, Washington, D.C.

69. Sherman, 34.

70. Ibid., paraphrasing Ms. Polikoff; see *Seebol v. Farie,* 16 *Florida Law Weekly* (Monroe Cty. Ct. 1991).

71. *A.C. v. C.B.,* 829 P.2d 660 (1992).

72. Hunter, 101.

73. Sherman, 35.

74. See, for example, William A. Henry III, "Gay Parents: Under Fire and on the Rise," *Time,* 20 September 1993, 66.

75. Roberta Israeloff, "Happy Families Are Not All Alike," *Parents,* March 1993, 129.

76. Ibid., 130, quoting Dr. Andrew I. Schwebel, professor of psychology at The Ohio State University in Columbus, and Dr. Teresa Peck, clinical psychologist in San Francisco, California.

77. Ibid., 130–32.

78. See Roger J. Magnuson, *Are Gay Rights Right? Making Sense of the Controversy* (Sisters, Ore.: Multnomah, Division of Questar, 1990).

79. Shaista-Parveen Ali, Comment, "Homosexual Parenting: Child Custody and Adoption," 22 *U.C. Davis Law Review* 1009, 1011–12 n. 22 (Spring 1989) (hereinafter, "Homosexual Parenting." The Comment cites the Uniform Marriage and Divorce Act § 402, which defines what constitutes the child's best interests:

    (1) the wishes of the child's parent or parents as to his custody;

    (2) the wishes of the child as to his custodian;

    (3) the interaction and interrelationship of the child with his parent or parents, his siblings, and any other person who may significantly affect the child's best interest;

    (4) the child's adjustment to his home, school, and community; and

    (5) the mental and physical health of all individuals involved.

    The court shall not consider conduct of a proposed custodian that does not affect his relationship to the child.

    Uniform Marriage and Divorce Act, Sec. 402, 9A U.L.A. 561 (1987); Steve Susoeff, Comment, "Assessing Children's Best Interests When a Parent Is Gay or Lesbian: Toward a Rational Custody Standard," 32 *U.C.L.A. Law Review,* 852, 861–66 (1985).

80. See *In Re Marriage of Birdsall,* 243 Cal. Rptr. 287, 289 (Cal.App. 4 Dist. 1988) ("The court may not . . . determine custody on the basis of sexual preference alone. Indeed, a parent is not unfit, as a matter of law, merely because he or she is homosexual"); *Guinan v. Guinan,* 477 N.Y.S.2d 830 (N.Y. App. Div. 1984) ("whether [female] defendant had sexual relationships with other women is not determinative of this custody dispute. A parent's sexual indiscretions should be a consideration in a custody dispute only if they are shown to adversely affect the child's welfare"); *accord, A.C. v. C.B.,* 829 P.2d at 664; *Williams v. Williams,* 591 N.Y.S.2d 872, 875; (N.Y. App. Div. 1992): *State Ex Rel. Human Services Dept. v. Jacinta M.,* 764 P.2d 1327, 1329–30 (N.M. Ct. App. 1988); *Stroman v. Williams,* 353 S.E.2d 704, 705 (S.C. Ct. App. 1987); *S.N.E. v. R.L.B.,* 699 P.2d 875, 879 (Alaska 1985); *Matter of Marriage of Cabalquinto,* 669 P.2d 886, 888 (Wash. 1983); *Doe v. Doe,* 452 N.E.2d 293, 296 (Mass. App. Ct. 1983); *D.H. v. J.H.,* 418 N.E.2d 286, 293 (Ind. Ct. App. 1981); *Bezio v. Patenaude,* 410 N.E.2d 1207, 1216 (Mass. 1980); *Kallas v. Kallas,* 614 P.2d 641, 645 (Utah 1980).

81. *Matter of Adoption of Evan,* 583 N.Y.S.2d 997 (Sur. 1992) ("The fact that the petitioners here maintain an open lesbian relationship is not a reason to deny adoption. New York law recognizes that a child's best interest is not predicated or controlled by parental sexual orientation"); 18 N.Y.C.R.R. § 421.16(h)(2) (specifically prohibiting sexual orientation discrimination in adoptions in New York).

82. See *White v. Thompson,* 569 So.2d 1181 (Miss.1990) (lesbian mother found to be morally unfit for custody, based on numerous factors, including her lesbianism; court never reached the question of *per se* unfitness); *J.P. v. P.W.,* 772 S.W.2d 786, 792–93 (Mo. Ct. App. 1989) ("It is appropriate to acknowledge that some states hold that the influence of homosexual behavior is a basis for restricting or denying visitation only when such an influence has adversely affected or is likely to affect the child in question. . . . That is not the law in this state. . . . 'The court does not need to wait, though, till the damage is done'" [quoting *N.K.M. v. L.E.M.,* 606 S.W.2d 179, 186 (Mo. Ct. App. 1980)]); *S.E.G. v. R.A.G.,* 735 S.W.2d 164, 166 (Mo. Ct. App. 1987) ("[the mother's homosexual] conduct can never be kept private enough to be a neutral factor in the development of a child's values and character. We will not ignore such conduct by a parent which may have an effect on the children's moral development"); *Roe v. Roe,* 324 S.E.2d 691, 694 (Va. 1985) (The father's continuous exposure of the child to his immoral and illicit relationship renders him an unfit and improper custodian as a matter of law; "We conclude that the best interests of the child will only be served by protecting her from the burdens imposed by [the father's homosexual] behavior"); *Constant A. v. Paul C.A.,* 496 A.2d 1, 10 (Pa. Super. 1985) ("We also find . . . that there are sufficient social, moral and legal distinctions between the traditional heterosexual family relationship and illicit homosexual relationship to raise the presumption of regularity in favor of the licit, when established, shifting to the illicit, the burden of disproving detriment to the children," rejecting approach of other states that require showing of concrete harm to child before effect of parent's sexual preference is evaluated); *Jacobson v. Jacobson,* 314 N.W.2d 78, 82 (N.D. 1981) ("we believe that because of the mores of today's society, because [the mother] is engaged in a homosexual relationship in the home in which she resides with the children, and because of the lack of legal recognition of the status of a homosexual relationship, the best interests of the children will be better served by placing custody of the children with [the heterosexual father]").

Typical restrictions placed upon the visitation rights of homosexual parents include requiring responsible adult supervision of the child's visit with the homosexual parent (*J.P. v. P.W.,* 772 S.W.2d at 794); the exercise of visitation outside the presence of the homosexual parent's lover (*White,* 569 So.2d at 1185; but see *Blew v. Verta,* 617 A.2d 31, 34, 36 (Pa.Super. Ct. 1992) (trial court abused discretion in restricting lesbian mother's partial custody to visits at her parents' home outside her lesbian lover's presence; one of the facts of the child's life "is that one of his parents is homosexual"; thus the child's "best interest is served by exposing him to reality and not fostering in him shame or abhorrence for his mother's non-traditional commitment"); *In Re Marriage of Diehl,* 582 N.E.2d 281, 294 (Ill.App. Ct. 1991) (reversing trial court's visitation restriction, which required that "any other female with whom [the mother] may be residing" not be present; trial court should have used the "serious endangerment" standard and not the "best interests" standard); *In Re Marriage of Walsh,* 451 N.W.2d 492, 493 (Iowa 1990) (reversing trial court's mandate that homosexual father's visitation only be exercised when "no unrelated adult" was present; father testifies that in no way will child be exposed to his lifestyle; therefore the visitation restriction must fall)); forbidding the child to remain overnight if the homosexual parent's lover was to so remain (*Pennington v. Pennington,* 596 N.E.2d 305 (Ind.App. 1 Dist. 1992); *Irish v. Irish,* 300 N.W.2d 739 (Mich.App. 1980)); placing restrictions on general overnight visitation even if not in the presence of parent's lover (*Chicoine v. Chicoine,* 479 N.W.2d 891, 894 (S.D. 1992) (requiring a home study to assure "that the children are not placed in an unsafe or unstable environment. Similarly, the trial court must provide adequate enforcement measures to assure compliance with any restrictions imposed should it persist in granting overnight visitation")); forbidding any sexual contact between the parent and the homosexual lover in the presence of the child (Ibid.); ordering the parent not to expose the child to homosexual rights rallies (*J.L.P. v. D.J.P.,* 643 S.W. 2d 865 (Mo.Ct. Appl. 1982)); and requiring that the parent not take the child to a homosexual church (id.; see generally, *Annotation, Visitation Rights of Homosexual or Lesbian Parent,* 36 A.L.R.4th 997 (1985 and Supp. 1992)); (hereinafter *Visitation Rights*). A former lover of a lesbian parent even sought visitation of the lesbian parent's child, but was refused (*Kulla v. McNulty,* 472 N.W.2d 175 (Minn.Ct. Appl. 1991) (former lesbian lover had burden of proving that visitation rights would not interfere in the relationship between lesbian mother and her child)). A parent's residence with a homosexual lover has been held to be grounds for a change of custody (*N.K.M. v. L.E.M.,* 606 S.W.2d 179 (Mo.Ct. Appl. 1980)).

For additional discussion and research sources on the relevance of a parent's homosexuality in custody/visitation disputes, see *Visitation Rights,* 36 A.L.R.4th 997 (1985 and Supp. 1992) and Annotation, *Initial Award or Denial of Child Custody to Homosexual or Lesbian Parent,* 6 A.L.R.4th 1297 (1981 and Supp. 1992).

83. *Matter of Adoption of Adult Anonymous,* 435 N.Y.S.2d 527, 106 Misc. 2d 792 (1981) (adoption permitted); *Matter of Adoption of Robert Paul P.,* 471 N.E. 2d 424 (Ct. App. 1984) (adoption not permitted).

84. *Adult Anonymous,* 435 N.Y.S.2d 527.

85. Ibid., at 530–31.

86. Ibid., at 531.

87. Ibid., at 530.

88. *Robert Paul P.,* 481 N.Y.S.2d at 653.

89. Ibid.

90. Ibid., at 655.

91. *Braschi v. Stahl Associates,* 74 N.Y.2d 201 (1989).

92. "Interview: John Money," conducted in Amsterdam by Joseph Geraci and Donald Mader in May 1990, reprinted in *Paidika: The Journal of Paedophilia* 2 no. 7 (Spring 1991), 3.

93. Ibid., 3, 12.

94. Michael Ebert, "Pedophilia Steps into the Daylight," *Citizen,* 16 November 1992, 8.

95. *Paidika: The Journal of Paedophilia* 1, no. 1, 2.

96. Judith Reisman, quoted in Ebert, "Pedophilia Steps into the Daylight," 8.

97. See John Leo, "Pedophiles in the Schools," *U.S. News & World Report,* 11 October 1993, 37.

98. Ibid.

99. David Von Biema, "For the Love of Kids," *Time,* 1 November 1993, 51.

100. Ibid.

101. Robert H. Knight, "Video 'On Being Gay' Twists the Facts," *Insight,* no. 14 (July 1993). Some of the largest corporations employ Mr. McNaught as a consultant.

102. Thomas A. Stewart, "Gay in Corporate America," *Fortune,* 16 December 1991, 44, 50.

103. "Straight Talk About Gays," 48.

104. See John W. Whitehead, *Religion and the Workplace: Rights and Responsibilities* (Charlottesville, Va.: Rutherford Institute, 1992).

105. "Kodak Gives Special Recognition to Homosexuals," *Journal of the American Family Association,* April 1993, 1.

106. See "Connections," AT&T Newsletter (1993).

107. Undated newsletter "LeAGUE Chapter Formed at WPD-Clemson" (1993), 1.

108. Ibid.

109. See Minutes of Regional Management Team Meeting, U.S. Forest Service, 3 February 1993.

110. Ibid.

111. Ibid.

112. Ibid.

113. Ibid.

114. Ibid.

115. See Harvard Law Review Association, "Developments in the Law: Sexual Orientation and the Law," 102 *Harvard Law Review* 1508, 1667–68 (1989) (hereinafter "Sexual Orientation and the Law"). At the time this Harvard article was published, "only Wisconsin [had] a comprehensive statute barring [homosexual] discrimination in employment."

116. See William A. Henry III, "Born Gay?" *Time,* 26 July 1993, 36, for an article describing the research as of July 1993 on this topic.

117. *City of Cleburne v. Cleburne Living Center,* 473 U.S. 432, 440 (1985).

118. 473 U.S. at 440–41.

119. 478 U.S. 186 (1986).

120. Id. at 194–96.

121. *High Tech Gays v. Defense Industrial Security Clearance Office,* 895 F.2d 563, 571 (9th Cir. 1990); *Ben-Shalom v. Marsh,* 881 F.2d 454, 464–65 (7th cir. 1989) ("If homosexual conduct may constitutionally be criminalized, then homosexuals do not constitute a suspect or quasi-suspect class entitled to greater than rational basis scrutiny for equal protection purposes. The Constitution, in light of *Hardwick,* cannot otherwise be rationally applied, lest an unjustified and indefensible inconsistency result"); *Woodward v. U.S.,* 871 F.2d 1068, 1076 (Fed. Cir. 1989) ("After *Hardwick* it cannot logically be asserted that discrimination against homosexuals is constitutionally infirm"); *Padula v. Webster,* 822 F.2d 97, 103 (D.C. Cir. 1987) ("It would be quite anomalous, on its face, to declare status defined by conduct that states may constitutionally criminalize as deserving of strict scrutiny under the equal protection clause. . . . If the Court was unwilling to object to state laws that criminalize the behavior that defines the class, it is hardly open to a lower court to conclude that state sponsored discrimination against the class is invidious. After all, there can hardly be more palpable discrimination against a class than making conduct that defines the class criminal").

122. See "Sexual Orientation and the Law," 102 *Harvard Law Review* at 1668 n. 51. (provides a listing, current through March 1989 only, of United States localities that have enacted homosexual antidiscrimination regulations).

123. 4 Colo. Code Regs. § 801-1, Policy 11-1, "State Personnel Prohibition of Discrimination because of Sexual Preference" (1992).

124. Cal. Labor Code § 1102.1(a) (West 1993 Pocket Part). It should be noted, however, that a section of this California provision exempts religious associations/corporations "not organized for private profit" from the proscription against homosexual discrimination (Ibid., at § 1102.1(b)(2)). Subsection (c) assures that this nondiscrimination provision does not affect marital status classifications (it does not change the marriage law to allow gay marriages). Subsection (d) states that no quotas or affirmative action is required or permitted under the section. It should be noted that this new addition to the labor code of California is simply a codification of already existing California law via court decisions handed down in *Gay Law Students Ass'n v. Pacific Tel. & Tel.,* 595 P.2d 592 (Cal. 1979) and *Soroka v. Dayton Hudson Corp.,* 235 Cal. App. 3d 654 (1991), *review granted,* Jan. 13, 1992, SO24102. Historical Note, Cal. Labor Code § 1102.1 (West Supp. 1993). Other states have enacted similar provisions, including Massachusetts, Wisconsin, and Minnesota.

   Massachusetts—Mass. Gen. Laws Ann. 151B § 4 (West Supp. 1993) (Labor and Industries Discrimination). The language protecting against sexual orientation discrimination was added to the general antidiscrimination provision of the Massachusetts code on November 15, 1989. It prohibits sexual orientation discrimination, but excludes from protection those "whose sexual orientation involves minor children as the sex object." § 4(1). The prohibition also does not apply if the reason for the discrimination is that the individual lacked a "bona fide occupational qualification." Id. Subsection (18) assures that nothing in the entire antidiscrimination section is to be "construed to bar any religious or denominational institution or organization, or any organization operated for charitable or educational purposes, which is operated, supervised or controlled by or in connection with a religious organization, from limiting admission to or giving preference to persons of the same religion or denomination or from taking any action with respect to matters of employment, discipline, faith, internal organization, or ecclesiastical rule, custom, or law which are calculated by such organization to promote the religious principles for which it is established or maintained."

In other words, if a church sought to deny a homosexual the position of, say, pastor or priest, it would have to show that denying the homosexual such employment is intended to promote the religious ideals and beliefs for which that church is established.

Wisconsin—Wis. Stat. Ann. §§ 111.31–111.36 (West 1986) ("Fair Employment"). These sections add homosexuals to the list of those who may not be lawfully discriminated against in employment. Section 111.31(3) forbids any kind of affirmative action pursuant to this section. Section 111.337(2)(am) (West Supp. 1990), added on March 17, 1988, does give some relief to religious organizations. Although there is not a special section set out to exempt religious organizations, the section does allow nonprofit religious associations, organizations, or corporations that are primarily controlled by religious associations to so discriminate, *if* "the job description demonstrates that the position is clearly related to the religious teachings and beliefs of the religious association." Id. Thus, there is no blanket exemption for churches, which likely means that in Wisconsin, churches may not legally refuse to hire, for example, a homosexual janitor, but may refuse employment to a gay pastor if their doctrine makes it clear that homosexuality is religiously objectionable to the church and its members.

Minnesota—1993 Minn. Sess. Law Serv. ch. 22 (H.F. 585) (WESTLAW). Minnesota has also added homosexuals to its list of protected classes in the employment discrimination context. Id. Subsection (1) exempts religious organizations from the proscription against sexual orientation discrimination *if* sexual orientation is a bona fide occupational qualification (BFOQ). In other words, like Wisconsin's provision, a church may be permitted to refuse employment to a minister, if being a heterosexual is somewhat of a "prerequisite," in religious terms, to leading their church. However, a church will be hard put to convincingly show a court that having the church janitors share in the church body's disapproval of homosexuality is so important to the mission of the church as to be somewhat of a prerequisite for janitorial employment.

125. D.C. Code Ann. § 1-2501: "It is the intent of the Council of the District of Columbia to secure an end in the District of Columbia to discrimination for any reason other than that of individual merit, including but not limited to, discrimination by reason of race, color, religion, national origin, sex, age, marital status, personal appearance, and *sexual orientation*" (italics added).

126. The legislative history of the statute notes the decision of the District of Columbia Court of Appeals in *Gay Rights Coalition v. Georgetown University,* 536 A.2d 1 (D.C. 1987), in which it was held that the government's compelling interest in the eradication of discrimination on the basis of sexual orientation outweighed any burden on Georgetown University's free exercise of religion. The university believed that homosexuality was sin, and that thus it did not want to allow a gay student group to meet on campus (*Georgetown,* 536 A.2d at 11). Although the court held that the university had to allow the group to meet, it refused to force the university to recognize officially the gay student organization, as this would be tantamount to "compelled expression in violation of the first amendment" (*Georgetown,* 536 A.2d at 21–22). The D.C. statute points to this decision as evidence that there exists no religious exemption from the homosexual antidiscrimination provision. See "Legislative history of Law 2-38," following D.C. Code Ann. § 1-2501; but cf., "Sexual Orientation," 102 *Harvard Law Review* at 1668–70 (even though the gay/lesbian group was allowed to meet, because Georgetown University was not forced to recognize the group officially, "the *Georgetown* decision may thus help perpetuate the unfounded belief that gay and lesbian students are unacceptable to campus life, and further divide students on the basis of sexual orientation").

127. The United States District Court for the District of Columbia, in *Clifton-Terrace Assocs. v. United Tech. Corp.*, 728 F.Supp. 24 (D.D.C. 1990), held that there exists an unlawful refusal to deal when four elements are proved: (1) plaintiff is a member of a protected class; (2) plaintiff applied for services it was qualified to receive; (3) services were denied to plaintiff; and (4) plaintiff's membership in the class was substantial factor in the refusal to deal.

128. On February 17, 1993, for example, Bill No. 1530 was introduced in the Florida State Senate (Florida 1993 Regular Session). This bill is intended to amend Florida's current antidiscrimination provision (Fla. Stat. Ann. § 760.60) to protect homosexuals against discrimination (Florida Senate Bill No. 1530). The religious exemption provided in the bill applies only to religious organizations "where business activity is not prevalent." Such an exemption seems unduly vague and prone to abuse and could be applied so

as to restrict the hiring freedoms of various religious ministries whose financial well-being, indeed whose very existence, depends upon the sale of such things as religious goods and literature.

129. Vt. Stat. Ann. tit. 9, ch. 139, § 4503 (Supp. 1992).

130. Ibid., at § 4503(a)(1). Cf. *County of Dane v. Norman,* 497 N.W.2d 714 (Wis. 1993) (landlord's policy of not renting to unmarried persons who intended to live together was not marital status discrimination). In *Norman,* the Wisconsin Supreme Court said that living together was "conduct" and not "status" (id., at 717), and thus was not proscribed as marital status discrimination. Thus, under Wisconsin law via *Norman,* a landlord may be able to refuse two unmarried homosexual lovers a rental unit, not on the basis of their homosexuality, but on the basis of both their unmarried statuses and their intention to live together, hence making the conduct and not the homosexual status the deciding factor.

131. Ibid., at § 4503(a)(2).

132. Ibid., at § 4503(a)(3).

133. Ibid., at § 4503(a)(4).

134. Ibid., at § 4503(a)(7).

135. Ibid., at § 4504(5).

136. Ibid. However, the churches may not so discriminate if the basis for the restriction is the race, color, or national origin of the individual seeking occupancy (id.).

137. Ibid.

138. Mass. Gen. Laws Ann. 151B § 4(7).

139. Ibid., at § 4 (7) (c).

140. Ibid., at § 4 (11) (3).

141. Nancie L. Katz, "Massachusetts Urges Sensitivity to Gay Kids," *Dallas Morning News,* 13 July 1993.

142. Ibid.

143. Deeann Glamser, "Gay Rights Debate Enters the Classroom," *USA Today,* 18 May 1993, 8A.

144. Hunter, 6.

145. Ibid., citing *Fricke v. Lynch,* 491 F.Supp. 381 (D.R.I. 1980), *vacated and remanded,* 627 F.2d 1088 (1st Cir. 1981).

146. Jerry Z. Muller, "Coming Out Ahead: The Homosexual Moment in the Academy," *First Things,* August/September 1993, 17–18.

147. May 17, 1993 letter from Core Course Coordinator, University of California, Santa Cruz, Kresge College.

148. Spring 1993 telephone conversation with Pennsylvania State Office of Residence Life.

149. Spring 1993 telephone conversation with Office of University Housing, University of Oregon.

150. February 9, 1993, letter from Larry I. Palmer, vice president of Cornell University, to Mr. P. W. Gifford.

151. July 1993 letter from Richard R. Eakin, chancellor of East Carolina University, to the members of the class of 1997.

152. Ibid.

153. See Hunter, Appendix C.

154. Chavez, 16.

155. "Stop Rutherford Institute," *This Week in Texas,* March 19–March 25, p. 28.

156. Cal Thomas, "Morality Demands That We Condemn Gays," *Detroit Free Press,* 28 April 1993, 11A.

CHAPTER 8: The End of Public Religion

1. David Mamet, *Writing in Restaurants* (New York: Viking, 1986), 80.

2. *Sherman v. Community Consolidated School Dist. 21 of Wheeling Township,* 980 F.2d 437, 447 (7th Cir. 1992).

3. Justin Kaplan, "How God Made It onto Religiously Neutral American Money," *Los Angeles Daily Journal,* 9 October 1992, quoting Mark Twain.

4. See Dennis Cauchon, "Debate Over Competing Principles," *USA Today,* 31 March 1993, cover story.

5. See generally John C. Miller, *The Wolf by the Ears: Thomas Jefferson and Slavery* (New York: Free, 1977).

6. Philip Elmer-Dewitt, "Cyberpunk!" *Time,* 8 February 1993, 60.

7. Ibid.

8. Ibid.

9. Richard N. Ostling, "The Church Search," *Time,* 5 April 1993, 47.

10. "Index of Leading Cultural Indicators," *Time,* 29 March 1993, 18.

11. Richard Brookhiser, "We Can All Share American Culture," *Time,* 31 August 1992, 74.

12. See Forrest McDonald, *E Pluribus Unum: The Formation of the American Republic 1776–1790* (Boston: Houghton Mifflin, 1965); Samuel E. Morison and Henry S. Commager and William Leuchtenburg, *The Growth of the American Republic,* 7th ed. (New York: Oxford Univ. Press, 1980).

13. See generally John W. Whitehead, *The Second American Revolution* (Westchester, Ill.: Crossway, 1982).

14. See Morris D. Forkosch, "Religion, Education, and the Constitution—A Middle Way," 23 *Loyola Law Review* 617, 626 (1977).

15. Ibid., 632.

16. Brookhiser, 74.

17. See Donald L. Drakeman, *Church-State Constitutional Issues* (New York: Greenwood, 1991), 81–91.

18. Winthrop S. Hudson, *Religion in America,* 4th ed. (New York: Macmillan, 1987), 224.

19. Ibid.

20. See Thomas T. Handy, *Undermined Establishment: Church-State Relations in America, 1880–1920* (Princeton, N.J.: Princeton Univ. Press, 1991).

21. Ostling, 46–47.

22. With respect to the "Christian nation" notion, Mark Twain once scoffed (though perhaps for different reasons): "If the United States is, indeed, 'a Christian country,' so is hell" (Mark Twain, quoted in Justin Kaplan, "How God Made It onto Religiously Neutral American Money," reprinted in the *Los Angeles Daily Journal,* 9 October 1992, 6).

23. "Mississippi Governor Criticized for 'Christian Nation' Remark," *Dallas/Fort Worth Heritage* 1, no. 7 (January 1993), 14.

24. Rob Boston, "The 'Christian Nation' Debate," *Church & State,* January 1993, 10 (10).

25. See, for example, Jill Smolowe, "Crusade for the Classroom," *Time,* 1 November 1993, 34.

26. See "What You Can Do About the Religious Right," *Church & State,* October 1993.

27. Clifford Goldstein, answer to letter, "The New Christian Right: Strategy for the Nineties," *Liberty,* March/April 1993, 2–3 (italics in original).

28. See, for example, Bill Turque, "Press '1' for the Christian Right," *Newsweek,* 8 February 1993, 28. Also see Marshall Fishwick and Ray B. Browne, eds., *The God Pumpers: Religion in the Electronic Age* (Bowling Green, Ohio: Bowling Green State Univ. Popular Press, 1987).

29. Charles Krauthammer, "How Conservatism Can Come Back," *Time,* 18 January 1993, 68.

30. Robert Wuthnow, *The Struggle for America's Soul* (Grand Rapids: Eerdmans, 1989), 120.
    However, Mr. Wuthnow writes that "no simple correlation can be suggested between the rise of religious television and the privatization of faith. Religious television certainly has a private dimension, but so does any kind of religion—we would not regard it a very profound sort of faith that did not. It may be useful, as I have suggested, to liken religious television to the devotional dimension of traditional religion. Rather than asking how religious television viewing differs from attending religious services in person, therefore, we might want to focus attention on the contrasts and similarities between religious television viewing and such long-standing devotional practices as Bible reading, prayer, and meditation" (ibid., 125).
    Nonetheless, Mr. Wuthnow concludes that "the question of passivity and activity is one of finding an appropriate balance. Religious television appears to tip the scale far in the direction of passivity, and thus gives rise for concerns about what kinds of more active devotional expressions should be encouraged. But some element of passive, externally guided behavior seems inescapable" (ibid., 129).

31. For a more detailed discussion of this position, see John W. Whitehead and Alexis I. Crow, "Beyond Establishment Clause Analysis in Public School Situations: The Need to Apply the Public Forum and Tinker Doctrines," 28 *Tulsa Law Journal* 150 (1992). See also Tim Stafford, "Move Over, ACLU," *Christianity Today,* 25 October 1993, 20.

32. John Whitehead, "Accommodation and Equal Treatment of Religion: Federal Funding of Religiously-Affiliated Child Care Facilities," 26 *Harvard Journal on Legislation* 573, 582 (1989).

33. *County of Allegheny v. American Civil Liberties Union,* 492 U.S. 573, 657–58 (1989) (Kennedy, J., concurring in part and dissenting in part).

34. For an essay expressing concern over this development, see Richard Brookhiser, "The Melting Pot Is Still Simmering," *Time,* 1 March 1993, 72.

35. Quoted in Brookhiser.

36. *Webster's New Collegiate Dictionary* (Springfield, Mass.: Merriam, 1975), s.v. "minority."

37. Charles Krauthammer, "Apocalypse, With and Without God," *Time,* 22 March 1993, 82.

38. Ralph Reed, "Christianity vs. Fanaticism," *Wall Street Journal,* 16 March 1993, A18.

39. "Interview with Nadine Strossen," *Rutherford,* December 1992, 9.

40. See *Roberts v. Madigan,* 921 F.2d 1047 (10th Cir. 1990), *cert. denied,* 60 U.S.L.W. 3878 (U.S. June 29, 1992).

41. *Lee v. Weisman,* 112 S. Ct. 2649, 2685 (1992) (Scalia, J., dissenting) (italics added).

42. Id. at 2656.

43. H. G. Wood, *Christianity and Civilization* (New York: Octagon, 1973), 2, quoting Sir Richard Livingstone in *The Future of Education,* 109.

44. Harold Berman, *The Interaction of Law and Religion* (New York: Abingdon, 1974), 21.

CHAPTER 9: The State of Modern Christianity

1. Michael Harrington, *The Politics at God's Funeral: The Spiritual Crisis of Western Civilization* (New York: Holt, Rinehart, Winston, 1983), 165. See generally, John W. Whitehead, *True Christianity* (Westchester, Ill.: Crossway, 1989).

2. Ibid.

3. George Gallup, Jr., and William Proctor, *Forecast 2000: George Gallup, Jr. Predicts the Future of America* (New York: William Morrow, 1984), 152.

4. Ibid., 153.

5. Richard Lovelace, *Dynamics of Spiritual Life: An Evangelical Theology of Renewal* (Downers Grove, Ill.: InterVarsity, 1979), 85.

6. Quoted in Malcolm Muggeridge, *Christ and the Media* (Grand Rapids: Eerdmans, 1977), 49.

7. C. S. Lewis, *God in the Dock: Essays on Theology and Ethics* (Grand Rapids: Eerdmans, 1971), 262.

8. Luke 15:1–2.
9. Luke 18:9–14.
10. Galatians 3:28.
11. John 17:15.
12. John R. W. Stott, *Christ the Controversialist* (Downers Grove, Ill.: InterVarsity, 1970), 183.
13. Ibid., 182.
14. Mark 13:32.
15. Stott, 188.
16. Erik Erikson, *Childhood and Society* (New York: Norton, 1963), 79–80.
17. Ephesians 6:12.
18. 2 Corinthians 10:4.
19. Neil Postman, *Amusing Ourselves to Death: Public Discourse in the Age of Show Business* (New York: Viking, 1985), 116–17.
20. Ibid., 118–19.
21. Ibid., 119–20.
22. Muggeridge, 60.
23. Ibid., 30.
24. Ibid., 23–42.
25. Postman, 123.
26. *National and International Religion Report* (14 December 1992), 3.
27. Ben Armstrong, *The Electronic Church* (Nashville: Thomas Nelson, 1979), 137.
28. Postman, 121.
29. Ibid., 117.
30. Ibid., 55–56.
31. Harry Blamires, *The Christian Mind* (Ann Arbor, Mich.: Servant, 1978), 3.
32. 1 Peter 4:17.

CHAPTER 10: The True God

1. Richard F. Lovelace, *Dynamics of Spiritual Life: An Evangelical Theology of Renewal* (Downers Grove, Ill.: InterVarsity, 1979), 85.
2. Romans 1:4.
3. Acts 13:33.
4. 1 Corinthians 15:14.
5. 1 Corinthians 15:45.
6. 1 Corinthians 15:47.
7. Revelation 1:5.
8. Malcolm Muggeridge, *Christ and the Media* (Grand Rapids: Eerdmans, 1977), 71.
9. 1 Corinthians 13:12.
10. Ephesians 6:12.
11. John 8:32.
12. Galatians 2:20.
13. Galatians 2:20.
14. Galatians 5:22–23.
15. Matthew 4:3.
16. See Fyodor Dostoyevsky, *The Brothers Karamazov* (New York: Bantam, 1970), 297–319.
17. Matthew 4:4.

18. Galatians 5:13–14.
19. Matthew 11:19.
20. Matthew 18:20.
21. See 1 Corinthians 12:13; also see Ephesians 4:1–16.
22. Romans 16:5.
23. Acts 20:7; 1 Corinthians 16:2.
24. Acts 6:1–6.
25. 1 Timothy 3:1–13; Titus 1:5–9.
26. See Acts 15.
27. See Francis A. Schaeffer, *The Church at the End of the Twentieth Century* (Westchester, Ill.: Crossway, 1985), 63–67.
28. 1 Timothy 3:15.
29. Acts 21:39.

CHAPTER 11: The Christian Mentality

1. John R. W. Stott, *Christ the Controversialist* (Downers Grove, Ill.: InterVarsity, 1970), 13–14.
2. Matthew 21:12–13.
3. Mark 11:16.
4. Matthew 28:18–20.
5. Stott, 18.
6. Acts 17:5.
7. Acts 17:6 (KJV).
8. Mark 11:18 (italics added).
9. Acts 17:16–21.
10. Acts 17:28.
11. Matthew 22:37.
12. John 14:15.
13. Matthew 22:39.
14. Matthew 5:13.
15. Matthew 5:14–16.
16. See *Webster's New Collegiate Dictionary* (Springfield, Mass.: Merriam, 1975), s.v. "radical."
17. William Barclay, *The Ten Commandments for Today* (Grand Rapids: Eerdmans, 1973), 9.
18. Ibid.
19. Joshua 2:11.
20. 1 Kings 2:28, 34.
21. Brother Andrew, *The Ethics of Smuggling* (Wheaton, Ill.: Tyndale, 1975), 18.

CHAPTER 12: The Political Question

1. See *Webster's New Collegiate Dictionary* (Springfield, Mass.: Merriam, 1975), s.v. "activism."
2. Romans 1:18 (KJV).
3. As quoted in John W. Whitehead, *The Second American Revolution* (Westchester, Ill.: Crossway, 1982), 164.
4. John 18:36.

5. Matthew 19:19.

6. For example, Rev. Pat Robertson, widely believed to be gearing up for a 1996 Presidential campaign, was shown on the 4 November 1993 issue of Ted Koppel's "Nightline" on ABC as saying:

> As a religious leader, as a teacher of the Bible, I would say, "Here's what the Bible says: Life begins at conception, life is precious, life is made in the image of God and the taking of life is wrong." And I would urge people, as a matter of *private choice,* not to choose abortion, because I think it's wrong. It's something else, though, in the *political arena,* to go out on a quixotic crusade when you know you will be beaten continuously. So I say let's do what is possible. [Italics added]

7. Luke 4:18.

8. See generally John W. Whitehead, *An American Dream* (Westchester, Ill.: Crossway, 1987).

CHAPTER 13: Cautious Radicalism and Civil Disobedience

1. See John W. Whitehead, *The Second American Revolution* (Westchester, Ill.: Crossway, 1982), 145–60.

2. As quoted in Alan Bullock, *Hitler: A Study in Tyranny* (New York: Harper & Row, 1962), 389–90.

3. See generally Whitehead, "Avoiding Religious Apartheid: Affording Equal Treatment for Student-Initiated Religious Expression in Public Schools," 16 *Pepperdine Law Review* 229 (1989).

4. See generally Whitehead, "Civil Disobedience and Operation Rescue: A Historical and Theoretical Analysis," 48 *Washington and Lee Law Review* 77 (1991).

5. Glenn Tinder, "Can We Be Good Without God?" *Atlantic Monthly,* December 1989, 83. See also Glenn Tinder, *The Political Meaning of Christianity* (Baton Rouge: Louisiana State Univ. Press, 1989).

6. Ibid., 84.

7. Ibid.

8. Ibid., 85.

9. Ibid., 82.

10. Francis A. Schaeffer, *A Christian Manifesto* (Westchester, Ill.: Crossway, 1981), 92.

11. See Whitehead, *The Second American Revolution,* 148–52.

12. Romans 13:4.

13. Mark 10:43.

14. 1 Timothy 4:6.

15. 1 Thessalonians 3:2 (KJV).

16. Ephesians 6:21.

17. Romans 13:6.

18. Romans 13:1.

19. 1 Timothy 2:1–4.

20. Whitehead, *The Second American Revolution,* 151.

21. Schaeffer, 93.

22. Alan F. Johnson, *The Freedom Letter* (Chicago: Moody, 1974), 196.

23. John 18:18–23.

24. Luke 13:32.

25. John 2:13–17.

26. Acts 23:1–5.

27. Acts 5:29.

28. Acts 5:42.

29. Acts 17:6 (KJV).

30. Johnson, 195.

31. J. S. Conway, *The Nazi Persecution of the Churches: 1933–45* (New York: Basic, 1968), 335.

32. As quoted in Peter Matheson, *The Third Reich and the Christian Churches* (Grand Rapids: Eerdmans, 1981), 26–27 (italics added).

33. Conway, 336.

34. As quoted in William Barclay, *The Ten Commandments for Today* (Grand Rapids: Eerdmans, 1973), 94.

CHAPTER 14: Pro-Life Strategies

1. See generally John W. Whitehead, *A Pro-Life Manifesto: Strategy on the Abortion Issue* (Charlottesville, Va.: Rutherford Institute, 1993).

2. *Casey v. Planned Parenthood,* 112 S.Ct. 932 (1992).

3. Doug Johnson, National Right to Life, telephone interview September 17, 1992.

4. Lisa Belkin, "Pro-Life vs. Pro-Choice: Buffalo Stampede," *Elle,* August 1992, 92.

5. Ibid., 96.

6. Michael Ebert, "What's Next for Operation Rescue?" *Citizen,* 21 September 1992, 10.

7. Ibid.

8. John Leo, "Not the Way to Stop Abortions," *U.S. News & World Report,* 29 March 1993, 17.

9. Ibid.

10. Ibid.

11. Ibid.

12. As reported in "Abortion Bias Seeps into News Media," *Citizen,* 15 October 1990, 10.

13. Ibid.

14. Ibid., 11.

15. Ibid.

16. Ibid.

17. Leo, 17.

18. See generally *Major Articles and Books Concerning the Detrimental Effects of Abortion* (Charlottesville, Va.: Rutherford Institute, 1990).

19. Ibid.

20. Ibid.

21. See, for example, *National Organization of Women v. Operation Rescue,* 726 F. Supp. 1483 (E.D. Va. 1989), *aff'd,* 914 F.2d 582 (4th Cir. 1990), *cert. granted. sub. nom. Bray v. Alexandria Clinic,* 1991 US LEXIS 1147, case restored to calendar for reargument 112 S.Ct. 2935; *Town of West Hartford v. Operation Rescue,* 726 F. Supp. 371 (D. Conn. 1989), *vacated,* 915 F.2d 92 (2d Cir. 1990); *Cousins v. Terry,* 721 F. Supp. 426 (N.D. N.Y. 1989).

22. See Randy Frame, "Time to Face the Consequences," *Christianity Today,* 10 September 1990, 48–51.

23. See "Abortion Clinic Worker Goes Long Way for Turkey Sandwich," *Rutherford,* December 1992, 4.

24. Ibid.

CHAPTER 15: The Family and the Human Element

1. See Ephesians 5:22–6:4.

2. 1 Timothy 5:8.

3. Ephesians 5:25.

4. Ephesians 5:28.

5. Urie Bronfenbrenner, "The Roots of Alienation," *Influences on Human Development,* Urie Bronfenbrenner, ed. (Hinsdale, Ill.: Dryden, 1975), 664.

6. Ibid.

7. Pete Hamill, "Crack and the Box," *Esquire,* May 1990, 64.

8. Ibid.

9. Ibid.

10. Ibid.

11. Malcolm Muggeridge, *Christ and the Media* (Grand Rapids: Eerdmans, 1977), 82.

12. Hamill, 65 (italics in original).

13. Malachi 4:6.

CHAPTER 16: The Bloody Face of History

1. Matthew 22:35–40.

2. John 13:34–35.

3. Francis A. Schaeffer, *The Complete Works of Francis A. Schaeffer,* vol. 4 (Westchester, Ill.: Crossway, 1982), 187.

4. Ibid., 187–88.

5. C. S. Lewis, *Mere Christianity* (New York: Macmillan, 1943), 81–82.

6. Romans 15:1.

7. Os Guinness, *The Dust of Death* (Downers Grove, Ill.: InterVarsity, 1973), 187.

8. John 15:18–19.

9. John 16:33.

10. Hebrews 2:10.

11. Acts 14:22.

12. 1 Peter 3:14.

13. Matthew 5:12.

14. 1 Corinthians 9:24.

15. Matthew 11:28–29; Hebrews 4:9.

16. Guinness, 391.

17. Quoted in Guinness, 364. For a different translation of this particular statement, see Albert Camus, *Resistance, Rebellion and Death,* trans. Justin O'Brien (New York: Knopf, 1961), 71–72.

18. Isaiah 6:8.

SELECT BIBLIOGRAPHY

"Abortion Bias Seeps into News Media." *Citizen,* 15 October 1990.

"Abortion Clinic Worker Goes Long Way for Turkey Sandwich." *Rutherford,* December 1992.

"Abortion TV Ads Catch on in Campaigns, Candidate Gets Graphic Images Past Censors." *Washington Post,* 20 July 1992.

Adler, Jerry. "Taking Offense." *Newsweek,* 24 December 1990.

Ali, Shaista-Parveen. Comment, "Homosexual Parenting: Child Custody and Adoption." 22 *University of California at Davis Law Review* 1009 (Spring 1989).

American Law Reports. "Visitation Rights of Homosexual or Lesbian Parent." 36 A.L.R. 4th 997 (1985 and Supp. 1992).

———. "Marriage Between Persons of the Same Sex." 63 A.L.R. 3d 1199 (1975 & Supp. 1992).

———. "Initial Award or Denial of Child Custody to Homosexual or Lesbian Parent." 6 A.L.R. 4th 1297 (1981 and Supp. 1992).

———. "Visitation Rights." 36 A.L.R. 4th 997 (1985 and Supp. 1992).

Anderson. "Political Correctness on College Campus: Freedom of Speech v. Doing the Politically Correct Thing." 46 *Southern Methodist University Law Review* 171 (1992).

Anderson, Kurt. "Big Mouths." *Time,* 1 November 1993.

Andrew, Brother. *The Ethics of Smuggling.* Wheaton, Ill.: Tyndale, 1975.

Anthony, Susan B. "Women's Right to Vote." In *The American Reader: Words That Moved a Nation,* edited by Diane Ravitch. San Francisco: Harper Collins, 1991.

"Are There No Limits?" *National Right to Life News,* 23 February 1993.

Arendt, Hannah. *On Revolution.* New York: Viking, 1965.

Aristotle. *Politics.* Cambridge: Harvard Univ. Press, 1932.

Armstrong, Ben. *The Electronic Church.* Nashville: Thomas Nelson, 1979.

Augustine, St. *The City of God.* 413–26. 2 vols. New York: Dutton, 1945.

Baer, Richard A., Jr. "The High Court's 'S' Word." *Christianity Today,* 8 September 1989.

Bailyn, Bernard, David Brian Davis, David Herbert Donald, John L. Thomas, Robert H. Wiebe, and Gordon S. Wood. *The Great Republic: A History of the American People.* Boston: Little, Brown, 1977.

Bainton, Roland. *The Travail of Religious Liberty.* Hamden, Conn.: Shoe String, 1971.

Barber, Noel. *Seven Days of Freedom: The Hungarian Uprising 1956.* New York: Stein & Day, 1974.

Barclay, William. *The Ten Commandments for Today.* Grand Rapids: Eerdmans, 1973.

Barth, Karl. *The Epistle to the Romans* (1919). New York: Oxford Univ. Press, 1933.

Belkin, Lisa. "Pro-Life vs. Pro-Choice: Buffalo Stampede." *Elle,* August 1992.

Berke, Joseph H. *The Tyranny of Malice: Exploring the Dark Side of Character and Culture.* New York: Summit, 1988.

Berman, Harold. *The Interaction of Law and Religion.* New York: Abingdon, 1974.

Blamires, Harry. *The Christian Mind.* Ann Arbor, Mich.: Servant, 1978.

Blanshard, Paul. "Three Cheers for Our Secular State." *The Humanist,* March/April 1976.

Bolt, Robert. *A Man for All Seasons.* New York: Vintage, 1960.

Book Review. "From Equal Opportunity to Affirmative Action—A Leap of Policy." 70 *Texas Law Review* 1525 (1992).

Boorstin, Daniel. *Image; or, What Happened to the American Dream.* New York: Atheneum, 1962.

Borisov, Vadim. "Personality and National Awareness." In Alexander Solzenitsyn et al., *From Under the Rubble.* Boston: Little, Brown, 1975.

Bork, Robert H. *The Tempting of America: The Political Seduction of the Law.* New York: Free, 1990.

Boston, Rob. "The 'Christian Nation' Debate." *Church & State,* January 1993.

Bradbury, Ray. *Fahrenheit 451.* New York: Ballantine, 1979.

Bredemeier, Havy C. and Richard M. Stephenson. *The Analysis of Social Systems.* New York: Holt, Rinehart & Winston, 1962.

Bridenbaugh, Carl. *Mitre and Sceptre: Transatlantic Faiths, Ideas, Personalities and Politics 1689–1775.* New York: Oxford Univ. Press, 1962.

Briggs, Ed. "Only 1 in 10 Held Deeply Committed." *Richmond Times-Dispatch,* 27 November 1982.

Broadus, Joseph E., and William B. Rubenstein. "Don't Ask, Don't Tell." *American Bar Association Journal,* October 1993.

Bronfenbrenner, Urie. "Socialization and Social Class Through Time and Space." *Reading in Social Psychology.* New York: Holt, Rinehart & Winston, 1958.

———. "The Roots of Alienation." *Influences on Human Development.* Hinsdale, Ill.: Dryden, 1975.

_____. *Two Worlds of Childhood: U.S. and U.S.S.R.* New York: Russell Sage Foundation, 1970.

Brookhiser, Richard. "The Melting Pot Is Still Simmering." *Time,* 1 March 1993.

_____. "The Cultural Right Is Here to Stay." *Time,* 31 May 1993.

_____. "We Can All Share American Culture." *Time,* 31 August 1992.

Bullock, Alan. *Hitler: A Study in Tyranny.* Rev. ed. New York: Harper & Row, 1962.

Burgess, Anthony. *A Clockwork Orange.* New York: Norton, 1963.

Burr, Chandler. "Homosexuality and Biology." *The Atlantic Monthly,* March 1993.

Bush, Barbara. Address to Wellesley, May 1992.

Byrne, J. "Anti-Parent Charter Worry." 22 *Australian Association for Adolescent Health Newsletter* (1990).

Calabresi, Guido. *Ideals, Beliefs, Attitudes and the Law: Private Law Perspectives on a Public Law Problem.* Syracuse, N.Y.: Syracuse Univ. Press, 1985.

Calvin, John. *The Institutes of the Christian Religion.* 2 vols. 1536–59. Reprint. Philadelphia: Westminster, 1960.

Camus, Albert. *Resistance, Rebellion and Death.* Translated by J. O'Brien. New York: Knopf, 1961.

_____. *The Rebel.* Translated by Anthony Bower. New York: Knopf, 1969.

Carlson, Allan. "Uncle Sam's Child." *Chronicles,* January 1993.

Carter, Stephen L. *The Culture of Disbelief.* New York: Basic, 1993.

Cauchon, Dennis. "Debate Over Competing Principles." *USA Today,* 31 March 1993.

Chadwick, Bruce A. and Tim B. Heaton, eds. *Statistical Handbook on the American Family.* Phoenix: Oryx, 1992.

"Challenges, 'Executive Disorders.'" *Life Insight.* NCCB Secretariat for Prolife Activities, February 1993.

Chandler, Walter M. *The Trial of Jesus.* Vol. 1. Atlanta: Harrison, 1972.

Chavez, Linda. "Homosexuality and the Moral Order." *First Things,* April 1993.

Chesterton, G. K. *Collected Works.* Vol. 1, *Heretics, Orthodoxy, and Blatchford Controversies.* San Francisco: Ignatius, 1986.

"Children in Crisis." *American Bar Association Journal,* October 1993.

Christensen, Mike, and Bob Dart. "Gay Advisor to Clinton Assails Nunn as 'Bigot.'" *Atlanta Journal and Constitution,* 27 March 1993.

Clark, Kenneth. *Civilisation: A Personal View.* New York: Harper & Row, 1969.

Clinton, Hillary Rodham. "Children Under the Law." 43 *Harvard Educational Review* 487 (November 1973).

Cohen, Carl. *Civil Disobedience: Conscience, Tactics and the Law.* New York: Columbia Univ. Press, 1971.

Cohn, Bob. "Discrimination: The Limits of the Law." *Newsweek,* 14 September 1992.

_____. "From Chattel to Full Citizens." *Newsweek,* 21 September 1993.

Coleman, James. *The Adolescent Society.* New York: Free Press of Glencoe, 1961.

Collier, James Lincoln. *The Rise of Selfishness in America.* New York: Oxford Univ. Press, 1991.

Colson, Chuck. "Can We Be Good Without God?" *Imprimis,* April 1993.

———. *Kingdoms in Conflict.* New York and Grand Rapids: William Morrow and Zondervan, 1987.

Commager, Henry Steele. *The Empire of Reason.* Garden City, N.Y.: Anchor Press-Doubleday, 1977.

"Committee Recommends House Reprimand Two for Sexual Misconduct." *Washington Post,* 15 July 1983.

"Connections." *AT&T Newsletter* (1993).

"Convention on the Rights of the Child." G.A. Res. 44/25, U.N. GAOR Annex, U.N. Doc. A/44/736 (1989), reprinted in 28 *International Legal Materials* 1456 (1989).

Conway, J. S. *The Nazi Persecution of the Churches: 1933–45.* New York: Basic, 1968.

Coontz, Stephanie. *The Way We Never Were.* New York: Basic, 1992.

Cox, Harvey. *Religion in the Secular City: Toward a Postmodern Theology.* New York: Simon & Schuster, 1984.

———. *The Secular City: Secularization and Urbanization in Theological Perspective.* New York: Macmillan, 1965.

———. *The Seduction of the Spirit.* New York: Simon & Schuster, 1973.

Crick, Francis. *Of Molecules and Men.* Seattle: Univ. of Washington Press, 1967.

Darwin, Charles. *Autobiography and Selected Letters.* 1892. Edited by Francis Darwin. New York: Dover, 1958.

———. *The Descent of Man, and Selection in Relation to Sex.* London: John Murray, 1871.

———. *The Illustrated Origin of Species.* New York: Hill & Wang, 1979.

———. *The Origin of Species by Means of Natural Selection, or the Preservation of Favoured Races in the Struggle for Life.* New York: D. Appleton, 1872.

———. *The Origin of Species by Means of Natural Selection, or the Preservation of Favoured Races in the Struggle for Life: A Variorum Text.* Edited by Morse Peckham. Philadelphia: Univ. of Pennsylvania Press, 1959.

Dennis, James S. *Christian Missions and Social Progress.* Old Tappan, N.J.: Revell, 1909.

Dewey, John. *A Common Faith.* New Haven: Yale Univ. Press, 1934.

"Divorce, Clinton-Style." *National Review,* 19 October 1992.

Dobson, James. "Are You There?" *Citizen* 6, no. 9 (21 September 1992), V-1.

"Doctor Recalls Starved Boy." *Dallas Texas Morning News,* 8 August 1992.

Dorros, Karen, and Patricia Dorsey. "Whose Rights Are We Protecting Anyway?" *Children Today,* May-June 1989.

Dostoyevsky, Fyodor. *The Brothers Karamazov.* 1879–80. Translated by Andrew MacAndrew. New York: Bantam, 1970.

Drakeman, Donald L. *Church-State Constitutional Issues.* New York: Greenwood, 1991.

Dromm, Daniel P. "America Needs This Curriculum." *The American Teacher* (The American Federation of Teachers), February 1993.

Dunlap. "The Lesbian and Gay Marriage Debate: A Microcosm of Our Hopes and Troubles in the Nineties." 1 *Law and Sexuality: Review Lesbian and Gay Legal Issues* 63 (1991).

Dunn, Robert. "Why Levi Strauss & Co. Stopped Funding the Boy Scouts." *Washington Times,* 28 August 1992.

Durant, Will. *The Story of Philosophy.* New York: Simon & Schuster, 1961.

Durant, Will and Ariel. *The Age of Faith.* New York: Simon & Schuster, 1950.

_____. *The Age of Napoleon: A History of European Civilization from 1789 to 1815.* New York: Simon & Schuster, 1975.

_____. *The Age of Reason Begins.* New York: Simon & Schuster, 1961.

_____. *The Lessons of History.* New York: Simon & Schuster, 1968.

_____. *The Life of Greece.* New York: Simon & Schuster, 1939.

_____. *The Story of Civilization.* 11 vols. New York: Simon & Schuster, 1954–75.

Ebert, Michael. "Pedophilia Steps into the Daylight." *Citizen,* 16 November 1992.

_____. "What's Next for Operation Rescue?" *Citizen,* 21 September 1992.

Einstein, Albert. "Why Do They Hate the Jews?" *Ideas and Opinions.* New York: Crown, 1954.

Ellul, Jacques. *The Meaning of the City.* Grand Rapids.: Eerdmans, 1970.

_____. *The Political Illusion.* New York: Vintage, 1972.

_____. *The Technological Society.* New York: Vintage, 1964.

_____. *The Theological Foundation of Law.* New York: Seabury, 1969.

Elmer-Dewitt, Philip. "Cloning: Where Do We Draw the Line?" *Time,* 8 November 1993.

_____. "Cyberpunk!" *Time,* 8 February 1993.

Ely, John H. "The Wages of Crying Wolf: A Comment on *Roe v. Wade.*" *Yale Law Journal* 82 (1973): 920.

Erikson, Erik. *Childhood and Society.* New York: Norton, 1963.

Erlich, Paul. *The Population Bomb.* New York: Ballantine, 1968.

"Expendable Lives." *First Things,* October 1993.

Farrell, John A. "Conservative Accuses Studds of Censorship." *Boston Globe,* 7 February 1993.

Farrell, Warren. *The Myth of Male Power: Why Men Are the Disposable Sex.* New York: Simon & Schuster, 1993.

FCC Mass Media Bureau Letter Ruling of August 21, 1992.

Fishwick, Marshall, and Ray B. Browne, eds. *The God Pumpers: Religion in the Electronic Age.* Bowling Green, Ohio: Bowling Green State Univ. Popular Press, 1987.

Fleming, Thomas. "Cultural Revolutions." *Chronicles,* January 1993.

———. "Puppets and Their Masters." *Chronicles,* October 1993.

Forkosch, Morris D. "Religion, Education, and the Constitution—A Middle Way." 23 *Loyola Law Review* 617 (1977).

Frame, Randy. "Time to Face the Consequences." *Christianity Today,* 10 September 1990.

Francis, Samuel. "Gay Activists Are Silencing Their Critics." *Human Events,* 12 December 1992.

Freed, Curt R., M.D. "Survival of Implanted Fetal Dopamine Cells and Neurologic Improvement 12 to 46 Months After Transplantation for Parkinson's Disease." *The New England Journal of Medicine* 327, no. 22 (26 November 1992).

Freedom of Choice Act, 1993 S. 25 and 1993 H.R. 25, §2(b).

Frend, W. H. C. *The Rise of Christianity.* Philadelphia: Fortress, 1984.

Freud, Sigmund. *Civilization and Its Discontents.* 1930. New York: Doubleday, 1958.

———. *The Future of an Illusion.* 1927. Garden City, N.Y.: Anchor, 1964.

———. *Moses and Monotheism.* 1939. New York: Knopf, 1949.

Friedan, Betty. *It Changed My Life.* New York: Random, 1976.

Galbraith, John Kenneth. *The Affluent Society.* Boston: Houghton Mifflin, 1958.

———. *The Age of Uncertainty.* Boston: Houghton Mifflin, 1977.

Galbraith, John Kenneth, and M. S. Randhawa. *The New Industrial State.* Boston: Houghton Mifflin, 1967.

Gallup, George, Jr., and William Proctor. *Forecast 2000: George Gallup, Jr. Predicts the Future of America.* New York: Morrow, 1984.

Gardner, Richard A. "Modern Witch Hunt—Child Abuse Charges." *Wall Street Journal,* 22 February 1993.

Gay, Peter, ed. *The Enlightenment.* New York: Simon & Schuster, 1973.

Geraci, Joseph, and Donald Mader. "Interview: John Money." *Paidika: The Journal of Paedophilia,* Spring 1991.

Gibbon, Edward. *The Decline and Fall of the Roman Empire.* 6 vols. 1776–88. Reprint. New York: Dutton, 1910.

Gilder, George. *Naked Nomads.* New York: Quadrangle-New York Times, 1974.

———. *Sexual Suicide.* New York: Quadrangle-New York Times, 1973.

———. *Wealth and Poverty.* New York: Basic, 1981.

Ginsburg, Faye. *Contested Lives: The Abortion Debate in an American Community.* Berkeley: Univ. of California Press, 1989.

Glamser, Deeann. "Gay Rights Debate Enters the Classroom." *USA Today,* 18 May 1993.

Glasow, Richard D. "D & X Kills Late-Term Unborn Babies By Sucking Out Brains." *National Right to Life News,* 23 February 1993.

Glendon, Mary Ann. *Abortion and Divorce in Western Law.* Cambridge, Mass.: Harvard Univ. Press, 1987.

Goldman, Lucien. *Le Dieu Cache.* Paris: Gallimard, 1955.

Goldstein, Clifford. "The New Christian Right: Strategy for the Nineties." *Liberty,* March/April 1993.

Gomulka, Eugene T. "Homosexuality in Uniform: Is It Time?" *First Things,* February 1993.

Goodavage, Maria. "Boy Scouts: No Gays Despite Bans at Schools." *USA Today,* 17 September 1991.

Gorman, Christine. "When AIDS Strikes Parents." *Time,* 1 November 1993.

Gottlieb, Scott. "A Mockery of Justice on Campus." *Wall Street Journal,* 27 September 1993.

Gould, Stephen Jay. *The Mismeasure of Man.* New York: Norton, 1981.

Grant, George. *Third Time Around.* Brentwood, Tenn.: Wolgemuth & Hyatt, 1991.

Grant, Michael. *History of Rome.* New York: Scribner, 1978.

Greer, Germaine. *Sex and Destiny.* New York: Harper & Row, 1984.

Grimal, Pierre. *The Civilization of Rome.* New York: Simon & Schuster, 1963.

Gross, Bertram. *Friendly Fascism: The New Face of Power in America.* New York: Evans, 1980.

Guinness, Os. *The Dust of Death.* Downers Grove, Ill.: InterVarsity, 1973.

Halberstam, David. *The Fifties.* New York: Villard, 1993.

Hall, Edward T. *The Hidden Dimension.* Garden City, N.Y.: Anchor, 1969.

Hall, Thomas Cuming. *The Religious Background of American Culture.* Boston: Little, Brown, 1930.

Hamill, Pete. "Crack and the Box," *Esquire,* May 1990.

Hammarberg, T. "The U.N. Convention on the Rights of the Child—And How to Make It Work." 12 *Human Rights Quarterly* 97 (1990).

Handy, Thomas T. *Undermined Establishment: Church-State Relations in America, 1880–1920.* Princeton, N.J.: Princeton Univ. Press, 1991.

Hanson, Mark. "Boy Wants 'Divorce' From Parents." 78 *ABA Journal* 24(1) (July 1992).

Harrington, Michael. *The Politics at God's Funeral: The Spiritual Crisis of Western Civilization.* New York: Holt, Rinehart & Winston, 1983.

Harvard Law Review Association. "Developments in the Law: Sexual Orientation and the Law." 102 *Harvard Law Review* 1508 (1989).

Harvey, Debra. "Note, *Zbaraz v. Hartigan:* Mandatory Twenty-Four Hour Waiting Period After Parental Notification Unconstitutionally Burdens A Minor's Abortion Decision." 19 *John Marshall Law Review* 1071 (1986).

Hax, Carolyn. "No Birth, No Pangs." *The Washington Post,* 21 March 1993, C1.

Haynes, Christine. "Taking America Back." *Chronicles,* January 1993.

Hegel, George W. F. *The Logic of Hegel.* New York: Oxford Univ. Press, 1892.

———. *Philosophy of Right.* New York: Oxford Univ. Press, 1962.

Heidegger, Martin. *Being and Time.* New York: Harper & Row, 1962.

Heimert, Alan, and Perry Miller, eds. *The Great Awakening.* Indianapolis: Bobbs-Merrill, 1967.

_____. *The Question of Being.* Boston: Twayne, 1958.

Henry, William A. III. "Born Gay?" *Time,* 26 July 1993, 36.

_____. "Gay Parents: Under Fire and on the Rise." *Time,* 20 September 1993.

_____. "Upside Down in the Groves of Academe." *Time,* 1 April 1991.

Hentoff, Nat. "Gregorian's Chant." *Washington Post,* 13 April 1991.

Hess-Mahan, Theodore M. "Human Fetal Tissue Transplantation Research: Entering a Brave New World." 23 *Suffolk University Law Review* 789 (1989).

Hewitt, Bill and Meg Grant. "The Home of His Choice." *People,* 12 October 1992.

Hill, Christopher. *The Century of Revolution 1703–1714.* New York: Nelson, 1961.

Hillerbrand, Hans J. *The Protestant Reformation.* New York: Walker, 1968.

Hitchcock, James. *What Is Secular Humanism?* Ann Arbor, Mich.: Servant, 1982.

Hitler, Adolf. *Mein Kampf.* 1925. New York: Houghton, Mifflin, 1971.

Hittinger, Russell. "What Really Happened in the *Casey* Decision?" *Crises,* September 1992.

_____. "When the Court Should Not Be Obeyed." *First Things,* October 1993.

Hoar, William P. "Emasculating the Military: The Legalized Homosexuality Edict." *The New American,* 8 March 1993.

"Homosexuals Make Babies." *Christian American,* February 1993.

Hopkins, Ellen. "Abusing the Rights of Parents." *Newsweek,* 18 October 1993.

Horowitz, Robert, J.D. (Associate Director, National Legal Resource Center for Child Advocacy and Protection, American Bar Association). "Tighten Standards for Termination of Parental Rights." *Children Today,* May-June 1989.

Hudson, Winthrop S. *Religion in America.* 4th ed. New York: Macmillan, 1987.

Hughes, Robert. *Culture of Complaint: The Fraying of America.* New York: Oxford Univ. Press, 1993.

Hunter, James Davison. *Culture Wars: The Struggle to Define America.* New York: Basic, 1992.

Hunter, Nan D. *The Rights of Lesbians and Gay Men.* Carbondale, Ill.: Southern Illinois Univ. Press, 1992.

Huntford, Roland. *The New Totalitarians.* New York: Stein & Day, 1972.

Hurlock, Elizabeth. *Child Development.* New York: McGraw-Hill, 1942.

Hurwitz, Howard L. "It Undermines Traditional Family Values." *The American Teacher* (American Federation of Teachers), February 1993.

Huxley, Aldous. *Brave New World.* 1939. New York: Bantam Books, 1968.

_____. *The Doors of Perception.* New York: Harper & Row, 1954.

_____. *Heaven and Hell.* New York: Harper & Row, 1956.

_____. *Science, Liberty, and Peace.* New York: Harper & Row, 1946.

Hyde, Douglas. *Dedication and Leadership*. Notre Dame, Ind.: Univ. of Notre Dame Press, 1966.

Hyde and Fishman. "The Collegiate Speech Protection Act of 1991: A Response to the New Intolerance in the Academy." 37 *Wayne Law Review* 1469 (1991).

"Index of Leading Cultural Indicators." *Time*, 29 March 1993.

Israeloff, Roberta. "Happy Families Are Not All Alike." *Parents*, March 1993.

Jaspers, Karl. *Man in the Modern Age*. New York: Doubleday, 1957.

———. *The Enchanted Loom: Mind in the Universe*. New York: Simon & Schuster, 1981.

———. *God and the Astronomers*. New York: Norton, 1978.

———. *Until the Sun Dies*. New York: Norton, 1977.

Johnson, Alan F. *The Freedom Letter*. Chicago: Moody, 1974.

Johnson, Ophelia D. "Parents Feel Besieged by Suspicions." *Richmond Times-Dispatch*, 3 May 1992.

Johnson, Paul. *A History of Christianity*. New York: Atheneum, 1976.

———. *Modern Times: The World from the Twenties to the Eighties*. New York: Harper & Row, 1983.

Jordan, Mary. "College Repeals Speech Code." *Washington Post*, 12 September 1993.

Kant, Immanuel. *Critique of Pure Reason*. 1781. Reprint. New York: Wiley, 1943.

———. *Gesammelte Schliften*. Berlin: George Reiner, 1911.

Kaplan, Justin. "How God Made It onto Religiously Neutral American Money." *Los Angeles Daily Journal*, 9 October 1992.

Katz, Nancie L. "Massachusetts Urges Sensitivity to Gay Kids." *Dallas Morning News*, 13 July 1993.

Key, Wilson Bryan. *The Age of Manipulation: The Con in Confidence, The Sin in Sincere*. Lanham, Md.: Madison, 1989.

Kimbrell, Andrew. *The Human Body Shop: The Engineering and Marketing of Life*. San Francisco: Harper, 1993.

Kirby, Douglas. "The Effect of School-Based Health Clinics in St. Paul on School-Wide Birthrates." *Family Planning Perspectives*, January/February 1993.

Knight, Robert H. "Video 'On Being Gay' Twists the Facts." *Insight*, July 1993.

Knight-Ridder. "Free Speech Ruling on Abortion Protest Seen Bound for Supreme Court." *Washington Post*, 24 October 1993.

Koch, H. W. *Hitler Youth: The Duped Generation*. New York: Ballantine, 1972.

"Kodak Gives Special Recognition to Homosexuals." *Journal of the American Family Association*, April 1993.

Koestler, Arthur. *Darkness at Noon*. New York: Bantam, 1968.

———. *The Ghost in the Machine*. New York: Macmillan, 1968.

Kramer, Michael. "Pulling the Plug." *Time*, 4 October 1993.

Krauthammer, Charles. "Apocalypse, With and Without God." *Time,* 22 March 1993.

———. "How Conservatism Can Come Back." *Time,* 18 January 1993.

Kung, Hans. *On Being a Christian.* Garden City, N.Y.: Doubleday, 1976.

Kurtz, Howard. "Gay Journalists 'Asserting Themselves in the Media.'" *Washington Post,* 12 September 1993.

Lader, Lawrence. *Abortion II: Making the Revolution.* Boston: Beacon, 1973.

Lancaster, John. "Clinton and the Military: Is Gay Policy Just the Opening Skirmish?" *Washington Post,* 1 February 1993.

Lapping, Brian. *Apartheid: A History.* London: Paladin, 1987.

Lasch, Christopher. *The Culture of Narcissism: American Life in an Age of Diminishing Expectations.* New York: Warner, 1979.

Lawrence. "If He Hollers Let Him Go: Regulating Racist Speech on Campus." *Duke Law Journal* 431 (1990).

"LeAGUE Chapter Formed at WPD-Clemson" (1993).

Leder, Lawrence H., ed. *The Meaning of the American Revolution.* Chicago: Quadrangle, 1969.

"Legisletter." American Life League, Inc., Winter 1993.

Leo, John. "Not the Way to Stop Abortions." *U.S. News & World Report,* 29 March 1993.

———. "Pedophiles in the Schools." *U.S. News & World Report,* 11 October 1993.

Levy, Leonard W. *Blasphemy: Verbal Offense Against the Sacred from Moses to Salman Rushdie.* New York: Knopf, 1993.

Lewis, C. S. *God in the Dock: Essays on Theology and Ethics.* Grand Rapids.: Eerdmans, 1971.

———. *Mere Christianity.* New York: Macmillan, 1943.

———. *Miracles.* New York: Macmillan, 1947.

———. *The Abolition of Man.* New York: Macmillan, 1947.

———. *The Discarded Image.* New York: Cambridge Univ. Press, 1964.

———. *The Great Divorce.* New York: Macmillan, 1946.

———. "The Humanitarian Theory of Punishment." In *God in the Dock.* Grand Rapids.: Eerdmans, 1971.

———. *The Problem of Pain.* New York: Macmillan, 1962.

———. *The Screwtape Letters.* New York: Macmillan, 1959.

Livingston, Derek Charles. "A Look Beyond the Inaugural." *March on Washington for Lesbian, Gay & Bi Equal Rights and Liberation.* Newspaper Project of the Committee for the March on Washington, Inc. (February 1993).

Locke, John. *Essay Concerning Human Understanding.* 1690. Reprint. Gloucester, Mass.: Peter Smith, 1973.

———. *On the Reasonableness of Christianity.* 1695. Reprint. Chicago: Henry Regnery, 1965.

Loftus, Elizabeth F., and Laura A. Rosenwald. "Buried Memories, Shattered Lives." *American Bar Association Journal,* November 1993.

Logue, Barbara J. *Last Rights.* New York: Maxwell Macmillan International, 1993.

Lovelace, Richard F. *Dynamics of Spiritual Life: An Evangelical Theology of Renewal.* Downers Grove, Ill.: InterVarsity, 1979.

Luker, Kristin. *Abortion and the Politics of Motherhood.* Berkeley: Univ. of California Press, 1984.

Luther, Martin. *Ninety-Five Theses.* 1517. Philadelphia: Fortress, 1957.

———. *Works of Martin Luther.* 6 vols. Grand Rapids: Baker, 1982.

Machen, J. Gresham. *The Christian Faith in the Modern World.* Grand Rapids: Eerdmans, 1965.

———. *The Origin of Paul's Religion.* Grand Rapids: Eerdmans, 1925.

Magnuson, Roger J. *Are Gay Rights Right? Making Sense of the Controversy.* Sisters, Ore.: Multnomah, 1990.

Mamet, David. *Writing in Restaurants.* New York: Viking, 1986.

"Mandatory Parental Consent to Abortion." *Journal of the American Medical Association* 269, no. 1 (6 January 1993).

Mangrum, R. Collin. "Religious Constraints During Visitation: Under What Circumstances Are They Constitutional?" 24 *Creighton Law Review* 445 (1991).

Mannix, Daniel P. *Those About to Die.* New York: Ballantine, 1958.

Marco. "Oppressed Minority, or Counterfeits?" *Citizen,* 20 April 1992.

Marcuse, Herbert. *One Dimensional Man.* Boston: Beacon, 1964.

Marius, Richard. *Luther: A Biography.* Philadelphia: Lippincott, 1974.

Marty, Martin E. *Modern American Religion.* Vol. 1, *The Irony of It All, 1893–1919.* Chicago: Univ. of Chicago Press, 1986.

Marx, Karl, and Friedrich Engels. *The Manifesto of the Communist Party.* 1848. Reprint. San Francisco: China, 1965.

Mason, D. "The Rights of Australia's Children in a Global Context." 15 *Children Australia* 6 (1990).

Matheson, Peter. *The Third Reich and the Christian Churches.* Grand Rapids: Eerdmans, 1981.

Matsuda. "Public Response to Racist Speech: Considering the Victim's Story." 87 *Michigan Law Review* 2320 (1989).

Maupin, Armistead. "Boycott Colorado." *New York Times,* 21 November 1992.

McLuhan, Marshall. "Cybernation and Culture." In *The Social Impact of Cybernetics,* edited by Charles R. Dechert. New York: Simon & Schuster, 1966.

———. *The Gutenberg Galaxy.* Toronto: Univ. of Toronto Press, 1962.

———. *Understanding Media: The Extension of Man.* New York: McGraw-Hill, 1964.

McDonald, Forrest. *E Pluribus Unum: The Formation of the American Republic 1776–1790.* Boston: Houghton Mifflin, 1965.

Milk, Leslie, and Harry Jaffe. "Saturday Night." *The Washingtonian,* September 1993.

Miller, Arthur R. *Miller's Court.* New York: New American Library, 1983.

Miller, John C. *The Wolf by the Ears: Thomas Jefferson and Slavery*. New York: Free, 1977.

Miller, Perry. *The Life of the Mind in America*. London: Victor Gallancz, 1966.

Minutes of Regional Management Team Meeting, U.S. Forest Service (3 February 1993).

"Mississippi Governor Criticized for 'Christian Nation' Remark." *The Dallas/Fort Worth Heritage*, January 1993.

Moberly, Sir Walter. *The Crisis in the University*. New York: Macmillan, 1949.

Mohr, James. *Abortion in America: The Origins and Evolution of National Policy, 1800–1900*. New York: Oxford Univ. Press, 1978.

Monaghan, Patrick. "'Substantively Due Processing' the Black Population." 4 *Lincoln Review* 45 (1983).

Morison, Samuel E., Henry S. Commager, and William Leuchtenburg. *The Growth of the American Republic*. 7th ed. New York: Oxford Univ. Press, 1980.

Morris, Leon. *The Apostolic Preaching of the Cross*. Grand Rapids: Eerdmans, 1955.

Muggeridge, Malcolm. *Christ and the Media*. Grand Rapids: Eerdmans, 1977.

_____. *Jesus Rediscovered*. Garden City, N.Y.: Doubleday, 1969.

_____. *Jesus: The Man Who Lives*. New York: Harper & Row, 1975.

Muller, Jerry Z. "Coming Out Ahead: The Homosexual Moment in the Academy." *First Things*, August/September 1993.

Myers, John E. B. "A Survey of Child Abuse and Neglect Reporting Statutes." 10 *The Journal of Juvenile Law* 1 (1986).

Myrdal, Gunnar. *Beyond the Welfare State*. New York: Bantam, 1967.

National and International Religious Report (14 December 1992).

Neier, Aryeh. *Defending My Enemy*. New York: Dutton, 1979.

Neuhaus, Richard J. *The Naked Public Square: Religion and Democracy in America*. Grand Rapids: Eerdmans, 1984.

Newman, Leslea. *Heather Has Two Mommies*. Boston, Mass.: Alyson Publications, 1989.

Nichols, Bill. "Clinton: Gay Policy 'Right.'" *USA Today*, 20 July 1993.

Niebuhr, Gustav. "Lesbian Ousted from the Military Is Hoping to Return as a Chaplain." *Washington Post*, 10 February 1993.

Nietzsche, Friedrich Wilhelm. *Thus Spake Zarathustra*. Vol. 1 of *The Philosophy of Nietzsche*. New York: Modern Library, 1937.

Noll, Mark A. *Christians in the American Revolution*. Washington, D.C.: Christian Univ. Press, 1977.

Note. "Fetal Experimentation: Moral, Legal, and Medical Implications." 26 *Stanford Law Review* 1191 (1974).

Novak, Michael. *The Experience of Nothingness*. New York: Harper & Row, 1970.

Orwell, George. *Animal Farm*. New York: Harcourt, Brace & World, 1946.

_____. *Nineteen Eighty-Four*. New York: Harcourt, Brace & World, 1949.

Ostling, Richard N. "The Church Search." *Time,* 5 April 1993.

Otlowski, Margaret, and B. Martin Tsamenyi. "Parental Authority and the United Nations Convention on the Rights of the Child: Are the Fears Justified?" 6 *Australian Journal of Family Law* 137 (1992).

Ozment, Steven. *Protestants: The Birth of a Revolution.* New York: Doubleday, 1992.

Phillips, D. "The Risk to Family Relationships from the U.N. Convention on the Rights of the Child." 60 *Light* 8 (1990).

Phillips, Kevin P. *Post-Conservative America: People, Politics, and Ideology in a Time of Crisis.* New York: Random, 1982.

Plato. *Republic.* New York: Basic, 1968.

Podgers, James. "Debate Grows Over Euthanasia." 78 *American Bar Association Journal* (May 1992).

Polanyi, Michael. *Personal Knowledge: Towards a Post-Critical Philosophy.* Chicago: Univ. of Chicago Press, 1958.

———. *The Tacit Dimension.* New York: Doubleday, 1967.

"Polynesian P.C." *Chronicles,* October 1993.

"Post-Abortion Fetal Study Stirs Storm," *Medical World News,* 8 June 1973.

Postman, Neil. *Amusing Ourselves to Death: Public Discourse in the Age of Show Business.* New York: Viking, 1985.

Powell, General Colin. Letter to Representative Patricia Schroeder, 8 May 1992. Reprinted in *Crisis,* July/August 1992.

Presser. "The Politically Correct Law School: Where It's Right to Be Left." *American Bar Association Journal,* September 1991.

Price, Deb. "First Gay Pal Serves as Bridge to Clinton." *Detroit News and Free Press,* 25 April 1993.

"Pro-Choice, Anti-Speech." *Wall Street Journal,* 30 November 1992.

Rabb, Theodore K. *Renaissance Lives: Portraits of an Age.* New York: Pantheon, 1993.

Rawls, J. *A Theory of Justice.* Cambridge: Harvard Univ. Press, 1971.

Reed, Ralph. "Christianity vs. Fanaticism." *Wall Street Journal,* 16 March 1993.

"Reinventing School: The Goals of Educational Restructuring." Charlottesville, Va.: The Rutherford Institute (January 1994).

Reisman, Judith Bat-Ada. "Freedom of Speech as Mythology, or 'Quill Pen and Parchment Thinking' in an Electronic Environment." 8 *New York University Review of Law and Social Change* 271 (1979).

"Reproductive Rights." Planned Parenthood of the Blue Ridge. Roanoke, Virginia (January 1993).

Revel, Jean-Francois. *How Democracies Perish.* Garden City, N.Y.: Doubleday, 1983.

———. *The Totalitarian Temptation.* Garden City, N.Y.: Doubleday, 1977.

Richard, Paul. "Scrawling in the Margins." *Washington Post,* 4 March 1993.

Rivenburg, Roy. "Of Boy Scouts and Boycotts." *Los Angeles Times,* 31 August 1992.

Roberts, J. M. *The Triumph of the West.* London: British Broadcasting Corporation, 1985.

Rofes, Eric E. "Mobilizing for a Freedom March in 1993." *March on Washington for Lesbian, Gay & Bi Equal Rights and Liberation.* Newspaper Project of the Committee for the March on Washington, Inc. (February 1993).

Rookmaaker, H. R. *Modern Art and the Death of a Culture.* Downers Grove, Ill.: InterVarsity, 1970.

Rosenstock-Huessy, Eugene. *Out of Revolution.* New York: William Morrow, 1938.

Rubin, Eva. *Abortion, Politics and the Courts.* 2d ed. New York: Greenwood, 1987.

Ruchlak. "Civil Rights, Confederate Flags, and Political Correctness: Free Speech and Race Relations on Campus." 66 *Tulane Law Review* 1411 (1992).

Rutherford, Samuel. *Lex, Rex; or, the Law and the Prince.* 1644. Harrisonburg, Va.: Sprinkle, 1980.

Sachs, Andrea. "Home Smoke, Free Home." *Time,* 25 October 1993.

Safire, William. *The First Dissident: The Book of Job in Today's Politics.* New York: Random, 1992.

Sagan, Carl. *Cosmos.* New York: Random, 1980.

Salholz, Eloise. "The Power and the Pride." *Newsweek,* 21 June 1993.

Sanger, Margaret. *An Autobiography.* New York: Dover, 1971.

Schaeffer, Francis A. *A Christian Manifesto.* Westchester, Ill.: Crossway, 1981.

———. *Back to Freedom and Dignity.* Downers Grove, Ill.: InterVarsity, 1972.

———. *Escape from Reason.* Downers Grove, Ill.: InterVarsity, 1968.

———. *Genesis in Space and Time.* Downers Grove, Ill.: InterVarsity, 1972.

———. *How Should We Then Live?* Old Tappan, N.J.: Revell, 1976.

———. *Pollution and the Death of Man: The Christian View of Ecology.* Wheaton, Ill.: Tyndale, 1970.

———. *The Church at the End of the Twentieth Century.* Westchester, Ill.: Crossway, 1985.

———. *The Complete Works of Francis A. Schaeffer.* Westchester, Ill.: Crossway, 1982.

———. *The God Who Is There.* Downers Grove, Ill.: InterVarsity, 1968.

———. *The Great Evangelical Disaster.* Westchester, Ill.: Crossway, 1984.

———. *The Mark of the Christian.* Downers Grove, Ill.: InterVarsity, 1970.

Schaeffer, Francis, and C. Everett Koop. *Whatever Happened to the Human Race?* London: Marshall, Morgan & Scott, 1980.

Schaeffer, Franky. *A Time for Anger: The Myth of Neutrality.* Westchester, Ill.: Crossway, 1982.

———. *Addicted to Mediocrity.* Westchester, Ill.: Crossway, 1981.

Scott, Kimberly. "Making Babies." *Washington Blade,* 23 October 1992.

Sedler. "The Unconstitutionality of Campus Bans on 'Racist Speech': The View from Without and Within." 53 *University of Pittsburgh Law Review* 631 (1992).

Sennett, Richard. *The Fall of Public Man.* New York: Knopf, 1977.

"Sexual Disorientation." Family Research Council, Washington, D.C. (June 1992).

Sherman, Rorie. "Gay Law No Longer Closeted." *The National Law Journal,* 26 October 1992.

Sherry, Suzanna. "Speaking of Virtue: A Republican Approach to University Regulation of Hate Speech." 75 *Minnesota Law Review* 933 (1991).

Shirer, William L. *The Rise and Fall of the Third Reich: A History of Nazi Germany.* New York: Simon & Schuster, 1960.

Shortall, James. "Hodgson v. Minnesota: Balancing the Competing Interests of the State, Parents and Minor—A Missed Opportunity?" 69 *Denver University Law Review* 539 (1992).

Simon, Julian L. *The Ultimate Resource.* Princeton, N.J.: Princeton Univ. Press, 1981.

Skinner, B. F. *Beyond Freedom and Dignity.* New York: Knopf, 1971.

Smolowe, Jill. "Crusade for the Classroom." *Time,* 1 November 1993.

_____. "New, Improved and Ready for Battle." *Time,* 14 June 1993, 48.

Solzhenitsyn, Aleksandr I. *August 1914.* New York: Farrar, Straus & Giroux, 1972.

_____. "Gulag Survivor Indicts Western 'Freedom,'" *Los Angeles Times,* 13 June 1976.

_____. *Lenin in Zurich.* Translated by H. T. Willetts. New York: Farrar, Straus & Giroux, 1976.

_____. *Letter to the Soviet Leaders.* Translated by Hilary Sternberg. New York: Harper & Row, 1974.

_____. *The Gulag Archipelago 1918–1956: An Experiment in Literary Investigation.* Translated by Thomas P. Whitney. New York: Harper & Row, 1973.

_____. *The Gulag Archipelago 1918–1956 (Two).* Translated by Thomas P. Whitney. New York: Harper & Row, 1978.

_____. *The Oak and the Calf: A Memoir.* Translated by Harry Willetts. New York: Harper & Row, 1980.

"Speech and Reason at GMU." *Washington Post,* 13 September 1993.

Speer, Albert. *Infiltration.* New York: Macmillan, 1981.

_____. *Inside the Third Reich.* New York: Macmillan, 1970.

_____. *Spandau: The Secret Diaries.* New York: Macmillan, 1976.

Spencer, Dennis D., M.D. "Unilateral Transplantation of Human Fetal Mesencephalic Tissue into the Caudate Nucleus of Patients with Parkinson's Disease." *The New England Journal of Medicine* 327, no. 22 (26 November 1992).

Stafford, Tim. "Move Over, ACLU." *Christianity Today,* 25 October 1993.

Stanley, Alessandra. "Militants Back 'Queer,' Shoving 'Gay' the Way of 'Negro.'" *New York Times,* 6 April 1991.

Stauffer, Ethelbert. *Christ and the Caesars.* Philadelphia: Westminster, 1965.

Stewart, George A. "Interpreting the Child's Right to Identity in the U.N. Convention on the Rights of the Child." 26 *Family Law Quarterly* 221 (1992).

Stewart, Thomas A. "Gay in Corporate America." *Fortune,* 16 December 1991.

"Stop Rutherford Institute." *This Week in Texas,* 19 March–25 March 1993.

Stott, John R. W. *Christ the Controversialist.* Downers Grove, Ill.: InterVarsity, 1970.

"Straight Talk about Gays." *U.S. News & World Report,* 5 July 1993.

Strauss, William, and Neil Howe. *Generations: The History of America's Future, 1584 to 2069.* New York: Morrow, 1991.

Strossen. "Regulating Racist Speech on Campus: A Modest Proposal." *Duke Law Journal* 484 (1990).

––––––. "Thoughts on the Controversy over Politically Correct Speech." 46 *Southern Methodist University Law Review* 119 (1992).

Susoeff, Steve. Comment, "Assessing Children's Best Interests When a Parent Is Gay or Lesbian: Toward a Rational Custody Standard." 32 *University of Los Angeles Law Review* 852 (1985).

The Abortion Report. November 2, 1992.

The Committee on Child Psychiatry, Group for the Advancement of Psychiatry. *How Old is Old Enough?: The Ages of Rights and Responsibilities.* New York: Brunner/Mazel, 1989.

"The Second Woman Justice." *American Bar Association Journal,* October 1993.

The Williamsburg Charter Survey on Religion and Public Life. Washington, D.C.: Williamsburg Charter Foundation, 1988.

Thomas, Cal. "Morality Demands that We Condemn Gays." *Detroit Free Press,* 28 April 1993.

––––––. *The Death of Ethics in America.* Waco, Tex.: Word, 1988.

Thompson, William Irwin. "'What's Past is Prologue,' The Past—What's That?" *New York Times,* 10 June 1976.

Tinder, Glenn. "Can We Be Good Without God?" *The Atlantic Monthly,* December 1989.

––––––. *The Political Meaning of Christianity.* Baton Rouge: Louisiana State Univ. Press, 1989.

Tocqueville, Alexis de. *Democracy in America.* 1835–40. Garden City, N.Y.: Anchor, 1960.

Toffler, Alvin. *Previews and Premises.* New York: Morrow, 1983.

––––––. *The Eco-Spasm Report.* New York: Bantam, 1975.

––––––. *The Third Wave.* New York: Morrow, 1980.

Tolins, Jonathan. "A Playwright's Insight—And Warning." *Time,* 26 July 1993.

Trescott, Jacqueline. "After Warning, WMZQ Airs Gay Alliance Ad." *Washington Post,* 22 October 1992.

Tribe, Lawrence. *Abortion: The Clash of Absolutes.* New York: Norton, 1990.

Turque, Bill. "Press '1' for the Christian Right." *Newsweek*, 8 February 1993.

Tuveson, Ernest Lee. *Redeemer Nation: The Idea of America's Millennial Role.* Chicago: Univ. of Chicago Press, 1968.

Von Biema, David. "For the Love of Kids." *Time,* 1 November 1993, 51.

Wadlington, Walter. *Cases and Other Materials on Domestic Relations.* Westbury, N.Y.: Foundation, 1990.

Walzer, Michael. *Exodus and Revolution.* New York: Basic, 1985.

Webster's New Collegiate Dictionary. Springfield, Mass.: Merriam, 1975.

Weiss, Rick. "The Ethics of Cloning: Who Decides?" *Washington Post Health,* 16 November 1993.

Weizenbaum, Joseph. *Computer Power and Human Reason: From Judgment to Calculation.* San Francisco: Walt Freeman, 1976.

Wells, H. G. *The Outline of History.* Garden City, N.Y.: Doubleday, 1971.

_____. *The Shape of Things to Come.* New York: Macmillan, 1945.

Wells-Petry, Major Melissa. *Exclusion: Homosexuals and the Right to Serve.* Washington, D.C.: Regnery Gateway, 1993.

"What You Can Do About the Religious Right." *Church and State,* October 1993.

"While We're At It." *First Things,* August/September 1993.

White, Robert J., M.D., "Fetal Brain Transplantation: Questionable Human Experiment." *America,* 28 November 1992.

Whitehead, Alfred North. *Adventures of Ideas.* New York: Macmillan, 1933.

_____. *Nature and Life.* New York: Greenwood, 1968.

_____. *The Principles of Natural Knowledge.* Cambridge, England: Cambridge Univ. Press, 1925.

_____. *Science and the Modern World.* New York: Macmillan, 1925.

Whitehead, Barbara DaFoe. "Dan Quayle Was Right." *The Atlantic Monthly,* April 1993.

Whitehead, John W. *The Second American Revolution.* Westchester, Ill.: Crossway, 1982.

_____. "Accommodation and Equal Treatment of Religion: Federal Funding of Religiously-Affiliated Child Care Facilities." 26 *Harvard Journal on Legislation* 573 (1989).

_____. "Avoiding Religious Apartheid: Affording Equal Treatment for Student-Initiated Religious Expression in Public Schools." 16 *Pepperdine Law Review* 229 (1989).

_____. *A Pro-Life Manifesto: Strategy on the Abortion Issue.* Charlottesville, Va.: The Rutherford Institute, 1993.

_____. *The Rights of Religious Persons in Public Education.* 2d ed. Wheaton, Ill.: Crossway, 1993.

_____. "Civil Disobedience and Operation Rescue: A Historical and Theoretical Analysis." 48 *Washington and Lee Law Review* 77 (1991).

313

_____. *Religion and the Workplace: Rights and Responsibilities.* Charlottesville, Va.: The Rutherford Institute, 1992.

_____. *An American Dream.* Westchester, Ill.: Crossway, 1987.

_____. *True Christianity.* Westchester, Ill.: Crossway, 1989.

Whitehead, John W., and Alexis I. Crow. "Beyond Establishment Clause Analysis in Public School Situations: The Need to Apply the Public Forum and Tinker Doctrines." 28 *Tulsa Law Journal* 150 (1992).

Whitehead, John W., and James J. Knicely. "Religious Freedom Restoration Act: Wolf in Sheep's Clothing?" Charlottesville, Va.: The Rutherford Institute, 1991.

Willhoite, Michael. *Daddy's Roommate.* Boston: Alyson, 1990.

Wills. "Peeling Off Political Labels." *Sacramento Bee,* 28 December 1990.

Wilson, James D. "Gays Under Fire." *Newsweek,* 14 September 1992.

Wingert, Pat and Eloise Salholz. "Irreconcilable Differences." *Newsweek,* 21 September 1992.

Wood, H. G. *Christianity and Civilization.* New York: Octagon, 1973.

Woodside, Moya. *Sterilization in North Carolina: A Sociological and Psychological Study.* Chapel Hill, N.C.: Univ. of North Carolina Press, 1950.

Woodward, Kenneth L., and David Gates. "How the Bible Made America." *Newsweek,* 12 December 1982.

Wuthnow, Robert. *The Struggle for America's Soul.* Grand Rapids: Eerdmans, 1989.

GENERAL
INDEX